Fatal Attractions

Edited by Lynne Pearce
and Gina Wisker

Fatal Attractions

Re-scripting Romance in Contemporary Literature and Film

Pluto Press
LONDON • STERLING, VIRGINIA

First published 1998 by Pluto Press
345 Archway Road, London N6 5AA
and 22883 Quicksilver Drive,
Sterling, VA 21066–2012, USA

British Library Cataloguing in Publication Data
A catalogue record for this book is available from
the British Library

ISBN 0 7453 1386 8 hbk

Library of Congress Cataloging in Publication Data
A catalog record for this book is available from
the Library of Congress

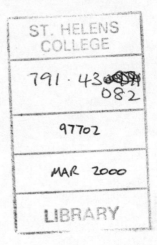
Designed and produced for Pluto Press by
Chase Production Services, Chadlington, OX7 3LN
Typeset from disk by Stanford DTP Services, Northampton
Printed in the EC by T.J. International, Padstow

Contents

Acknowledgements

As is often the case with edited collections, this volume has taken several years to achieve publication, and we would therefore like to thank all our contributors for their stalwart patience and good humour. Our desire to keep the volume as topical and 'state-of-the-art' as possible has inevitably meant that we have had to ask for late revisions, and we very much appreciate the efforts of those concerned. Thanks, too, to the new contributors who have delivered their copy so promptly.

On a more personal note, Gina would like to thank Alistair, Liam and Kitt for their continued support and patience and Isabel King for her invaluable administrative assistance; and Lynne would like to thank Jackie Stacey and Rowena Murray for offering valuable comment and direction on the Introduction, Chapter 7, and romantic discourse in general.

Final thanks must go to Anne Beech and Pluto Press for their commitment to a topic that is, we believe, as politically urgent today as it has ever been.

Lynne Pearce and Gina Wisker
October 1997

Lynne Pearce and Gina Wisker

Rescripting Romance: an Introduction

As Phyllis Creme's chapter for this volume signals, 'love transforms'. Across centuries, across cultures – and allowing, as we must, for the wide range of specificities and differences which attend such a claim – romantic love is perceived to be an emotional event with the power to change the lives of all those it touches. The key question we are concerned with in this volume, however, is: can love, itself, *be transformed*? That is to say, does the changing representation of romantic love in contemporary culture reflect and/or constitute significant changes in the role and function of romance in our lives? Is romantic love being *rescripted* at the same time as it is being retold, and if so, what is the *extent* of the subversion taking place?

This volume, focusing on the representation of romance in contemporary literature and film, would seem to provide keen evidence that significant changes have taken place, though with varying degrees of subversion. Whilst the essays signal an extremely inventive range of ways in which romance is being *renegotiated* in our postmodern culture (and in the wake of 'antagonistic' political movements such as feminism and socialism), only occasionally do we find texts/productions which rock the foundations of this most enduring of 'grand narratives'.[1] Our thesis here, based on the evidence supplied by this rich sample of contemporary texts, is that the radical potential of such reworkings – the point, indeed, at which a 'retelling' *becomes* a 're-scripting' – lies *not only* in the extent to which they alter the codes and conventions of traditional romance (e.g., the sexuality of the lovers; the nature of the obstacles they face; the order in which key episodes take place), but whether or not they *actively* interrogate and destabilise the institutions in which those conventions have become embedded (e.g., heterosexuality, marriage, monogamy, the family or the prescription for same-race relationships). In this respect, recent advances in queer and postcolonial theory have been instrumental in helping us think through how these cultural orthodoxies have been dependent upon a process of 'othering' and 'abjection', and nowhere is this more evident than in the arena of our romantic and sexual relations.[2] According to this rationale, it could be argued that the truly subversive romance is the one that somehow severs the 'necessary' connection between the archetypal structures of desire (as set out in the various psychoanalytic/structuralist accounts of self–other relations: see below) and the institutions that have appropriated those structures (and their attendant narratives) in the service of various cultural orthodoxies. Romantic subversion is not, therefore, simply a question of retelling the same story with different players, or a different plot, or in a different context, but of more radically disassociating the psychic foundations of desire from the cultural ones *in such a way that the operation of the orthodoxy is exposed and challenged.* Some queer theorists would argue, indeed, that this is the difference between a text like Jane Rule's *Desert of the Heart* (1964) which leaves the cultural institution of heterosexuality relatively untouched, and Angela Carter's *The Passion of New Eve* (1977) which works to expose the means by which the hetero- and homosexual binaries have been produced.[3] Whilst the love of Ann and Vivian is seen to be negotiating a space/place within the traditional romance, that between Tristessa and 'New Eve' shows how it is through the 'othering' of gay and other 'deviant' relationships that the institutions of heterosexuality and marriage have been sustained. To the extent, then, that heterosexual marriage (the traditional closure of the romance narrative) has depended upon the othering of non-permissive relationships, a gay appropriation of that institution is paradoxical to say the least. With even a minimal awareness of the 'logic' of queer theory, it should be clear that the codes and conventions of traditional romantic courtship/marriage are something that non-heterosexuals can *imitate* but never '*do*'; moreover, this realisation should quickly point to the fact that heterosexuals can never really *do* them either.[4] Romance, in this respect, is an agent of a cultural orthodoxy that has worked by and through the othering of certain groups and elements to the extent that the bonding of 'two souls' (frequently perceived as sexless, genderless and otherwise 'unmarked' in socio-cultural terms) is really anything but. Here the old chant of 'you and me against the world' begs the question 'but who *is* this world that has to be shut out?'. The truly subversive romantic texts, according to this logic, are the ones that make explicit the cultural inscription of all our desires and all our stories of desire: which is not to say that they should (or could) abandon either the desires or the stories.

But this last point is also crucial. What past research has shown, and what many of the texts considered in this volume confirm, is that there remains a significant gap between the ostensibly liberating destabilisation of all gendered and sexual identity associated with some strains of queer theory, and our longing for more *permanent* identities, whether heterosexual or gay *or* queer.[5] With respect to the cultural reproduction of romance this means that we cannot, and should not, expect all contemporary texts to explode the foundations of self and society in the way that queer 'logic' (or the 'popular' version thereof) would seem to demand. Whilst poststructuralist theory has been consummately successful in persuading us of the 'mythical' (discursive) origins of all identities and the institutions which create/sustain them, the fact remains that the *desire* for such coherence is psychically and structurally inscribed (see discussion following) and therefore not easily relinquished.

In the review of the different types/levels/degrees of romantic subversion featured in this volume which follows, we therefore avoid the assumption that the most subversive texts/discussions in terms of the queer logic just outlined are necessarily the most interesting or most 'important'. In the final analysis romance is, and will always remain, a discourse predicated upon 'convention' (in every sense of the word) and the subtle, as well as the major, deviations from its norms (not to mention its whole-hearted *re*inscriptions) must remain our concern.

The Formation/s of Romantic Love

Before we move on to consider the different categories, and degrees, of subversion present in contemporary rescriptings of romance it is necessary that we open with a brief review of the foundations of romantic love as 'told' by certain theorists: those aspects of 'the story', in other words, that we should expect *not to change* regardless of their appropriation by dominant or oppositional cultural groups. Responses to the question of *why* romantic love, and its associated cultural representations, should have endured all philosophical and political attempts to discredit it, can be broadly separated into the psychoanalytic and the structural although each, as we shall see, is closely implicated in the other.

Both Freudian and Lacanian psychoanalytic theory tell a similar story about why human adults sustain an apparently insatiable appetite both for 'falling in love' and seeing the experience represented in their culture(s). The emotional drive we experience as 'desire' is predicated upon a 'lack' set up in early childhood, either through the imperfect resolution of the Oedipal crisis and the creation of the unconscious (Freud), or through the loss of plenitude and agency associated with the 'Imaginary' phase of infant development (Lacan). Whilst we feel it unnecessary to chronicle either of these models in detail since this has now been done repeatedly elsewhere, it is interesting to reflect some more on what they have in common in terms of *narrative structuration*, especially with respect to the way this is used to explain the dynamics of adult relationships.[6] We have consequently chosen to reproduce two short extracts from recent works on the cultural representation of romantic love: in the first (from the introduction of *Romance Revisited*, 1995), Jackie Stacey explicates Freud's explanation for the insatiability of adult desire, whilst in the second, Catherine Belsey (*Desire*, 1994) offers us Lacan's version of the same story.

(1) Although Freudian, Lacanian and object relations theory all vary enormously in their accounts, all three are nevertheless concerned with the relationship between the self and the ideal, with the role of fantasy in the development of sexuality, and with the importance of early childhood experiences in the formation of adult desires.

An obstacle is required in order to heighten libido: and where natural resistances to satisfaction have not been sufficient, men [sic] have at all times erected conventional ones so as to be able to enjoy love. (Freud, 1912: 256–7)

Freud's description of the cultural production of romantic love thus stresses the necessity of its narrativity to the function of libido: the measure of love depends upon the satisfaction of overcoming the barriers to it; in their absence, a story invents them. This process of 'erecting' obstacles (to ensure delayed gratification) makes the other person special, unattainable, or 'ideal', in so far as their status grows proportionally to the difficulty of attainment. A central characteristic of romantic love, then, is *idealisation*: the overvaluation of the 'love object' (as in the phrase 'love blinds'). According to Freud, the patterns of adult love (such as the over-investment in another person) can be explained by early psychosexual development (see Mitchell, 1975). The Oedipal attachments to parent figures involve many of the key ingredients of romantic love in later life, Freud argues; these include both the initial idealisation and obsession and the accompanying rivalry and jealousy (in which the child believes the parent to be the source of all knowledge, the solution to all problems and the 'meeter' of all needs), as well as the gradual disillusionment, resentment or hatred (as the child separates from the parents and eventually rejects them).[7]

(2) Desire is the effect of lost needs: loss returns and presents itself as desire. Desire is not *the same as* need: analytic experience certainly demonstrates 'the paradoxical, deviant, erratic, eccentric, even scandalous character' which distinguishes desire from anything that could possibly be *necessary* (Lacan 1977: 286). The erotic capabilities of the human animal are way in excess of nature's reproductive imperative. In any case, the needs in question were a matter of survival, not sex. What returns as desire is quite other than the repressed needs that are its cause ...

... The cause of desire, Lacan's *objet à*, is the lost object in the unknowable real. Desire is thus 'a relation of being to lack. This lack is a lack of being properly speaking. It isn't the lack of this or that, but the lack of being whereby the being exists'. (Lacan 1988: 223) Desire is a metonym (a displaced version) of the want-to-be that necessarily characterizes a human life divided between the unmasterable symbolic and the unreachable, inextricable real ... (Lacan 1977: 284) ...

... How absurd in these circumstances to suppose that desire can be met by 'leaving it to the virtue of the "genital" to resolve it through the maturation of tenderness' (Lacan 1977: 287). Lacan has nothing but contempt for the view that true love leading to happy marriage is the project of desire, since desire precisely exceeds the dualism of sensuality and affection, resides both beyond need and demand.[8]

Despite the fact that Belsey's understanding of the Lacanian 'lack' disassociates it from *any* external 'others' who have their 'originals' in our parents, and identifies it, instead, as a product of the 'splitting of the self' brought about by a complex relay of signification and difference, the model is predicated upon the same *dynamic* as Freud's. Reduced to their bare bones, both accounts see adult desire (the emotion that our culture(s) have dressed up as 'romantic love') as the *effect* of a loss produced in our early psychosexual development. Our tendency, in adult life, is to seek to redress the loss in, or through, another person; and rather than identify the loss itself as the (effectively irreversible) obstacle to our desire, we make the person the substitute object of our desire and the obstacle anything that stands in the way of our possessing them. Strung out in this way, it is clear how the 'origins' of desire, psychoanalytically conceived, are *instantly narrativised.* If all adult desire can be traced back to a state of being, or relationship, that has been lost, then any attempt to redeem it will inevitably take the form of a narrative quest: a 'love story' or 'romance'. The fact, moreover, that in both the Freudian and Lacanian accounts the initial loss is construed differently for male and female children matters little to this fundamental principle. While such differences most certainly *do* impact on how these losses are negotiated in adult life, psychoanalysis requires us to *begin* from the assumption that (to quote Tennyson) 'loss is common to the human race', male and female alike.[9]

Set out in this way, it will probably seem that we concur with these psychoanalytic explanations of 'why' romantic love (as the re/production of infantile human desire) and romance (as the cultural representation of that desire) persist and endure across history, cultures and all political attempts to undermine them. This, we agree, is possibly the simplest option; though another is to take the 'will-to-story' – *the desire to narrativise desire* – as the generating principle. Instead of believing, in other words, that the psychosexual processes of early childhood development are the catalyst for the romance narrative, we might argue that it is the archetypal patterns of storytelling in Western culture(s) – or, indeed, as we have already hinted, the 'will-to-story' itself – that have *produced* such persuasive accounts of desire as an expression of lack, or loss.

Pursuing this thesis is not difficult. Directly we turn to the work of the early structuralist theorist, Vladimir Propp (*Morphology of the Folktale*, 1928), we see that 'liquidation of a lack' heads up Propp's list of the thirty-one functions he sees structuring *every* classic folktale or fairy-story.[10] Although initially hard to credit, Propp and his followers such as Greimas (1966) and Levi-Strauss (1958) have made a convincing case for this structural homogeneity which has also been adopted, with minimal modification, by feminist theorists of popular romance such as Janice Radway (1984) and Tania Modleski (1982).[11] In so far as the classic romance narrative can be seen to derive – in part, at least – from the fairy-tales of European culture, then a textual and intertextual 'answer' to why romance endures is readily available. Some theorists of the fairy-tale like Bruno Bettleheim (1968) have gone on to argue, not surprisingly, that the archetypal nature of these functions and their agents (the heroes, villains, donors and so on that Propp describes as 'spheres of action') can themselves be explained only in psychoanalytic terms.[12] This remains debatable, however, and it is, we feel, possible to make a perfectly good case for such 'classic stories', and/or the desire to tell them, being acceptable as an explanation for the endurance of romance in their own right.

These structuralist 'explanations' of romance have also been persuasively reworked in the context of poststructuralism where discourse theory supports the notion that desire *begins* life as a text. It is 'always already' a story, and it is simply because it is a *good story* that it has, and will, endure. Working within a Foucauldian rationale, feminist scholars like Stevi Jackson have argued that it is the fact that romantic love *does not have* a single psychic or structural 'origin', but is instead fed (produced, reproduced and sustained) by multiple, and competing, cultural and textual sources, that has made it so enduring.[13] Whilst this will be the preferred argument for most scholars who have been poststructurally trained, ourselves included, this excellent account of how romance grows and circulates nevertheless fails to account for the narrowness, simplicity and apparent immutability of the narrative (desire/loss, quest and redemption) at its heart. Whilst we therefore agree that the psychoanalytic and structuralist 'explanations' *could* be challenged further, we have preferred, for the purposes of the wider thesis being pursued in this Introduction, to accept, at least, their 'claim to truth'. Is this not, perhaps, a narrative kernel too tough to be cracked? The blasting apart of this central core might thus be as impossible as splitting the atom (was thought to be?!), and we should content ourselves – as we have already suggested – by looking for our subversions elsewhere: in particular, in the *disarticulation* between love's narrative core and its cultural inscription.

Rescripting Romance

Irony and Satire
In this and the following sections we aim to offer some reflections on how romantic love is being rescripted in contemporary literature and film, including an assessment of its subversive potential. These discussions will be linked to the texts and theses presented in the following chapters, but will not be confined to them, since it is our aim to make this chapter a discussion piece in its own right.

If asked to name a contemporary text which 'subverts' romantic love, we are likely to reach first for some sort of comic example. Notwithstanding the fact that romance and comedy are generically linked in literary history, or the fact that many of the most popular contemporary romances are those with a decidedly 'light touch', we are also aware that such comedy is sometimes (or to a certain extent) made the bearer of a more serious interrogation and critique. In texts and productions as wide-ranging as David Lodge's burlesque 'comedy of (academic) manners', *Small World* (1983), to *When Harry Met Sally* (1989), to Fay Weldon's 'gothic' satire, *The Life and Loves of a She-Devil* (1983) or Angela Carter's carnivalesque 'masquerades', romantic love is clearly *exposed* as an ideological and/or psychological 'trap' with the power to make fools of us all.

The way in which comedy has been invoked in feminist interrogations is especially interesting here, since it helps us assess the 'success' of this form of subversion *vis-a-vis* a clear political agenda. Implicit in such reasoning is, of course, the recognition that a good deal of romantic comedy – even that inclining towards *heavy* irony and satire – has no real wish to challenge either romance or its supporting institutions. Love might, indeed, make fools of all of us, but it is still 'the best of life' (and of human nature): a 'madness' that we should continue to believe in.[14]

Whilst plenty of contemporary feminists would seem to share this sentiment (Jeanette Winterson, for example: see discussion following), a few have invoked various inflections of irony and satire in order to make visible the cruel and nasty 'other side' of romantic love. Fay Weldon and Margaret Atwood are two authors who have spilt a good deal of blood in (or from) this particular vein. Weldon's *The Life and Loves of a She-Devil* (1983) has assumed a particular seminal status in this respect because of its self-reflexive commentary on the pleasures and dangers of popular romance literature for women.[15] Like Atwood's *Lady Oracle* (1982), it features a character who is herself the author of popular romance and who is seen to be both the perpetrator and ultimately the victim of the ideology in which she trades. What is most dark about this text (like Atwood's) is that *no one* is allowed to escape their ideological programming with respect to either the desire for love or the version of femininity that is supposed to 'achieve' it. Whilst many student readers resist this

implication in their desire for Ruth to be an out-and-out heroine, it is clear
that her 'engagement' of the various institutions (the family, the church,
the law) that obstruct her own right to romance is not with a view to their
overthrow. Ruth's desire for revenge on the 'Mary Fishers' of this world
goes no further than her desire to *become* 'Mary Fisher'. Her 'obstacles'
to true love and happiness are not the corrupt value systems which have
made romance the reward of the young, the conventionally beautiful and
the feminine, but simply the things (personal and social) that stand in the
way of *her* realising them: 'I am no revolutionary. Since I cannot change
them, I will change myself' (1983: 203). By making the sections of the
novel told from Mary Fisher's standpoint a pastiche of the romantic fiction
she, herself, manufactures, Weldon cleverly enables us to see this discourse
in the making. Thus the black heart of this text is not simply the grotesque
extremes that Ruth is prepared to put herself through in order to take up
her place in the Fisher fiction, but the fact that it does not allow either
characters or readers a space from which to 'opt-out'. In some respect,
and to some degree, we all carry Ruth's monstrous desire to 'conform'
around with us.

Not surprisingly, such a conclusion causes problems when we come
to consider whether or not this is a *feminist* text. The satire makes it
superficially 'anti-romance', certainly, but it fails to offer us any clear
possibilities for resistance. This in itself is, of course, consonant with what
many feel to be the inherently conservative politics of satire in general:
namely, that it is the rhetoric of impotence.[16] Whilst this must remain
debatable, in terms of the thesis that has been advancing here, it could
be said that texts like Weldon's and Atwood's show considerable subversive
power to the extent that they unflinchingly *expose* the institutions and
cultural orthodoxies that have laid claim to romance. Where they 'fail',
is in the process we have named 'disarticulation'; namely, in creating some
significant slippage between the core narrative and its institutional
appropriation which would then *become* the site of possible resistance. We
will return to an examination of how this might be achieved in the later
sections of this Introduction.

Vis-a-vis the present volume, Flora Alexander's chapter supplies ample
evidence of the different ways in which satire has been deployed by
novelists such as Atwood, Weldon and Margaret Drabble in order to
problematise romance, even if this amounts to a relatively modest
subversion. Her discussion points, in particular, to the various ways in
which these authors use satire in order to 'implicate' their readers.[17] It
is clearly significant, for example, that all the texts in question deploy
multiple narrators and points of view in their texts, and that many of the
speakers/protagonists are explicitly self-ironising. We should conclude,
therefore, that this satire is invoked *not* to ridicule and/or 'other' a
particular cultural group, but to reveal the power and inescapability of
discourses in which we *all* participate, no matter how critically aware.

The ironic self-awareness of so many of the voices and characters prevents us, as readers, from thinking we can assume a more critical perspective somewhere 'outside the text'. Alexander's chapter also sets up a significant distinction between these still relatively conservative subversions and the deeper challenges by authors like Angela Carter (1977, 1980, 1994) and Aretha van Herk (1989) who attempt to rescript romantic love through various cultural disarticulations (see below) at the same time as exposing its mechanisms.

Sublimation

Whilst the preceding discussions will have suggested that irony and satire have only a limited subversive potential as far as a radical 'rescripting' of romance is concerned, it is clear that many other contemporary texts sidestep the feminist politics of their political project entirely through a process of *sublimation*. Under this heading we must include texts and productions whose apparently radical or liberated reworking of the romance plot and/or protagonists cloaks a highly conservative and reactionary move.

Our first example of this trend is Jeanette Winterson's fiction, which, whilst celebrated for its depiction of non-standard relationships (her novels abound with 'queer couplings': see below), together with its playful mix of modernist and postmodernist narrative modes, nevertheless abides by a deeply conservative humanist philosophy as far as romantic love is concerned. Despite the fact that her characters represent a veritable rainbow of historical, sexual, and other cultural difference, this gesture towards specificity is seriously undermined by the fact that – when it comes to 'love' (the Great Universal) – the differences no longer seem to be of consequence. This point is illustrated very explicitly in *Written on the Body* (1992) in which the ambiguity surrounding the sex of the central protagonist has been taken as a sign of 'what does it matter?'.[18] Readers have been encouraged to believe that what Lothario and Louise share is somehow 'above' gender, sexuality, class, race, time – or any other kind of difference. In one fell swoop, then, the discourse of humanism can be seen to effectively wipe out any cultural disarticulation being attempted by the text. Whilst many of Winterson's stories do, indeed, pursue a 'queer trajectory' by manufacturing alliances between characters from both inside and outside the cultural orthodoxy, this politics tends to be neutralised by the fact their differences are in some way *immaterial*. As a result of this sublimation, the institutions upholding heterosexuality, the family, and so on, are left relatively unproblematised and untouched.

This particular move towards humanist sublimation is not, of course, exclusive to Winterson. It has become very much *the* favourite way of dealing with homosexual, mixed-race, and other 'deviant' relationships in the cultural mainstream. In both films and television soaps such as *Emmerdale* and *Brookside*, gay and other (non-orthodox) romances are effectively 'made safe' by being rendered 'just the same'.[19] In such scenarios, it is clear that romantic love is being used to shore up the cultural orthodoxy rather than being deployed as a site of radical interrogation.

An interesting variation on this species of humanist sublimation are those texts dealing with Aids. As Maria Lauret shows in her chapter, Hollywood cinema's response to the challenge of how to make sex safe 'in the age of Aids' has been to render romantic love 'virtual' or (literally) 'disembodied'. Whilst in *Ghost* (1990) romance is only allowed to 'prove itself' 'across the final boundary of Sam's death' (see p. 22), in *When Harry Met Sally* (1989) 'true love proves itself ... in the lack of any passion at all' (see p. 22). In both instances, the institutions of cultural orthodoxy are upheld by deferring, side-stepping, or literally transcending the traditional closure (of heterosexual penetrative sex) associated with the classic romance narrative. As Lauret shows, this is assisted by the fact that in earlier, classic romance this consummating 'act' was not represented 'on screen' anyway. When it comes to 'retelling' the stories of love in a new, and 'safe', way, there is no shortage of generic precedents that can be drawn upon and combined. But such 'retelling' is *not* a 'rescripting' in the way we have been defining it here: *both* the key conventions of the narrative and the cultural orthodoxies that have annexed them remain protected, and what emerges from the subtext is not 'subversion' but a particularly hysterical form of homophobia.

Whilst Aids might not be explicitly 'named' in such texts, it has become the perfect site on which to displace centuries' worth of 'horror' associated with the non-heterosexual (or otherwise deviant) 'other'. Therefore, although films like *Ghost* and *When Harry Met Sally* are by no means 'queer' texts, they most certainly do invite 'queer readings'. They are, indeed, 'love stories for our times': stories which reveal the extent to which our cultural institutions and orthodoxies have depended upon romance narratives that literally and figuratively 'close' themselves against the undesirable 'other' (and the extent to which those 'others' are 'closing-in'). This is turn links them, quite explicitly, with the new genre of *femme fatale* movies dealt with by Gina Wisker in her chapter, 'If Looks Could Kill', and Barbara Creed in her discussion of *Basic Instinct* in Chapter 12. What, in psychoananalytic terms (see note 2), might be thought of as the *abjection* of all sorts of undesirables in such texts (the homoerotic, the 'raced', the diseased and/or dying body) makes it clear to what extent that orthodoxy has depended upon the exclusion of such 'others'. In the final analysis, the union of a 'normal' man and a 'normal' woman in an act of romantic closure must be seen as a union *against* all manner of other terrifying possibilities including homosexuality, mixed-race sex, incest, polygamy, promiscuity, nymphomania and sado-masochism (see again Wisker on the *femme fatale*) and celibacy. In texts like *Ghost* and *When Harry Met Sally* what we have is therefore a most effective double-sublimation: first, a notionally traditional closure which brings a man and a woman together in what appears to be a transcendent humanist reprieve, air-brushing out the problematic differences of gender, class, race and so on; and then a sublimation or othering of the act of sex itself so that the threat of Aids (and all the deviance Aids signifies) is also magically 'disappeared'.

A final sort of sublimation featured in the chapters which follow, and a product of the readings as much as the texts they engage, is one that chooses to see romantic love as something other than 'an end in itself': an attempt to argue, for example, that romantic or sexual desire has become the vehicle for exploring other forms of growth, development and self-actualisation. This means of legitimating romance texts by side-stepping the gendered and other politics of the genre is the focus of attention in the chapters by Phyllis Creme and Lynne Pearce. With reference to both the film *Frankie and Johnny* (1991) and the British TV soap *EastEnders*, Creme draws on D. W. Winnicott's (1971) account of ego development and individuation to explain the 'transformations' that happen to the characters in these texts when they fall in love. Working within Winnicott's psychoanalytic framework she makes a convincing case for how romantic encounters are about our continuing search to 'find ourselves in the look of another' (p. 138): a look which replicates that of the mother who 'bestowed on the baby its identity and sense of self'. In this way, the successive romances of a character like Michelle from *EastEnders* bring about 'small and progressive transformations' in her personality (p. 138): there is more to romance, in other words, than (in this case) 'boy meets girl'. The 'hero' is most emphatically an agent of self-actualisation rather than the lost or missing 'other'. Similarly, in her chapter on 'The Chronotope of Romantic Love in Contemporary Feminist Fiction', Lynne Pearce argues how contemporary feminist novelists have exploited the romantic encounter ('being in love') as a space/place 'outside' of everyday time/space to explore other possibilities of 'being', identity and lifestyle. For such texts, the protagonist's 'object of desire' is no more than a springboard for a much more expansive, existential journey, and may be ultimately *less* significant than the literal and symbolic 'space' he or she occupies. As with Creme's examples, the sexual dimension of romantic love is displaced and sublimated in a process of self-actualisation which is 'in excess of the love relationship itself'. Whilst Lacanian theorists (see previous section) could easily show *why* this is the case (what we search for is our own lost 'Imaginary'), it is striking that so many contemporary texts go so far towards decentring and sublimating the 'agent' once thought of as the 'hero' of the text. In her chapter, Pearce nevertheless insists that the romance chronotope is far from an 'empty' time/space in which the material problems of self/other relations are magically swept away. In its most positive construction, the romance chronotope thus offers a distance and a perspective from which such things can be *confronted*.

In other words, it is sublimation put to a political purpose. Whether or not this amounts to a 'subversion' in the sense we have been developing here remains, however, debatable: the focus on the individual in such texts and readings tends once again to leave the institutions upholding the cultural orthodoxy of romance itself untouched. The discourse is recontextualised rather than rescripted.

Subjugation and Casualisation

A review of the texts dealt with in the following chapters has revealed two other interesting tendencies in the contemporary renegotiation of romance that we have described as 'subjugation' and 'casualisation'. The first of these refers to the way in which romance has been 'driven underground' in the fashionable, postmodern texts of the 1980s and 1990s as authors and film-makers have sought for a way of allowing the pleasures of the romance narrative to persist in a world in which all certainty, salvation and comfort have ostensibly been lost. In as much as romance has been *the* 'grand narrative' most likely to satisfy our desire for order ('sequence') and closure, it is not surprising that we should find it performing the role of a subjugated discourse in texts as various as *Pulp Fiction* (1994) and *Jurassic Park* (1993). Marginalised or ironised, these romantic subtexts nevertheless play an important structuring and ideological role that is, we would suggest, quite in excess of the 'sexual interest' they more obviously contribute. The role such subjugated romance narratives now play in the margins of postmodern, anti-humanist, nihilist or otherwise 'millenial' texts could well be *more* significant than the simultaneous flourishing of the genre *per se*. From the time of the first, grand epistemological upheavals of the mid-nineteenth century, it would seem that the more apparently complex and chaotic 'Human Life' and its supporting universe become, the more weight romantic couplings are made to bear. Think, for example, of Matthew Arnold's desperate cry of 'Ah love, let us be true to one another!' in the poem, 'Dover Beach' (1867), and the way this image of two souls clinging together against a metaphorical backdrop of alienation, chaos and confusion has been replicated in any number of late twentieth-century films. Such covert displacement of romance into a new, tough arena not immediately thought of as romantic is also the focus of discussion in Derek Longhurst's chapter which disputes the traditional generic separation of 'women's romance' and 'men's adventure text (film and fiction)' on the grounds that the figure of the 'quest' frequently *combines* the public and the private (emotional) aspects of heroism.

What seems to be emerging, then, is that the subjugation of the romance narrative in all such texts is enabling both film-makers and audience to have their cake and eat it too. Whilst, on the one hand, the postmodern and/or humanist kudos of the text is maintained in as much as it is 'about' the grand existential questions of the late twentieth century (and is most definitely *not* a 'chick's movie'), on the other it offers us the covert, almost guilty hope of a small personal salvation.

This movement of the romance narrative from main text to subtext may also be seen as a way of appeasing the politics of movements like feminism and socialism. As long as romantic love is not seen to be 'the whole' of a woman's life, then it might be more acceptable: a rationale that accords with the penchant for 'sublimated' texts and readings dealt with in the last section. This logic might also be applied to developments in contemporary gay and lesbian fiction (see Paulina Palmer's chapter) where there has been a decided trend away from 'the coming out' novel towards a literature which is about women/feminists who are shown to be living their lives as lesbians in a more 'everyday' fashion. In such texts (some of them 'queer', some of them more grounded in terms of their identity politics: see above), romantic love is not exactly incidental, but neither is it the central identity of either the text or its protagonists. This displacement of romance has also been achieved by the mixing of genres: lesbian/feminist crime fiction, for example, contains a good deal of romance, though this is ostensibly subjugated to the subplot, and certain series (for example, Sue Grafton, Val McDermid and Mary Wings) will signal this by making sure that their sleuths do not fall in love in every volume.[20]

The subjugation of the romance narrative as we have described it here easily slips into the cognate strategy we have named 'casualisation'. By this we mean the way in which a romantic narrative is allowed to remain at the forefront of a text, but on condition that it is somehow made incidental. A popular example that comes to mind here is the early 1990s film, *Go Fish* (1994), which was heralded as one of the first lesbian movies to break with the 'coming out' narrative and make the sexuality of its protagonists a more integral part of their lives. Such casualisation could also be said to be the means (along with the humanist sublimation discussed earlier) by which TV soaps (such as the recent and immensely successful *This Life*) have coped with romantic relationships erstwhile deemed 'deviant'. Love stories are told using the same codes and conventions as previously, but with a new casualness which comes from an emphatic contextualisation of the action. Once again, there is a sense that romantic love is being legitimated by being downsized.

It should be clear that neither subjugation nor casualisation can be thought of as particularly radical subversions of romance in terms of the logic of the species of queer theory invoked at the beginning of this chapter. They are certainly interesting developments in the evolution of romance culture, however, and whilst often appearing to reinvest in the institutions involved in the maintenance of normative sexual relations and/or 'the family' (remember *Jurassic Park*!), sometimes effect a partial dislocation. This is most noticeable in those texts/subtexts trading in a 'deviant' sexuality which is casualised and 'naturalised'. Here the archaic structures of romance remain a central point of reference, whilst having undergone a serious refurbishment.

Narrative Rearticulation
In the preceding sections we have already seen several examples of the way in which the classic romance plot has been adjusted, either in terms of the ordering of the 'functions' or in the designation of the roles/identities of the characters and their 'spheres of action' (Vladimir Propp: see discussion above). As we have noted, the challenges to traditional gender roles and sexualities that are central to so many contemporary rewrites of the romance have made it increasingly hard to decide who the hero, heroine and other narrative 'agents' are. Similarly, the 'functions' (events) might happen in a completely different order from the ones we were familiar with in classic romance.[21] One particularly interesting rearticulation that we have noted here is the strategic deferral or side-stepping of the text's closure/consummation as a response to 'the Aids threat' (see Maria Lauret's chapter), whilst Flora Alexander shows how feminist authors have 'defamiliarised' the traditional plot through parody and satire: in particular, through having different voices 'retell' the classic story in a self-consciously ironizing way. Similar, often small but significant, reworkings, are the subject of Patsy Stoneman's fascinating survey of the many and various new versions of Charlotte Brontë's *Jane Eyre* (1847). In this chapter Stoneman argues that Jane's 'most significant legacy lies not in her attainment of the object of her desire – experience or love – but in her control of the process of writing'. Once again, then, we have a situation in which the narrative is revised and subverted not through a reordering or restructuring *per se* but in the *way* in which it is (re)told. By seeing *Jane Eyre* as a text 'about' textual rather than sexual autonomy, and by reproducing the agency of Jane's own narrative voice in many of the rewrites, a new story arises out of the ashes of the old.

The phoenix metaphor is also invoked in Judy Simon's chapter on Daphne du Maurier's *Rebecca* (1938), though Simon is rather less sanguine about the *extent* of the subversion achieved in the act of rereading/rewriting. Exploring the way in which a text like *Rebecca* effectively 'dramatises' the 'act of (re)reading' through the persona/consciousness of 'the second wife' (it is she who puts together the 'story' of Rebecca and simultaneously rewrites the script of *Jane Eyre*), Simon nevertheless concludes that her vicarious participation in, and her unravelling of, the Rebecca narrative does not achieve a lasting catharsis or 'new start'. Like the readers of popular romance, the second Mrs de Winter is not able to transform the romance with which she has so powerfully engaged into something that will her assist her own 'real-life' marriage.

Another chapter to deal with subversion as a species of narrative rearticulation is Maroula Joannou's on Anita Brookner's fiction. Joannou shows that although Brookner's texts are ostensibly extremely conservative, avoiding the parodic and carnivalesque turns of writers like Atwood or Carter, they make their own small protest by focusing on love affairs *which come to nothing*. This is a strategy which, we would suggest, belongs to the strong and powerful tradition of fictional 'anti-romance': all those courtship novels from the time of Jane Austen onwards which undermine the 'happy endings' of the main plot with instances of loveless marriage or isolated spinsterhood. Whilst such texts (Brookner's included) *may* be read as wistful and tragic in as much as they presuppose that *somewhere* the successful relationship does exist, a more subversive feminist reading is to see them *embracing* the unsatisfactory closure as a means of exposing a harmful and disempowering ideology.[22] Thus Edith Hope, the heroine of Brookner's *Hotel du Lac* (1984), may be seen as a demystifying as well as a tragic figure.

With such reasoning we are back, once again, with a model of romantic rescripting which most certainly delivers a powerful critique of romance and its attendant institutions but falls short of offering any serious alternatives. This distinction, as we have argued, must rest with the texts/theories that not only expose the cultural orthodoxies that have laid claim to romance but which also *destabilise* them. How such a destabilisation might be effected is the topic of the following, final section.

Cultural Disarticulation
Throughout this Introduction we have been purposefully precise in our use of the term 'rescripting' in an attempt to uphold our opening hypothesis that for a text to be fully subversive it must do much more than 'retell' the stories of classic romance, even if that retelling contributes to a critique of the discourse and its cultural (re)presentation. We have suggested that a thorough-going romantic *rescripting* will interrogate not only the structural components of the romance narrative, but also its articulation with/within the discourses and institutions in which it is produced/reproduced. Further, to be truly radical and liberatory it must suggest a way in which the processes of 'othering' performed in the service of the cultural orthodoxies must be turned on their heads by 'queer couplings': alliances between subjects from the dominant and oppositional groups. In contemporary Western culture the two principle orthodoxies governing relationships are that they should be heterosexual and same-race, which is why romances that cross these boundaries have been so symbolically powerful.[23] Once again it is important to emphasise, however, that a 'deviant' coupling is not, *in itself*, subversive: a full disarticulation depends upon at least one of the parties retaining the mark/sign of cultural orthodoxy at the same time as their action shatters the foundations on which it stands.[24] The subversion depends, in other words, on both deconstruction and transformation occurring *simultaneously*.

Reviewing the novels and films discussed in the preceding sections of this Introduction it is possible to point to a number of texts which fall just short of this full subversion. Looking back to Weldon's *The Life and Loves of a She-Devil*, for example, we have a fine example of a text which delivers a powerful punch at the institutions which have made romantic love the puppet of various cultural orthodoxies, without finally destabilising them. What we mean by cultural disarticulation might have been achieved, in this instance, through a scenario in which Ruth fell *seriously* in love with one of the agents of cultural orthodoxy (e.g., the Judge) in a way that undermined both his symbolic power and her cultural disadvantage simultaneously. In such a rescripting, romantic love is set loose from its orthodox *inscription* in such a way that its pleasures and heartaches may be enjoyed by subjects from 'both sides of the tracks'.

The most 'queerly romantic' texts, then, must of necessity be those (like the Hanif Kureshi novel discussed in David Oswell's chapter) which make visible the institutional appropriation of romance not only by substituting orthodox with 'othered' subjects (the gay or lesbian; the diseased or mutilated subject; the partner of another race/religion), but also by insisting on the needs/rights of the 'othered' to such utopian desires. In the most ambitious rescriptings, like those of Kureshi and Angela Carter, these 'rights' are clung to against bizarre and overwhelming odds: something attested by the fact that readers are always 'surprised' to find the consummation of the relationship between Tristessa and 'New Eve' in *The Passion of New Eve* so 'moving' whilst it is also so 'unlikely'.

Conclusion

This last point brings us to the conclusion that we should not simply be looking for queer relationships (of whatever kind: and, as throughout, we are not thinking simply of the hetero/homo binary) to expose the phobic othering of 'straight' relationships, but a far more radical insistence that *romantic desire* (for union, merger, closure and so on) *can* be disassociated from the *institutions of romance* (heterosexuality, marriage, same-race relationships). Romantic love 'itself ', in other words – the apparently indestructable, irreducible kernel of narrative and psyche discussed at the beginning of this chapter – should, like wilderness, be the 'property' of everyone. This is not to say that we can look forward to a time (in the near future at least) when the orthodoxies which have appropriated it for so long, will magically disappear – but simply that a more open struggle may ensue.

In its attempt to advance a strong and, we hope, thought-provoking thesis on the changing characterisation of romantic love in contemporary literature and film, this chapter has chosen to define 'subversion' in a very specific way: one that is very much in line with the politics of *some* strands of queer thinking, although, as we have also acknowledged (see note 24) there is more than a little Althusserian Marxism mixed in. As part of our conclusion, however, we also wish to return readers to the equally important perspective noted at the beginning of the chapter: namely that the majority of romantic texts will continue to be as interesting/pleasurable/valuable in their *failure* to achieve this sort of ultimate transgression as the few that do.

In as much as romance continues to function as an ideology/discourse by which we are all inscribed (no matter how great our resolution otherwise), it is hardly surprising that we should continue to enjoy texts which 'retell' as well as those which 'rescript'. In this spirit, too, we would probably do well to show continued respect for those texts/productions which are effecting small, cosmetic changes rather than rocking the foundations of the various establishments. Sanitised and humanised as they might be, the various non-standard relationships that now proliferate in films and soaps around the world are certainly helping to gain 'acceptance-through-familiarity' for the minorities concerned. Whilst this may, according to some versions of queer (as well as gay and lesbian) politics, be seen as an ineffectual – and possibly retroactive – liberalism, there are those who would claim otherwise. In the final analysis, romantic love (and its cultural representations) is probably the last glasshouse that any of us throw stones in. As the saying goes, for a person to change they have got to *want* to change, and whilst a few inspired artists, theorists and individuals are offering us new models of how we might live out our relationships, the majority of us continue to be entranced (even despite ourselves!) by more conservative, less transgressive, desires.

Notes

1 'Grand narratives': the concept touted by the French postmodernist theorist Jean François Lyotard to describe those 'explanatory' and totalising discourses which have been undermined by the forces of postmodernism (see Jean François Lyotard, *The Postmodern Condition: a Report on Knowledge*, trans. G. Bennington and B. Massunni, (Manchester: Manchester University Press: 1984)). The role of feminism (itself another 'grand narrative') in challenging the value of romantic love in women's lives is discussed in the Introduction to *Romance Revisited*, Lynne Pearce and Jackie Stacey (eds) (London: Lawrence and Wishart, 1995), pp. 11–15. Further page references to this volume are given after quotations in the text.

2 'Queer and postcolonial theory': see, in particular, Judith Butler, *Gender Trouble: Feminism and the Subversion of Identity* (London and New York: Routledge, 1990) and *Bodies that Matter* (London and New York: Routledge, 1993); Eve Kosofsky Sedgwick, *Epistemology of the Closet* (Hemel Hempstead: Harvester Wheatsheaf, 1991) and *Tendencies* (London and New York: Routledge, 1994); Anne McClintock, *Imperial Leather: Race, Gender and Sexuality in the Imperial Contest* (London and New York: Routledge, 1995); Elspeth Probyn, *Sexing the Self: Gendered Positions in Cultural Studies* (London and New York: Routledge, 1993). As the theoretical/political movement talked rather loosely about as 'queer' expands, it becomes increasingly dangerous to

refer to all of its associated 'names' as though they shared the same beliefs and values. Indeed, several of those most associated with the development of queer concepts (e.g., Judith Butler) have eschewed personal identification with the label. To clarify our own usage, we should therefore explain that for the purposes of this chapter we are focusing on one axis of so-called queer thought (central to the early work of Butler and Sedgwick: see above): namely, the belief that the privileged 'norms' of society (e.g., whiteness, heterosexuality) are totally dependent upon the visible presence of their binary opposites (e.g., blackness, homosexuality). This 'othering' has also been linked to the psychoanalytically defined process known as 'abjection' which describes the subject's repulsion from things which symbolically threaten his/her bodily and psychic boundaries (such as bodily fluids). The abject is thus associated with the 'bad part' of the self which the subject desires to expel from his/her person and/or project on to another. Please note that David Oswell's chapter also provides a good overview of recent developments in queer theory.

3   Jane Rule, *Desert of the Heart* (London: Pandora Press, 1986); Angela Carter, *The Passion of New Eve* (London: Virago, 1977).

4   See in particular Judith Butler's readings of authors like Willa Cather in which homosexual subtexts are used to defamiliarise the apparently orthodox relationships in the texts and reveal all the characters to be involved in elaborate 'masquerades' of identity (see Butler, *Gender Trouble*, pp. 143–66).

5   See Pearce and Stacey, *Romance Revisited*, pp. 11–45, for further discussion of this thesis.

6   See, for example, Elizabeth Wright *Psychoanalytic Criticism: Theory in Practice* (London: Methuen, 1984) and *Feminism and Psychoanalysis: A Critical Dictionary* (Oxford: Blackwell, 1992); Judith Mitchell, *Psychoanalysis and Feminism* (Harmondsworth: Penguin, 1975).

7   Stacey, 'Introduction', p. 29. Sigmund Freud, *On Sexuality*, Vol. 7 in the Penguin Freud Library (Harmondsworth: Penguin, 1977).

8   Catherine Belsey, *Desire: Love Stories in Western Culture* (Oxford: Blackwell, 1994), pp. 57–61. Jacques Lacan, *Écrits*, trans. A. Sheridan (London: Tavistock, 1977).

9   For a detailed account of how the Freudian Oedipal complex is differently resolved for male and female children see Wright, *Feminism and Psychoanalysis*, pp. 290–6. It is worth noting, moreover, that all psychoanalytic theories regard the mother as the primary love object, and that most consider the task of 'separation' to be harder and more convoluted for female children because they do not bear the visible sign of difference (i.e., the penis) on their own bodies.

10 Vladimir Propp, *Morphology of the Folktale* ([1928] Austin and London: University of Texas Press, 1958).

11 A.J. Greimas, *Semantique Structurale* (Paris: Larousse, 1966); Claude Levi-Strauss, *Structural Anthropology*, trans. C. Jacobson and B. Grundfest Schoepf ([1958]) London: Allen Lane, 1968); Janice Radway, *Reading the Romance; Women, Patriarchy and Popular Literature* (Chapel Hill and London: The University of Carolina Press, 1984); and Tania Modleski, *Loving with a Vengeance: Mass-Produced Fantasies for Women* (London: Methuen, 1982).

12 Bruno Bettleheim, *The Uses of Enchantment: The Meaning and Importance of Fairy Tales* (New York: Alfred A. Knopf, 1976).

13 Stevi Jackson, 'Women and heterosexual love: complicity, resistance and change', in Pearce and Stacey, *Romance Revisited*, p. 49–62.

14 This tradition of 'foolishness' is certainly built into the structure of many 'classic' romances beginning with texts like Shakespeare's *A Midsummer Night's Dream.*

15 Fay Weldon, *The Life and Loves of a She-Devil* (London: Hodder and Stoughton, 1983).

16 There is an excellent discussion of the conservative limitations of irony in Linda Hutcheon's *Irony's Edge: The Theory and Politics of Irony* (London and New York: Routledge, 1994).

17   'Implicate the reader': in the Introduction to *Feminism and the Politics of Reading* (London: Edward Arnold, 1997) Lynne Pearce outlines a theory of what she describes as 'implicated reading'. This is contrasted with the 'hermeneutic reading' we practice as professional feminist scholars.

18   Jeanette Winterson, *Written on the Body* (London: Jonathan Cape, 1992). See Chapters 5 and 6 of Pearce, *Feminism and the Politics of Reading* for further discussion of this point *vis-à-vis Written on the Body*. In a number of media interviews Winterson maintained that the sex of the central protagonist was left ambiguous because it was of no signficance.

19   See Louise Allen's *The Lesbian Idol: Martina, kd and the Consumption of Masculinity* (London: Cassell Academic, 1997) for a discussion of this tendency in contemporary popular culture.

20   See for example: Val McDermid, *Report for Murder* (London: Women's Press, 1987); Sue Grafton, *K is for Killer* (London: Pan Books, 1995); Mary Wings, *She Came Too Late* (London: Women's Press, 1986). Each of these authors has other titles in their series.

21   See Pearce and Stacey, *Romance Revisited*, p. 24 for further discussion of this point.

22   See Joan Forbes's chapter on 'Anti-romantic discourse as resistance', in Pearce and Stacey, *Romance Revisted*, pp. 293–305, and also this author's unpublished PhD thesis 'Resisting romance: anti-romantic discourse in women's courtship fiction 1780–1820' (Lancaster University, 1997).

23   See Felly Nkweto Simmonds's chapter in Pearce and Stacey, *Romance Revisited*, pp. 210–22.

24   Although our concept of 'cultural disarticulation' has been developed with specific reference to queer theory, this concluding discussion on texts which make visible the dominant ideologies by which they have been constructed (perhaps at the same time as delivering an oppositional point of view) recalls Louis Althusser's concept of *internal distantiation*, as discussed in his 'Letter on Art'. See Louis Althusser, *Lenin and Philosophy and Other Essays*, trans. Ben Brewster (London: New Left Books, 1971).

Filmography

Basic Instinct (dir. Paul Verhoeven, 1991).
Bram Stoker's Dracula (dir. Francis Ford Coppola, 1992).
Frankie and Johnny (dir. Garry Marshall, 1991).
Ghost (dir. Jerry Zucker, 1990).
Go Fish (dir. Rose Troche, 1994).
Jurassic Park (dir. Steven Spielberg, 1993).
Pulp Fiction (dir. Quentin Tarantino, 1994).
When Harry Met Sally (dir. Rob Reiner, 1989).

2

Maria Lauret

Hollywood Romance in the Aids Era: *Ghost* and *When Harry Met Sally*

Straight sex is not always safe sex. (*Adrian Lyne*)[1]

And words like 'love' and 'hate' and 'faith' and 'history', 'pain' and 'joy', 'passion' and 'compassion' – the depth words drawn up like ghosts from a different dimension – will always come back in the 11th hour to haunt the Second World and those who want to live there in the Now. (*Dick Hebdige*)[2]

How can film represent an invisible virus whose transmission cannot be seen and whose carriers have been subject to hostile surveillance and revelation? (*Paul Julian Smith*)[3]

Watch this:

a woman in a restaurant demonstrates to her male friend, in full view and hearing of all the other customers, that he can't tell a fake orgasm from a real one. She begins slowly, with a few gentle moans, then leans back, hands clawing through her hair, getting louder: oh, oooh, ooh God, ooooh, oh God, and builds up to full crescendo: oooooh! Oh my God! ooh right there, oh oh oh, Yes! Yes! Yes! aaaah! ah! oh! (her hand banging the table), and ends with a few softly sighed satisfied aaaahs. She then smiles at her friend and resumes eating. Gradually, fellow guests do the same; male friend looks put out. (*When Harry Met Sally*, 1989)

Or this:

an attractive young woman in a New York apartment is sitting at her potters' wheel in the middle of the night. Her male lover joins her.

Focus on the Wurlitzer, which begins to play the Righteous Brothers' *Unchained Melody* ('O, my love/my darling/ I hunger for your touch' etcetera). Together they erect, slowly, a massive phallus-like object, stroking, caressing, close-up of how she massages the tip of it into shape, their hands entwined, the material responsive to their touch. As the music (rather like Ravel's *Bolero*) works up to full lyrical rhythm and the voice reaches dizzying heights, male lover sweeps the woman up in his arms and foreplay begins. As the record ends, they land on the sofa, entwined in missionary position. (*Ghost*, 1990)

True Love, False Sex

Two scenes from two popular films about romance, both produced on the threshold of the 1990s in Hollywood's dry-dream factory. Two scenes which are memorable as sex scenes, because they are more explicit, possibly, than the rampant heterosex dished up in later films such as *Basic Instinct* (1991) or earlier ones like *Fatal Attraction* (1987), and more uncomfortable to watch, certainly. In each case, voyeuristic unease with watching a mock-pornographic scene that you couldn't quite have seen coming, quickly dissolves into laughter as the woman at the next table to Sally tells the waitress 'I'll have what she's having', and as in *Ghost* the erect phallus dissolves into the mound of clay it always was. Sally's performance of a fake orgasm for Harry's benefit is so convincing that his previously penetrating male gaze, which purports to know her better than she knows herself, is disabled from that moment on. And Meg Ryan's performance of a fake orgasm is so convincing that you can't tell it from a real film orgasm; as a moment of cinematic self-parody Ryan achieves a double fake – and a double take on the part of the audience.

What, we may ask, is all this in aid of ? Why are these images of sexuality, fake and flaunting it, so memorable? What is the satisfaction of ersatz? To ask these questions is to imply another one: what happens to screen romance in the Aids era?

In an interview with Louise Tanner, the director of *Fatal Attraction* Adrian Lyne explained that that film was intended as a cautionary tale, with the moral 'straight sex isn't always safe sex'. But if safe sex is immediately associated with the prevention of Aids, this was not Lyne's primary concern. Instead, *Fatal Attraction* warns against the danger for heterosexual family men of getting involved with single women whose so-called biological clocks are ticking away like time bombs; it warns against the hidden violence of women and against their power to make – or break up – family life.[4]

I want to suggest that the fake sex in Rob Reiner's *When Harry Met Sally* and Jenny Zucker's *Ghost* echo Lyne's message about straight sex and safe sex, albeit in different ways. What they convey, in effect, is that fake sex is the safest sex of all, or, to put it in more academic terms, changes in the possibility of heterosexual romance in both films are significant changes, because they can be read in the light of anxieties about Aids in the popular imagination. A whole cluster of metaphors, visual puns and connotations presents itself which revolves around intercourse, as a source of transmission equalling a death sentence, and around promiscuity, which fosters fears of exposing oneself to contagion and invasion by an alien (anti)body. In *Ghost*, true romance can only prove itself across the final boundary of Sam's death, as an out-of-the-body experience. Sam declares his love for Molly for the first time in so many words at the end of the film – something he could not do whilst still alive, still in the body. This is love *at last sight*, as it were, a love which will last forever but has nowhere to go: it can, precisely, not be consummated in marriage or continue to exist in the real world.

In *When Harry Met Sally* by contrast, true love proves itself not in undying (albeit disembodied) passion, but in the lack of any passion at all. No love at first sight, no infatuation or courtship, but a paradoxical conjunction of history and fate brings the lovers together at the end. If it is clear from the first frame that Harry and Sally are destined for each other, it still takes them twelve years to get it on, and even then nothing is simple. Those twelve years, we are asked to believe, are years of self-delusion and yet necessary as an incubation period, a testing time in which each keeps track of where the other has been. Twelve years to establish trust and intimacy, and to learn to forsake all others: an apprenticeship to love – as safe sex.

Clearly, what we have here are not conventional romantic narratives, although both films incorporate enough of romance's vital ingredients to be recognisable as such. In her classic book on romantic fiction *Loving With a Vengeance*, Tania Modleski sketches the conventional romance plot thus:

> ... a young, inexperienced, poor to moderately well-to-do woman encounters and becomes involved with a handsome, strong, experienced, wealthy man, older than herself by ten to fifteen years. The heroine is confused by the hero's behaviour since, though he is obviously interested in her, he is mocking, cynical, contemptuous, often hostile, and even somewhat brutal. By the end, however, all mis-understandings are cleared away, and the hero reveals his love for the heroine, who reciprocates.[5]

This push me/pull me narrative of classic romance characterises *When Harry Met Sally* rather better than it does *Ghost*. Harry's behaviour is that of Modleski's hero, and the film's visual formula which employs multiple echoes and mirrorings of his 'n' hers scenes (Harry with his buddy Jesse; Sally with her friend Marie) underwrites the rigid binary division of sexual and gender roles that typifies the conventional romance. *Ghost*'s figuration of sexual difference has the more old-fashioned contrast between a man-of-the-world hero (Patrick Swayze) and waif-like heroine (an androgynous-looking Demi Moore, pre-implants) that Reiner's film lacks, whilst Sam and Molly's relationship across death is an extreme and literalised version of the classic unrequited *Love Story* (1970) (or indeed the newly topical *Romeo and Juliet* (1996), Hollywood style). Despite these elements of the conventional, however, both films break the generic mould as well. *Ghost* combines romance with thriller, tragedy and comedy – even farce. The romance plot is played out not between two but three people: Oda May (Whoopi Goldberg) as a spiritual medium can put Sam and Molly in ethereal touch with each other, and becomes a necessary third party.

Reiner's film, based on Nora Ephron's spiky script, is a soufflé whipped up from Woody Allen's stock ingredients: New York's middle class in perpetual interpersonal crisis, and served with a liberal sprinkling of quotations from other films.[6] And in true Allen style it is so centrally concerned with spelling out the trials and tribulations of modern love, post-sexual innocence and post-divorce, that it can be described with equal justification as an anti-romance which is merely masquerading as romantic comedy. Neither film entirely guarantees the satisfaction of a happy ending. In *When Harry Met Sally* eventual happiness is, as Pam Cook notes, tinged with melancholy, and *Ghost*'s conclusion of love eternal and justice done cannot quite compensate for the final separation of the romantic couple.[7]

Changes in the genre of romantic fiction are of course in themselves nothing to write home about. In her article 'Romantic readers', Helen Taylor explains that '... the genre of romance is a complex one with many sub-genres within it'. Taylor sees a role for romance, as an ersatz genre *par excellence*, especially for the late 1980s because of '... the look-don't-touch atmosphere of Aids panic and *Fatal Attraction*'s (1987) warning to would-be adulterers'.[8] In a similar vein, Pam Cook remarks in her review of *When Harry Met Sally* that the '... recent Hollywood revival of romantic ... comedies with their will they/won't they deferral of consummation narratives smacks of contemporary sexual angst'.[9] Taylor points to changes in woman-authored and woman-read romantic fiction, which now give their heroines more worldly power and independent wealth than they used to, and hold out a fantasy of having it all. Whilst Hollywood heroines like Sally and Molly are also of this kind, the fantasy scenarios in popular cinema tend to pose the possibility of losing it all: screen romances are not so much dreams as morality plays for postmodern life, aimed at a mixed audience. Despite all the trappings of consumer culture and a Yuppie lifestyle (terms which date these films exactly in the period between recessions at the turn of the decade), films such as *Ghost* and *When Harry Met Sally* provide little of the wish fulfilment that the written romance genre still has to offer. Romance must, by definition, be removed from everyday life, yet in neither film can the emphasis on and valorisation of true love – the designer interior of psychic life, as it were – provide adequate shelter from the exigencies of contemporary existence. What constantly threatens the elegant order and safety of domestic as well as psychic space and the emotional economy of affluent composure is what is 'out there' – and invisible. In *Ghost* 'out there' is where Sam gets killed, on the streets of Manhattan which, in the style of *The Bonfire of the Vanities* (1990) and *Fatal Attraction*, exude the violence and racial tension of the 'urban jungle' (itself a racist term, of course). *Ghost* is a tale of the city, but as such it could not be further removed from Armistead Maupin's San Francisco where a fabled community of city dwellers can be found behind an anonymous urban facade.[10] New York stories are different: aggressive, competitive and dangerous; murderers lurk in dark corners; street people shout abuse at everybody and at nobody in particular, because – like Sam – everyone has their own phantoms to fight.

In *When Harry Met Sally* 'out there' is also the city, but the city as sexual marketplace: a jungle of hunters and those being hunted, of mating and dating out in the open: hard work for little reward. 'I got married to stop dating', complains Harry to Jesse after his marriage has failed; 'Tell me I'll never have to go out there again', says Marie in recently wedded bliss to her husband, bemoaning Harry and Sally's fate as single people.

It is this representation of 'out there' as well as, of course, the solutions *Ghost* and *When Harry Met Sally* pose in terms of 'in here' which lend both films their reactionary status as cautionary tales. Anxieties about contemporary life (instability, violence, social divisions, sexual angst) are first raised and fostered, only to be ultimately assuaged in ways which seem radically at odds with the dismal world in which they are framed. A closer look at each film's narrative may give a clearer picture of just how dismal this world is, and why its redeeming features have to be fetched from so far and so wide.

Ghost: Race, Romance and Revenge

Ghost is the story of Sam Wheat's premature death, just after he and his lover Molly, a sculptor, have moved in together. The Soho warehouse which they have converted into a stylish apartment-cum-studio represents a utopian space perched high above the mean streets of downtown New York. After a night out at the theatre (*Macbeth* – another ghost story) Sam is murdered by a mugger, Willie Lopez, on the commission of Sam's best friend and colleague at a Wall Street bank, Carl Bruner, who is laundering drugs money. In an out-of-the-body experience Sam watches himself die in Molly's arms. As a ghost who is physically impotent (but nevertheless present on screen throughout as his old all-American self) Sam is desperate to protect Molly from the danger that Bruner now also represents to her. More or less by accident he finds an ally in the real world in Oda May Brown, an African-American con artist who makes money out of people's desire to contact the dead. To her own surprise Oda May is receptive to Sam and can indeed communicate with him; she has 'the gift' after all and is able to help Sam and warn Molly. Together they manage to overcome the latter's disbelief and mistrust and they convince Molly both of Oda May's superior powers and of Sam's existence as a ghost. By way of proof, Sam 'borrows' Oda May's body in order to hold Molly once more. After Sam has learned (from another ghost in the underworld of the subway) that he can regain some of his physical strength through sheer concentration of rage, the three defeat Lopez and Bruner, who die bloody but righteous deaths and are dragged off to hell. Sam vanishes into a starburst of light, his mission on earth accomplished.

It is significant that in this ostensibly ludicrous story the premature death of a young white male is not treated solely as a lovers' tragedy (as, for example, in Anthony Minghella's more or less contemporaneous *Truly, Madly, Deeply* (1991), which is about the process of mourning) but also as a tale of revenge: this death is unjust and unnatural. Sam's rage at the betrayal of his best friend and his patriarchal desire to protect Molly from a similar fate fuel the plot, whilst Oda May's mistrust of white people and their foibles holds it up – and provides comic relief. Even so, it is the inter-racial alliance which makes revenge possible and which shifts attention away both from the heterosexual romance and from the homosocial betrayal. In other words: as bonds between Sam and Carl and Sam and Molly are broken, another (with Oda May) is forged. An early scene at the Wall Street bank prepares the ground for Carl's treachery and raises the spectre of Aids as a subtext, when Sam and Carl perform a comedy double act in the lift. It begins with Carl coughing and ends with all the other passengers moving away from the pair in fear and disgust as Sam extracts from Carl the information that he has a 'highly contagious' disease, which has 'spread to the genitals, everywhere really'. When they leave the lift laughing, Carl says to Sam, who initiated the joke: 'you're sick'.

In her essay 'Pictures of sickness' Martha Gever writes that it is '... the imagery and language of *sickness* – mental, moral, and medical – [that] link the perception of Aids and gay maleness' which the friends enact, by way of a joke, in the lift.[11] Within the logic of the film homosocial 'intercourse' then leads to murder, whereas in real life the major cause of death in young white males in New York City is Aids (street violence kills African-American men in staggering numbers, more than Aids does). Although we all know that Hollywood has little to do with real life, I do think that here, in *Ghost*, we have an example of how it cannot help itself: however studiously avoided as overt subject matter, anxieties about HIV transmission begin to corrode the possibilities of heterosexual romance.

They may be read as explaining why the phallus collapses 'into an ominous heap' (in the words of a reviewer), why male bonding is associated with betrayal and premature death, and why heterosexual love cannot endure except to the exclusion of actual physical intercourse.[12]

The phallic power of all-American Sam Wheat is unequal to the perfidy of his (Jewish, naturally) banker friend and his underworld (Puerto Rican) associates. He has to enlist a black woman in his service, depicted as a bag-lady who talks incessantly to herself (though really, as we know, to our invisible hero), in order to fulfil his patriarchal mission. The triangulation of romance, racial difference and the return of the white male avenger then is steeped in racial and gender stereotyping. As Oda May Brown, Whoopi Goldberg tries hard to be bigger than her part in this lily-white romance. In repeating the performance she gave in *Jumping Jack Flash* (1986), where she parodied stereotypical images of the African-American woman by improvising and ad-libbing, Goldberg highlights the status of her comedy as self-conscious minstrelsy.[13] Within the limits of this film text, however, such self-parody becomes rapidly self-defeating; the subversive potential of her persona gets lost in the course of the narrative and is sutured into a conciliatory ending in which racial difference is transcended. *Ghost*'s ideological charge as a narrative of patriarchal romance with homophobic Aids-related overtones then is, in fact, gradually displaced on to the sphere of race relations and turned into a 'race romance' in which new alliances are possible.[14] As Patrick Swayze says in the promotional interview which precedes the video version of the film: 'It doesn't matter who you are, black or white, love is what's important.' Nor is it insignificant that in that promotional interview, it is not Swayze and Moore but Goldberg and Swayze who are billed as the stars of *Ghost*. Preaching the film's message of belief in life after death and eternal love, it is they who are portrayed as the romantic couple – a marketing ploy which pre-interprets the video version as a 'race romance' in a way that was absent from the film's cinema release. At the end of the interview, the screen goes blank and we hear Whoopi Goldberg's voice: 'It'll make you *feel* better.' But what should *Ghost* make 'us' feel better *about*, exactly? A world of intimate betrayal for material gain, street violence, no-go areas in the city where you live and murderous intrigue in your place of work? Belief in ghosts or 'lurve' seems hardly an adequate cure for such ills. On the face of it *Ghost*, like Mills and Boone's romantic fiction, is, in Germaine Greer's words, merely 'dope for dopes': it'll make you feel better, before it makes you feel worse.

In *The Political Unconscious* Fredric Jameson critiques such a reading of mass culture which sees the viewer as 'some inert and passive material' manipulated by the ideological machinations of a hegemonic culture industry. Jameson continues:

Yet it does not take much reflection to see that a process of compensatory exchange must be involved here, in which the henceforth manipulated viewer is offered specific gratifications for his or her consent to passivity. In other words, if the ideological function of mass culture is understood as a process whereby otherwise dangerous or protopolitical impulses are 'managed' and defused, rechanneled and offered spurious objects, then some preliminary step must also be theorized in which these same impulses – the raw material upon which the process works – are initially awakened within the very text that seeks to still them ... the function of the mass cultural text ... must necessarily involve a complex strategy of rhetorical persuasion in which substantial incentives are offered for ideological adherence. We will say that such incentives, as well as the impulses to be managed by the mass cultural text, are necessarily Utopian in nature.[15]

I am using Jameson's ideas here to explain the massive popularity of films like *Ghost* and *When Harry Met Sally* and also to dig a little deeper into the 'otherwise dangerous and protopolitical impulses' that he mentions. I have already suggested that the representation of urban life 'out there' in both films is so riddled with anxieties that they may qualify as symptoms of such protopolitical impulses, but I have also indicated that in *Ghost* there is something rather more specific at stake, which displaces issues of Aids and mourning on to those of race and revenge. In so doing, it cannot help but show how circumscribed the possibilities for heterosexual romance have become in the Aids era.

When Harry Met Sally: It Had to be They in the Old-fashioned Way

Where *Ghost* is a good example of a mass culture text which awakens fears at the same time as it tries to still them (through the revenge motif and what I have termed the 'race romance'), *When Harry Met Sally* purports to offer a prophylactic for such spilling over of Aids fears into heterosexual romance. Reiner's film heralds the return to a reactionary sexual morality which is supposed to shield against the dangers of the sexual world outside marriage – dangers which we may read as HIV 'incontinence'. The narrative is simple: after graduation from the University of Chicago in 1977 Harry and Sally meet for the first time when, by way of a 'marriage of convenience', they drive home to New York together and discuss life, sex and future plans only to find that they disagree about everything. They part and get on with their lives. Five years later they meet accidentally on an aeroplane, rehearse the same arguments once again, and part again. Over the next five years Harry gets married and divorced, Sally engaged and split up. Gradually the two – now both living in New York – develop an intimate friendship in which they encourage and support each other in their exploits on the sexual playing field, until their own best friends marry each other and they are left out on a limb ('out there', as yet unmated). Eleven years after their first meeting in Chicago (we are now in 1988) they have sex for the first time and decide it 'destroys the friendship'; a year on they are both convinced that 'it had to be you' (the insistent theme song for the film) after all and all along.

Straightforward enough: boy meets girl and the rest is history, except that here it takes a little bit longer than usual. But there is more. Harry's and Sally's meetings and partings in what is essentially a conventional sexual comedy mode turned awry ('a problematic love story in which the couple concerned wouldn't know romance if it hit them in the face' ((Martin Sutton)) are interspersed with very short, very different scenes in which unidentified older couples of their parents' generation talk on camera about how they met, and how their love has endured.[16]

These love stories present several varieties of what remains, nevertheless, it-had-to-be-you classic romance: love at first sight; marrying a high school sweetheart after a 34-year delay; marrying the same person twice; growing up on the same block but meeting only twenty years later in another city, and so on. The mock-autobiographical simplicity and documentary directness of these interludes makes Harry's and Sally's narrative look artificial and needlessly complicated. Several of the reviewers of the film read them as ironic contrasts between old-fashioned, innocent or – conversely – knowing romance and the difficulty and evanescence of 1980s' relationships.[17] But this contrast, as it turns out, is a false one. What happens in the end and after all is that Harry and Sally are sutured into this 'authentic' autobiographical space of true love as an endurance test. The implication is that *this* – passing the test – is the happy ending: not whirlwind romance, passion and sexual pleasure but monogamy, stability and shelter. This is significant as a version of romance for the Aids era. For it is not as if Harry and Sally learn anything new (about themselves, the world or each other) in their twelve years of apprenticeship to love as safe sex. It is, rather, a time for them to get desperate enough so that they finally give in to each other, having established a long history in which they discover that sex isn't everything, that there is nothing and nobody else worthwhile 'out there'.

In *When Harry Met Sally* our ideological adherence to the idea of a romantic, enduring monogamous marriage is purchased at the price of the utopia of the sexual revolution, of diverse and exploratory sexual relationships on the continuum of Armistead Maupin's community of friends and lovers. It seems that *When Harry Met Sally* offers, in Jameson's terms, mere 'gratification in return for submission to passivity' in the comfort of knowing that there is no alternative: it had to be you, you, nobody else but you. And, as Pam Cook wryly comments: 'Why fake orgasms should even exist is the awkward question lurking beneath this film's light-hearted veneer.'[18]

Yearnings: Is That All There Is?

The comfort of monogamous marriage in *When Harry Met Sally* or justice and eternal love in *Ghost* are, however, not quite enough in an era which has known alternatives within living memory and which continues to dream of a world in which real connections (within and across gender, race and class divisions beyond romantic coupledom) are possible. In both films it is, I believe, that desire for connection which, however deeply buried under a thick layer of platitudes and conventional wisdom about life, love and death, can be unearthed as Jameson's Utopian impulse. In *Ghost*, unearthing is the appropriate term in the sense that the film very consciously plays on the spiritual longings of a secular age. Its impossible love affair leaves a sadness which goes beyond nostalgia for the good old days of 1980s advertising when a true Yuppie romance could be enjoyed untainted by the pressures and the violence, indeed the *disease*, of contemporary urban life.[19] The sadness also elicits, above and beyond consumerism and sentimentality, a yearning for what Dick Hebdige calls in his seminal article on postmodernism, 'The bottom line on Planet One', the 'depth words' like love and hate and faith and history, words which 'will return like ghosts'. Hebdige characterises the difference between postmodernity (Planet Two) and modernity (Planet One) in the by now familiar terms of word versus image, signified versus signifier, depth versus surface. But with the metaphor of monogamy versus cruising he then delineates the same difference in ways of seeing and reading: by cruising, the 'reader' can take pleasure in a text without being obliged at the same time to take marriage vows and a mortgage on a house. And this separation of pleasure/use value from any pledge/commitment to 'love honour and obey' the diktats of the text constitutes the 'epistemological break' which divides Planet One from Planet Two and which sets up a field of alternating currents of attraction and repulsion between them.[20]

In both *Ghost* and *When Harry Met Sally* we have, I think, instances of such alternating currents of attraction and revulsion between Planets One and Two. And this is more than just a matter of the reader's freedom, or 'choice', to see a sex comedy and a revenge narrative rather than cautionary tales about Aids and life in the inner city. It is, rather, a case of Utopian impulses in both films which try to bridge the gap between postmodern *anomie* and outmoded value systems by articulating a desire for connection in inter-racial bonding and stable heterosexual romance.

In *When Harry Met Sally* the older couples speak the depth words of Planet One, whilst Harry and Sally are firmly located on Planet Two where such words have little meaning. It is only when they gain a certain materiality as *history* however, in their tried and tested partnership against what is 'out there', that the depth words can resurface – like Hebdige's ghosts – and gain a significance in the 'Now' and the 'in here'. Whatever its reactionary connotations, Harry and Sally's flight into monogamous marriage is also the signifier of a Utopian desire for continuity and connection between two eras or generations (theirs and their parents', post- and pre-Aids) as much as between two individuals.

In *Ghost*, as I have already indicated, this Utopian impulse lies rather more complicatedly in a desire for racial conciliation as well as heterosexual romance. Oda May Brown, the African-American medium, mediates not only between the dead and the living but also between the white man and the white woman, and indeed between the different worlds of hellish, street-level Brooklyn and Manhattan's lofty interior spaces where the beautiful people dwell. In the scene where Sam 'borrows' Oda May's body to touch and hold Molly once more, the African-American woman becomes literally the conduit of sexual and emotional energies which can no longer be transmitted by real, white, heterosexual bodies. And that notion of transmission first of all conjures up the earlier scene in the lift between Sam and Carl, and second, it stands in contrast to those episodes where Carl tries to get close to Molly and which always signal danger. The other woman, Oda May, is by this means designated safe, whilst the other man (Bruner or Lopez) is always unsafe. A reading which focuses purely on this scene's homophobic avoidance of a lesbian embrace by placing Oda May out of the frame and substituting Sam's image for hers, therefore ignores two important things. What you get, here, is rather more than what you see: Oda May 'becomes' Sam, but by the same token Sam is 'really' Oda May – the image of the black and white woman's hands entwined is a reminder of this. Second, the enactment of a white man 'invading' a black woman's body, with all the connotations of inter-racial rape and miscegenation that entails, is refused just as is the lesbian embrace.[21] We can then read Sam's 'borrowing' of Oda May's body to touch Molly as the literalisation of *Ghost*'s race/gender romance, rather than see it merely as the unambiguously homophobic and racist image that most reviewers and critics have taken it to be.

Oda May's permeable body is only one of a whole series of images of crossable boundaries in the film. From the demolition work at the beginning (in which Sam, Molly and Carl are seen breaking down walls and ceilings with unmistakable sexual connotation, whilst wearing surgical masks and gloves) and Sam's walking 'through' a subway gate (which goes 'through' him) to Willie Lopez' breaking into Molly's apartment and stalking her with the implied threat of sexual assault, *Ghost* is full of images of vulnerable bodies and buildings, of breaking and entering. Oda May's appearance in the Wall Street bank is in a way another instance of it, since it is quite clear that as a black woman from Brooklyn she 'has no business being there'.[22] Sam and Oda May enter into each other's homes and territories and this, we are led to believe, fosters the bond between them. The one who remains isolated, indoors and intact is Molly who, as the stereotypical white-woman-on-a-pedestal, has to be shielded from both the world of money (Carl) and that of street violence represented by Willie Lopez, the Puerto Rican male Other. Molly thus echoes the frail, domesticated figure of Miss Ann, the white mistress of slavery times. It is Oda May who through her eventual friendship with Molly diverts the narrative from its covertly racist track and turns it into its opposite: a race romance clinched in the image of white and black women's hands entwined.

Although it is clear that the friendship will not endure and is indeed little more than a temporary alliance enabling Sam to finish his unfinished business on earth, Oda May fulfils narratively the same role that the angel statue of the beginning of the movie plays symbolically. This statue, which sweeps in through the window and is perilously embraced by Sam hovering on the ledge, is the guardian angel of Christian lore. It is, as such, already connected to Oda May through a spiritual association of ancient religious tradition and wisdom, part of Hebdige's 'depth dimension'. At the symbolic and metaphysical level then, *Ghost* reconciles, in a typically postmodern move, not only African-American women with whites but also the Christian religious tradition of heaven and hell with that of African-American folk spirituality. The film here draws on the African-American belief (which also underlies Toni Morrison's *Beloved* (1989)) that the spirit of a murder victim can find no rest until it has avenged itself for the injustice done to it. The outmoded and childish idea of a guardian angel is here revamped for a contemporary, secular and heterogeneous audience (which sees the angel first introduced as nothing more than a fixture of interior decoration) with the help of an equally ancient but 'exotic' belief system to enable its work of vengeance and protection.

Ghost begins to tell a story in which 'sickness', premature death, greed and violence are collapsed together as threats which cross material and physical boundaries and unsettle the security of segregated affluent existence. But in the unbeatable combination of (Sam) Wheat and (Oda May) Brown, Christian and African-American lore then pushes it back into a conventional narrative in which those boundaries are reassuringly restored and made solid again. Carl's death, straddling the windowsill, pierced by an enormous shard of glass, not only mirrors Sam's position in 'rescuing' the angel statue, it also sums up his status as originary evil perched on the edge between inside and outside, destroyed by the very invisible barrier which he broke in the first place. The spectre of AIDS, raised earlier in the film in connection with Carl and already displaced by the revenge motif, is by this means at once reasserted and dispelled for good.

Paul Julian Smith asks in a review of Derek Jarman's Aids film *Blue* (1993): 'How can film represent an invisible virus whose transmission cannot be seen and whose carriers have been subject to hostile surveillance and revelation?'[23] In arthouse cinema, *Blue* is one answer (a blank, blue screen), but in popular film what happens in *Ghost* and *When Harry Met Sally* is another: subtext, metaphor and displacement on to the 'depth dimension' of ancient romantic and spiritual traditions. I think that, at some subliminal level, *Ghost* as a revenge narrative makes it possible for young audiences living in a profoundly materialistic and secular, but also deeply insecure, culture, to rehearse the scenario of seeing friends and lovers die before their time and project it on to a familiar narrative of villainy versus innocence. As a film of impossible romance and temporary inter-racial solidarity as well as mourning and loss, however, it confronts viewers also with metaphysical yearnings they might not know they had and which their postmodern life experience has not prepared them for; yearnings which, like ghosts, 'come back in the 11th hour to haunt the Second World and those who try to live there in the Now'.[24]

Hollywood in the Aids Era. Crisis? What Crisis?

In her contribution to the special issue of *October* devoted to Aids, Paula Treichler explores the multiple connotations of the Aids epidemic in the continuum of popular and bio-medical discourse, and gives examples of what she calls 'the epidemic of signification' around Aids. Treichler notes how HIV, in its punitive associations as an act of God, 'has come to represent the moment of truth for the sexual revolution', how it has come to be seen by the popular media as a 'Viral Terminator'.[25] It is no accident that Treichler uses a cinematic reference here; Hollywood has been a significant factor in the Aids debate for several years now, if only because of its sins of omission. The furore which greeted films about serial killers in the early 1990s for example (*Silence of the Lambs* (1990)), *Basic Instinct* (1991)) was inspired by Hollywood's homophobia and its willing association of homosexuals/transsexuals/lesbians with serial murder. The discursive link, much as film-makers would like to deny it, lies in the HIV virus as a 'serial killer'. Besides, as Leo Bersani points out in *October* (citing Simon Watney), gay men are themselves widely perceived as killers in that 'their behaviour is seen as the source and cause of Aids'.[26]

    Gay protests against such films as *Silence of the Lambs* and *Basic Instinct* have highlighted, besides negative stereotyping, Hollywood's refusal to address the Aids crisis at all. On one hand this is not surprising, since Hollywood has always been sluggish in dealing with contemporary social issues (it took fifteen years for films about Vietnam to be made, for example), but on the other hand it is all the more reprehensible because Aids has taken more than its proportionate toll upon people working in the film industry. Yet to date Aids has largely been addressed in documentary and educational films, distributed on video, mostly independently produced by gay activists. The same is true of features like *Buddies* (Arthur Bressan Jr., 1985), *Parting Glances* (Bill Sherwood, 1985) and *Long-time Companion* (Norman Rene, 1990) which, made-for-TV, were the first to reach a wider audience. Hollywood productions on Aids such as Jonathan Demme's *Philadelphia* (1993) were released in

1993–4, ten years after the potential scale of an Aids epidemic first became clear.

Yet to note that Hollywood's homophobia has led it to skirt around Aids is not to say that audiences, reviewers and critics have not been aware of its implicit presence in popular cinema. *Fatal Attraction* was widely (and rather unconvincingly) reviewed as one of the first mainstream films to be surreptitiously 'about' Aids; *Dracula* was read in no uncertain Aids terms.[27]

I have suggested here that there was a moment in popular cinema in 1989/90 which was haunted by the spectre of AIDS in a rather different way – unstated, unacknowledged, highly implicit yet there for all to see – if you wanted to see it. Popular film, in my view, started to take its cues from the Aids crisis, including the crisis in representation, long before it would openly acknowledge it. This took two forms, broadly speaking, organised around the themes of monogamy on one hand and mourning on the other. First of all was the moralistic and culturally conservative message that the gains of the sexual revolution were now exacting punishment, of which Aids was one. The remedy: sexual restraint, monogamy, and real loving relationships. This, as we have seen, is the message of *When Harry Met Sally*'s romantic anti-romance, in which Aids is never mentioned. That no one has made that connection is largely due, I suspect, to its generic conformism (its 'light-hearted veneer' in Pam Cook's words), but also to the fact that Rob Reiner in his round of publicity interviews for the film insisted on its autobiographical meanings: *When Harry Met Sally* was purportedly based on his and Nora Ephron's experiences of being 'between marriages' (tellingly, this is what being single means). Furthermore, in an interview with *American Film* Billy Crystal, who plays Harry, is also drawn into this orbit of autobiographical signification. Such publicity strategies tend to close the circle of possible readings and limit them to a prurient interest in actors' and directors' private lives.[28] Intertextually, however, this ploy does not quite succeed. For audiences familiar with Larry Kramer's play *The Normal Heart*, which issued a similar monogamic message to the gay community, *When Harry Met Sally* has a different inflection. The film plays, after all, with models of sexual pleasure and fulfilment which are not confined to heterosexual practice: Harry, the would-be playboy, has more in common with a gay cruising style of sexuality than with Sally's supposedly feminine ideal of sex-in-a-loving-relationship. He has to learn not so much the rewards of monogamy as the danger of and 'emptiness' of its opposite: promiscuity, just like the men in Kramer's play.[29]

Second, implicit Aids representation took the form of a fascination with premature death and mourning. There was a whole spate of films at the turn of the decade which speculate about life after death and out of the body experiences. In *Ghost*, in the British productions *Truly, Madly, Deeply* (1991) and *Dead Again* (1991), as well as in *Flatliners* (1990), young white and heterosexual people (predominantly, but not exclusively males) die prematurely or experiment with death as the final frontier which has to be conquered, tested, crossed and recrossed. In *Ghost* and *Truly, Madly, Deeply* (one of whose 'ghosts' is indeed an Aids victim) the theme of mourning the death of a lover is intertwined with an idealised view of (true) love, as if the truth of romance can only be proven from beyond the grave. This was more than just a variation on a familiar theme (or, as one reviewer said about *Ghost*: 'an object lesson in how to breathe new life into moribund material').[30] These films were, after all, not much like the conventional Gothic or horror movie; in *Ghost* the 'suspense' blast of loud music which accompanies the credit sequence is completely misplaced, since the ensuing narrative does not fulfil any such expectation of shock horror. When read in the context of the Aids crisis, the 'benevolent ghost' films make sense not just as genre entertainment but as symptoms of how Hollywood suffers from, and deals with, the 'epidemic of signification' surrounding Aids.

It is by contrast with films such as *Long-time Companion*, which does not attempt to repress, displace or reach for spiritual transcendence, that *Ghost* and *When Harry Met Sally* come into perspective as romances which are affected by the Aids crisis, but whose immune systems to the pressures of the real world go into overdrive without quite succeeding in warding off infection. *Long-time Companion* follows a fictional set of gay characters in California, from the early days of 'gay plague' scare stories through to the late 1980s, when the circle of friends is significantly diminished as a result of the ravages of Aids. The work of mourning is here represented as beginning long before people die a painful and undignified death. And it is represented *as work*, inextricably connected with caring for the sick and coming to terms with the loss of lovers and friends – as well as one's own life, potentially. Whatever the legitimate criticism which can be levelled at *Long-time Companion* as an idealised and glamorised view of the gay community, its appearance on national television was a welcome and important counter-balance to Aids reporting in the non-gay press.[31] What is, perhaps, most striking about *Long-time Companion* is its treatment of collective responsibility and care; this is a romance of 'community' which allows diverse modes of relationship from monogamous coupling to sexual friendship, serial monogamy and cruising, and which does not shirk the hard times of physical deterioration, dependency and death – including the death, in effect, of the pleasure culture.

Long-time Companion came out of gay culture, but also addresses itself to a heterosexual audience and confronts the so-called general public with a positive image – in spite of the film's subject matter – of sexual pleasure, kinship and friendship on the kind of continuum which is entirely absent from films such as *Ghost* and *When Harry Met Sally*. This is no mean achievement. By comparison then, *Ghost* has little to say about mourning except in the most facile of ways ('love lasts forever'), whilst the long-drawn-out build-up to monogamous resolution in *When Harry Met Sally* does nothing more than refashion passionlessness in love as safe sex. But, as Douglas Crimp points out: 'monogamy per se provides no protection against a virus that might already have infected one partner in a relationship'; the question of what love's got to do with it may have a negative answer.[32]

As cautionary tales *Ghost* and *When Harry Met Sally* avoid the real issue of HIV education, solidarity, and the legacy of the sexual revolution; each seeks the ideological consent on the part of its audience to a view of the world in which individualism reigns supreme and socio-political problems cannot be confronted, but only 'transcended' in the sphere of romantic and spiritual fantasy. Nor can this, of course, be a surprise, but it is worth stating that both films are products of popular culture which address contemporary anxieties around (hetero)sexuality in a way which both evokes romantic conventions and rewrites them at the same time, but under pressure. Neither can confront the Aids crisis explicitly, yet both can be read as informed by Aids' 'epidemic of signification' spilling over into heterosexual Hollywood romance. Whilst remaining committed to true love, this love is always already circumscribed by a view of the contemporary world as alien, violent and suffused with invisible dangers, lurking 'out there'.

Our earlier question of what the ersatz satisfaction that the fake sex of *Ghost* and *When Harry Met Sally* affords might be in aid of is finally answered by Sander L. Gilman when he states:

It is in the world of representations that we manage our fear of disease, isolating it as surely as if we had placed it in quarantine. But with such isolation, these icons remain visible to all of us, proof that we are still whole, healthy and sane; that we are not different, diseased or mad.[33]

Notes

1 Cited in Louise Tanner, 'Adrian Lyne and Patricia Rozema', *Films in Review* (December, 1987) p. 599.
2 Dick Hebdige, 'The bottom line on Planet One', in Philip Rice and Patricia Waugh (eds) *Modern Literary Theory: a Reader* (London: Edward Arnold, 1989), p. 281.
3 Paul Julian Smith, 'Review of Derek Harmnan's *Blue*', *Sight and Sound* (October, 1993), p. 18.
4 For a discussion of *Fatal Attraction* in relation to 1980s' media scares about women's biological clocks, see Susan Faludi's *Backlash: The Undeclared War Against Women* (London: Chatto and Windus, 1992) Chapters 4 and 5 (pp. 99–170).
5 Tania Modleski, *Loving With a Vengeance: Mass-Produced Fantasies for Women* (London: Methuen, 1982), p. 36.
6 For example: the split screen technique which is used several times in *When Harry Met Sally* is taken from *Pillow Talk* (1959), then pastiched as the screen splits four ways

instead of just two. There are several references to Allen's *Annie Hall* (1977) and, in particular, *Manhattan* (1979). And of course there are Harry and Sally's own discussions of that classic movie of ambivalent romance, *Casablanca* (1942).

7   Pam Cook, 'Review of *When Harry Met Sally*', *Monthly Film Bulletin*, Vol. 56, No. 671 (December, 1989), p. 378.

8   Helen Taylor, 'Romantic readers', in Helen Carr (ed.), *From My Guy to Sci Fi: Genre and Women's Writing in the Postmodern World* (London: Pandora, 1989) pp. 59, 58.

9   Pam Cook, 'Review of *When Harry Met Sally*', p. 378.

10 Armistead Maupin, *Tales of the City*, (London: Corgi, 1980). There are four further books in this series.

11 Martha Gever, 'Pictures of sickness: Stuart Marshall's *Bright Eyes*', *October*, No. 43 (Winter, 1987), p. 165.

12 Tom Milne, 'Review of *Ghost*', *Monthly Film Bulletin* Vol. 57, No. 681 (October, 1990), p. 296.

13 See also Tania Modleski's discussion of Goldberg in Chapter 7 of *Feminism without Women: Culture and Criticism in a 'Postfeminist' Age* (London: Routledge, 1991), pp. 131–3.

14 Interestingly, in Jonathan Demme's *Philadelphia*, which is about a gay white man with Aids who sues his law firm for unfair dismissal and has his case successfully fought by a black lawyer, we see a similar conjunction between (what is in the film constructed as) a revenge narrative enabled by an inter-racial alliance. In this case also the film cannot actually address the reality of Aids suffering (even if it purportedly forces us to stare it in the face in the shape of Kaposi's syndrome in endless and oppressive close-up of Tom Hanks) but displaces the issue on to the racial and homosocial dynamics of the relationship between Tom Hanks and Denzel Washington.

15 Fredric Jameson, *The Political Unconscious: Narrative as a Socially Symbolic Act* (London: Methuen, 1981), p. 287.

16 Martin Sutton, 'Review of *When Harry Met Sally*', *Films and Filming*, No. 422 (December, 1989), p. 50.

17 Martin Sutton writes for example in his review that the older couples 'can see love for what it is' and that the interludes provide images of 'steadfast, mature and battle-scarred affection which only old people have arrived at'. (p. 50) Pam Cook reads the interludes differently and remarks, rather more accurately than Sutton, that 'aged couples testify to the enduring power of love'. Even so, she concludes that the film demonstrates that the 'age of the romantic couple is over', which overlooks Sally and Harry's only mildly ironic regression to that age in the final sequence of the film (when we see them as a 'mature' couple): Pam Cook, 'review of *When Harry Met Sally*', p. 378.

18 Pam Cook, 'Review of *When Harry Met Sally*', p. 378.

19 *Ghost* uses many of the images and styles of 1980s' advertisements (specifically those drawing upon Gothic conventions), for example in the pottery scene which looks as if it was modelled on a Levi's commercial.

20 Dick Hebdige, 'The bottom line', p. 267.

21 This is significant, especially by contrast with an earlier occasion in Oda May's shop, when a black man *is* seen to invade, as a spirit, Oda May's body.

22 The same is true of Sam's forays into her and Willie Lopez' neighbourhood, but nothing is made of that: the white man has a 'right' to be anywhere.

23 See note 3.

24 Hebdidge, 'The bottom line'.

25 Paula Treichler, 'Aids, homophobia, and biomedical discourse: an epidemic of signification', *October*, No. 43 (Winter, 1987), p. 67.

26 Leo Bersani, 'Is the rectum a grave?', *October*, No. 43 (Winter, 1987), p. 211.

27 See for a good survey of Hollywood's treatment of gay issues in the late 1980s and early 1990s the Channel 4 documentary *Homophobia in Hollywood*, broadcast in 1992.

28   Marianne Gray, 'Interview with Rob Reiner', *Films and Filming*, No. 422 (December 1989), p. 14–17; Robert Lloyd, 'Interview with Rob Reiner and Billy Crystal', *American Film*, Vol. 14, No. 9 (July/August, 1989), pp. 28–33, 48.

29   See for a discussion of Kramer's sexual politics in *The Normal Heart*, Douglas Crimp, 'How to have promiscuity in an epidemic', *October*, No. 43 (Winter, 1987), pp. 246–8.

30   Tom Milne, 'Review of *Ghost*, p. 296.

31   Jan Zita Grover, for example, critiques the very phrase 'gay community' because 'the people characterized as the *gay/homosexual community* are too diverse politically, economically, demographically to be described meaningfully by such a term'. Jan Zita Grover, 'Aids: Keywords', *October*, No. 43 (Winter, 1987), p. 24. In 'Modern diseases: gay self-representation in the age of Aids' Bryan Bruce complains that gay self-representation is also often stereotyped; the gay-produced video *Chance of a Lifetime* for example has only white, middle-class, hedonistic characters and uses heterosexual romantic coupling as a model. To some extent, that criticism could be levelled at *Long-time Companion* too. Bryan Bruce, 'Modern diseases: gay self-representation in the age of Aids', *Cine Action!*, No. 15 (Winter, 1988–9) p. 34.

32   Douglas Crimp, 'How to have promiscuity', p. 247.

33   Sander L. Gilman, 'Aids and Syphilis: the iconography of disease' *October*, No. 43 (Winter, 1987), p. 107.

Filmography

Annie Hall (dir. Woody Allen, 1977).

Basic Instinct (dir. Paul Veerhoeven, 1992).

Blue (dir. Derek Jarman, 1993).

Bonfire of the Vanities (dir. Brian de Palma, 1990).

Bram Stoker's Dracula (dir. Francis Ford Coppola, 1992).

Casablanca (dir. Michael Curtiz, 1942).

Dead Aagin (dir. Kenneth Branagh, 1991).

Fatal Attraction (dir. Adrian Lyne, 1987).

Flatliners (dir. Joel Schumacher, 1990).

Ghost (dir. Jerry Zucker, 1990).

Jumpin' Jack Flash (dir. Penny Marshall, 1986).

Long-time Companion (dir. Norman Rene, 1990).

Love Story (dir. Arthur Hiller, 1970).

Manhattan (dir. Woody Allen, 1979).

Philadelphia (dir. Jonathan Demme, 1993).

Pillow Talk (dir. Michael Gordon, 1959).

Romeo and Juliet (dir. Baz Luhrman, 1996).

Silence of the Lambs (dir. Jonathan Demme, 1990).

Truly, Madly, Deeply (dir. Anthony Minghella, 1991).

When Harry Met Sally (dir. Rob Reiner, 1989).

3

Patsy Stoneman

Jane Eyre in Later Lives: Intertextual Strategies in Women's Self-Definition

'No one who had ever seen Catherine Morland in her infancy would have supposed her born to be a heroine.' The opening of Jane Austen's *Northanger Abbey* (1818) offers a challenge to an earlier literary convention that a heroine should be beautiful, good and accomplished, an ideal to be aspired to rather than the real, dirty, ignorant girl Catherine Morland proves to be. The debate was still vigorous in the 1840s when Charlotte Brontë protested to her sisters that she would take a heroine as small and plain as herself and make her as interesting as the most beautiful and accomplished heroine of conventional fiction.[1] Both the 'idealist' and the 'realist' approaches to literature, however, are based on a mirror-like concept of the reading process. The 'idealists' assumed that the reader, by identifying with an image of perfection, would become more perfect herself. The 'realists', on the other hand, assumed that readers needed above all confirmation of their own imperfect existence.

Ideals, of course, are themselves subject to historical change; Charlotte Brontë's 'realist' heroine has become an ideal of non-conformity for later readers. Valerie Grosvenor Myer argues that 'Jane Eyre has been an inspiration and example to generations of clever girls ... She is the first defiantly intellectual heroine in English literature.'[2] Her defiance, moreover, is as important as her intellect. The playbill for a Children's Theatre Company production of *young jane eyre* in Minneapolis (1988) reads:

> ... ten-year-old Jane is thrust into a frightening ... orphanage. But the waif's spirit does not succumb. A passionate testament to the courage and fortitude of youth, the power of love, and the eternal promise of a brighter tomorrow.[3]

This 'testament', moreover, speaks beyond the white Anglo-Saxon world. Patricia Duncker quotes O. C. Ogunyemi as evidence that *Jane Eyre* as a 'feminist utopia is for white women only'; but Maya Angelou writes:

... when I read the Brontës, I was a small black girl in the dirt roads of Arkansas during the depression. The society was against me surviving at all, but when I read about Heathcliffe [sic] and Jane Eyre, white society in that mean town had no power against me.

Tsitsi Dangarembga's heroine Tambudzai, a black child in Rhodesia, also 'read everything from Enid Blyton to the Brontë sisters, and responded to them all ... Thus', she says, 'began the period of my reincarnation'. In the Brontë Parsonage Museum at Haworth there is a hand-written comment from a Japanese woman called Hideko Maki on a Japanese stage production of *Jane Eyre*; she likes the production because the woman director, Kazue Kontaibo, 'has the same feeling on Jane Eyre, Charlotte Brontë as I have: She respects and loves Jane (Charlotte)'s dauntless, bracing way of life'. Barbara T. Christian, a black Caribbean woman, shares this response:

Disturbed as I was by Brontë's portrayal of Bertha, I nonetheless loved *Jane Eyre* and identified with plain Jane ... Despite the cultural differences between her world and mine ... I saw that her life too was sharply constrained ... Jane and I shared something in common, even as the mores of her society, even as the physical geography of her world were alien to me.[4]

The need for identification with literary models lies behind the 1970s phase of feminist literary criticism known as 'Images of Women' criticism. Arlyn Diamond, in *The Authority of Experience*, asks for 'authentic' pictures of women's lives, because she cannot 'recognise [her]self, or the women I know' in the female characters of male writers. 'Authenticity', however, easily shades into idealism: Cheri Register, writing in 1975, asks that 'A literary work should provide *role-models*, instill a positive sense of feminine identity by portraying women who are "self-actualising, whose identities are not dependent on men"'.' Maurianne Adams, in *The Authority of Experience*, actually quotes a famous passage of *Jane Eyre* – 'women feel just as men feel; they need exercise for their faculties and a field for their efforts as much as their brothers do' – to prove precisely this point. This 'authentic realism' movement was partly discredited in the 1980s by post-structuralist critics who found the 'mirror theory' of literature naive. Toril Moi, for instance, compares it with the misguided aims of socialist realism: 'instead of strong happy tractor drivers ... we are now presumably, to demand strong happy *women* tractor drivers'.[5]

Maurianne Adams's model of reading is not, however, a static one: 'Every time we rethink and reassimilate *Jane Eyre*', she writes, 'we bring to it a new orientation.' Adult rereading of *Jane Eyre* is 'unnerving', she says, because we do not encounter the same novel which 'we were engrossed by in our teens or preteens, when we saw in Jane's dreadful childhood ... our own fantasies of feeling unloved and forever unloveable'. As adult women, for instance, we have to come to terms with the precise kind of 'happy ending' offered by the novel. Each of the women I quoted as making Jane Eyre her heroine has, in fact, made a complicated negotiation between recognition and 'unnerving' difference. Pat Macpherson, for instance, considers how Jane can be a 'heroine' both for her and for her students twenty years later; she concludes that:

> ... what [my students] and I shared in *Jane Eyre* was a reading of ourselves, present-to-future, that half-described and half-prescribed our course out of lost girlhood to the resting place of fulfilled womanhood ... From real women we learn ... the limits of female space and power in the world as it presently is constituted ... From fiction, we learn how far we might push the limits of our own space and power.

For Barbara T. Christian this negotiation of sameness and difference extends over race and culture as well as over time:

> ... to read is not only to validate the self but also to participate in 'the other's' view of the world, the writer's view. Or why read? Writing and reading are means by which we communicate with one another, as Audre Lorde would say, 'bridge the joinings'.[6]

Maggie Berg, in her book, *Jane Eyre, Portrait of a Life*, argues that *Jane Eyre* itself provides a model for this process of negotiation. 'In the red-room', Berg argues, 'Jane sees herself as a rebellious slave, a hunger striker, the "scape-goat of the nursery" ... "No doubt", says the autobiographer [Jane] in retrospect, "I was a precocious actress".' Jane's 'self-dramatisation' here is equivalent to her looking into literary mirrors for an image of herself, just as Angelou, Dangarembga, Maki, Kontaibo, Christian and Macpherson look into *Jane Eyre*. 'This first identification of oneself in a mirror', Berg goes on,

> is regarded by Jacques Lacan as the most decisive stage in human development, constituting the awareness of oneself as an object of knowledge. Although the reflection is a misrepresentation, because static, it nevertheless confers the mark of adulthood: self-consciousness.

It is from this position of self-consciousness, achieved through repeated part-mirrorings of her self, that Jane is able to contribute to the symbolic construction of her identity. As Berg puts it, 'that Jane is the author of her own story is the single most important yet most neglected aspect of the novel'.[7]

In the rest of this chapter I want to argue that although readers may not consciously register the importance of Jane's status as author of her own story, the control of narrative plays a crucial part in the process of self-definition in those women's texts in which *Jane Eyre* functions as 'intertextual archetype', and that this is true whether we look at relatively sophisticated examples of twentieth-century texts by women or more popular writing.[8] All the texts I shall discuss confirm Maggie Berg's perception that Jane's significant legacy lies *not in her attainment of the object of her desire – experience or love – but in her control of the process of writing.* Moreover, they suggest that women's self-definition is a process in which the 'mirrors' which they look for in older texts sometimes turn monstrous, so that the writer must use language to separate herself from these mothers or sisters who are at the same time too much like themselves and too horribly unlike what they want to be. The aggressive aspects of this process are present even without reference to Bertha Mason, Jane's mirror and monster within Charlotte Brontë's text. Bertha does not figure in this chapter because my focal texts do not themselves refer to her. This 'not-said' is of course important, but to say it would make a different argument.

The Game, by A. S. Byatt (1967), and *The Waterfall* by Margaret Drabble (1969), were each written by a woman who, like Charlotte Brontë, shared a childhood fantasy world with siblings. Byatt and Drabble are sisters who appear, fictionally transformed, in each other's novels; in Byatt's novel one of the fictional sisters also writes a novel about a fictional family fantasy. The connections between 'life' and 'fiction' are here unusually convoluted, but it is commonly accepted that intertextuality is not confined to the printed page. John Hannay, in *The Intertextuality of Fate*, argues that the knowledge of generic plots like that of romance fiction constitutes a modern sense of 'fatedness': 'we "know what comes next"', he says, 'because we recall analogous stories and so discern the proleptic logic of the one we are reading' – or living. In each of these texts, Jane Eyre functions as a 'generic plot', transmitted both direct and by means of an intertextual chain, which for A. S. Byatt included another Brontë-inspired text, *The Brontës Went to Woolworths* by Rachel Ferguson (1931). 'I read *The Brontës Went to Woolworths*', Byatt writes,

> when I was ... a very well-read schoolgirl whose imaginary life was considerably livelier, more populated and more interesting than her real one. I was intrigued by the title, which seemed to suggest some impossible meeting of the urgent world of the romantic imagination and the everyday world of (in my case) Pontefract High Street.[9]

For all these writers 'the urgent world of the romantic imagination' offered more than 'the everyday world'; moreover, it was a world shared with siblings.

For Charlotte Brontë, the family fantasy which she describes in a poem, 'We wove a web in childhood ...', lasted well into adult life. At the age of twenty, she knew her Angrian characters as well as her brother and sisters; her daydreams were a resource so valuable that she provides it for her heroine in *Jane Eyre*. As a governess in Thornfield Hall, Jane describes how 'my sole relief was ... to open my inward ear to a tale that was never ended – a tale ... quickened with all of incident, life, fire, feeling, that I desired and had not in my actual existence'. Like Antonia Byatt on Pontefract High Street, Jane Eyre's daydreaming stems from an unsatisfying life, and she was not alone. The heroine of Julia Kavanagh's 1850 novel, *Nathalie*, also

> listened invariably to the wonderful and endless romance, which her own thoughts had framed from the dreams that haunt the brain and trouble the heart of longing and ardent youth ...[10]

In fact Freud, in *Creative Writers and Day-Dreaming* (1908), argues that 'every single phantasy is the fulfilment of a wish, a correction of unsatisfying reality'. Florence Nightingale made the same observation in the 1850s; in her essay, 'Cassandra', she imagines a Victorian family group and asks, 'Mothers, how many of your sons and daughters are *there*, do you think, while sitting round under your complacent eye? ... Is not one fancying herself the nurse of some new friend in sickness; another engaging in romantic dangers ...?' Nightingale sees that 'it is the want of interest in our life which produces' daydreaming. Moreover, like Freud, she sees its connection with creative writing: 'what are novels?', she asks. 'What is the secret of the charm of every romance?' Her answer is two-fold: novels provide scope for thoughts and feelings, and they liberate the heroine from 'family ties'. Nightingale has perceived what the Marxist-Feminist Literature Collective put in rather different terms in 1978; in women's Victorian writings, they say, 'the devised absence of the father represents a triple evasion of ... class structure, kinship structure and Oedipal socialisation'.[11]

Both Nightingale and the Marxist-Feminist group argue like Jane Eyre that 'human beings ... must have action; and they will make it if they cannot find it'.[12] On the other hand, Jane's dreams seem to be satisfied by Mr Rochester, just as Elizabeth Barrett Browning writes,

> I lived with visions for my company,
> Instead of men and women, years ago ...
> ... Then THOU didst come ... to be,
> Beloved, what they seemed ...
> (*Sonnets from the Portuguese*)[13]

Freud, too, argues that while men's fantasies are mostly ambitious, women's are mostly erotic. For Rachel Ferguson's heroine of the 1930s, the fear that Jane Eyre's ambition is just a smoke-screen for erotic desire – which leads, of course, straight back to domesticity – makes Jane into a 'monster' rather than a 'mirror'. Deirdre Carne, the first-person narrator of *The Brontës Went to Woolworths*, is a bright young thing who, like Ferguson herself, earns her living as a journalist. She seems to have achieved Jane Eyre's dream of reaching 'the busy world, towns, regions full of life'. Yet she and her sisters, just like Elizabeth Barrett, 'live ... with visions ... instead of men and women'. Their fantasy life is much more 'real' than the office she never describes. It seems that they have escaped the private house of the past only to be repelled by 'the public world ... with its jealousy, its pugnacity, its greed'. Virginia Woolf described women of this period as 'between the devil and the deep sea', and for the Carne sisters, the Brontës represent 'the devil' which they must and cannot escape.[14] Judith Kegan Gardiner argues that 'twentieth-century women writers ... often ... communicate a consciousness of their identity through paradoxes of sameness and difference', and *The Brontës Went to Woolworths* is paradoxical in this way; the Carne sisters copy the Brontë sisters by inventing 'a tale that was never ended', but they also fear them as spinsters ruled by erotic compulsions. The youngest sister's governess, Miss Martin, who dreams of marrying the curate, is a cruel parody of Charlotte Brontë, and when the sisters visit Haworth the Brontës, as table-tapping ghosts, appear really menacing. It is, I think, the modern women's fear of regression which allows the Brontës to figure as monsters in a text which also mirrors their fantasy lives; they occupy the position which, in more recent women's fiction, is taken by a 'bad mother'. Judith Kegan Gardiner argues that 'the mother-villain is so frightening because she is what the daughter fears to become'. In intertextual terms, the Carne sisters fear being 'characters' in a story in which they 'know what comes next', in which the 'bad mother' is their 'author'. Their self-authored fantasies are thus a more vital aid in gaining control over their lives than the work they do in the 'busy world'. Refusing the Brontës as authors, they use them as characters in their own stories. The Brontës 'go to Woolworths' because only in that way can the Carne sisters be authors of their own lives.[15]

This apparently whimsical story has a disturbing side to it which shows intertextuality not as an academic concept but as a battlefield where writing subjects struggle for control. A. S. Byatt's *The Game* has a similarly sinister atmosphere, but whereas in Ferguson's novel modern sisters use their shared fantasy against the Brontë threat, in Byatt's novel a childhood game shared by sisters becomes an adult fight to the death. Freud suggests that:

a phantasy ... hovers ... between ... the three moments of time which our ideation involves ... some provoking occasion in the present ...

which ... arouse[s] one of the subject's major wishes ... a memory of an earlier experience ... in which this wish was fulfilled; and ... the future which represents a fulfilment of the wish.[16]

In *The Game* the 'provoking occasion' is a television series, seen separately by both sisters, presented by a man who had been part of their youthful game; but neither their memories nor their 'wishes' are at all clear. Linda Anderson argues that Freud's sense of connection between past and present was much more complex than his 'daydreaming' essay suggests; he 'came to believe that memories were [themselves] ... phantasies, constructed out of wishes and their repression'. Thus 'the neurotic for Freud was someone who could not tell their own story'.[17]

In *The Game*, Cassandra, the elder sister, is an Oxford don; Julia a successful novelist. Cassandra is celibate; Julia is married; but their desires cannot be reduced to Freud's categories of erotic or ambitious wishes. Freud himself concedes that the categories are 'often united', and Jacques Lacan, developing Freud's theory of 'displacement', argues that objects of desire are always relatively arbitrary, since desire is a process of infinite deferral.[18] Since the gap between the subject and the object of desire is bridged, if at all, by language, it is appropriate that the sisters in Byatt's *The Game* strive not for specific objects but for transient victories in the battle for self-representation. Judith Kegan Gardiner argues that 'literary identifications ... derive some of their undoubted power from analogy with earlier mental states' such as 'infantile identifications with parental figures', and in *The Game*, the academic Cassandra finds a literary 'mother' in Charlotte Brontë, who 'had seen the Duke of Zamorna leaning against a school mantel-shelf and had felt exhilarated and faint'(p. 219). Cassandra's sister Julia, however, uses both Cassandra and Charlotte Brontë not as 'mothers' but as 'daughters' in her own novel, in the sense that Gardiner suggests, that 'the hero is her author's daughter'. Ironically, a fictional reviewer praises Julia's 'sympathy for her central character, Emily, the lady don', whose 'imaginative life' suggests 'Charlotte Brontë's passion for the Duke of Zamorna'. Julia's 'sympathy', however, has left no space for Cassandra to 'write herself'. If, as Gardiner argues, 'female identity is a process', Cassandra's use of Charlotte Brontë had been a strategy in that process; but Julia's novel 'identifies' her sister in the sense of fixing her to that image. Cassandra's mirror turns into a monster. 'There is', she knows, 'nowhere I shall not drag this grotesque shadow' (p. 230). So she kills herself. Julia is not unscathed – 'all her life Cassandra had been the mirror ... that proved her existence; now, she had lost a space and a purpose'(p. 235) – but she has won the battle for reality, which proved to be a battle of words. Cassandra's real death comes in the final sentence where, 'closed into crates, unread, unopened, Cassandra's private papers bumped and slid' (p. 238).[19]

In Fay Weldon's stage adaptation of *Jane Eyre*, Branwell, Emily and Anne are on stage throughout, helping Charlotte to write her story. Charlotte becomes Jane from time to time and the staging also identifies young Jane, her pupil, Adèle, and all the orphans of Lowood. The audience is thus made to feel that Jane's sense of isolation is an illusion, for all round her are girls and women each separately sharing the same experience. In *The Private Self*, Susan Stanford Friedman suggests that women's autobiography is characterised by this same sense of sharing. Drawing on Nancy Chodorow's theories, Friedman argues that whereas male autobiography requires 'a conscious awareness of the singularity of each individual life', women's autobiographies 'often explore their sense of shared identity with other women', feeling themselves 'very much *with* others in an interdependent existence'. This theoretical perspective raises a problem for the texts I am dealing with. Friedman acknowledges that women's 'sense of shared identity ... exists in tension with a sense of their own uniqueness', and Gardiner points out that 'the word "identity" is paradoxical in itself, meaning both sameness and distinctiveness'. The Fay Weldon play foregrounds this paradox by representing to us as similar women who, in the 'mother-text', are separate. In each of my texts, however, 'sameness' itself is the threat. In Margaret Drabble's novel, *The Waterfall*, the heroine, Jane, feels that her cousin Lucy is 'my sister, my fate, my example: her effect on me was incalculable'; but she is 'tired of all this Freudian family nexus'. Similarly Cassandra in *The Game* feels that she and Julia have been 'too real to each other, sharing the same thoughts ... In an ideal state they should be no more and no less real to each other than anyone else.'[20]

Carol Gilligan, in her book about women's ethical decision making, provides an explanation for this troubling unsisterliness. Like Susan Friedman, Gilligan uses Chodorow as her theoretical base, but unlike Friedman she argues that women, precisely *because* they have more fluid ego-boundaries than men, tend to experience ethical problems with individuation, whereas men experience problems with relationship. Interviews show that the women who feel happiest with their lives are those who feel that they have made their own decisions – even if afterwards they feel they were wrong – rather than being 'a character in someone else's story'. This could explain both the unpleasantly aggressive strategies by which my fictional sisters free themselves from the 'grotesque shadow' of their monstrous symbioses, and the fact that the novels end on a fairly positive note.[21] Even Jane Gray, in *The Waterfall*, who begins as 'the heroine of a life that has no story', stealing Charlotte Brontë's story to depict herself as suffering in 'some Brussels of the mind', ends by writing 'a very good sequence of poems' from her fear that her lover was dying.[22] The fact that he doesn't die underlines the extent to which our stories can be liberated from our lives – or vice versa. The generic texts of tragic love, of comic romance, are each susceptible to interception, and, like Derrida's postcard, can be diverted to other destinations.

Although these texts consistently confuse Jane Eyre with Charlotte Brontë, there are important differences between them. Jane, a fictional heroine, writes her own life; she is happy with the decisions she has made and sees herself as a character in her own story. If Charlotte Brontë had written her autobiography, it is likely that she would have written not of her passionate desire but of her life as a dutiful daughter. When Robert Southey gave his famous advice that 'literature cannot be the business of a woman's life', Charlotte replied that her ambition had all been 'senseless trash' – but she also began writing *Jane Eyre*. Stevie Davies describes this as a process 'whereby words (a sign in themselves of loss...) are liberated from their original conditions to be inscribed in the form of a homeopathic ... remedy for the very conditions they record'. Charlotte Brontë did not write her life, she wrote her daydream, composed of Freud's three elements: the memory of loss, of mother, sisters, lover; the present 'provoking' fear that her father too would die; and her future wish for a lover embodying mother, sisters, father. But we may note that, in Charlotte's daydream, Jane's 'sisters' (Diana and Mary) stay at a distance. Fay Weldon, rewriting *Jane Eyre* as a modern woman, sees sisters everywhere; Charlotte Brontë dreams herself as an orphan. Nancy Friday, in *My Mother My Self*, suggests that what we need is precisely sisters (or mothers) 'at a distance'. We need the 'web' of relatedness but we also need to be authors of our own stories. Charlotte Brontë's daydream, anchored in the past but launched into the future, becomes our past, the mirror by which we know ourselves, but, read as our future, the mirror turns monstrous. 'We wove a web in childhood', Charlotte Brontë wrote; but 'the web is sticky', wrote Antonia Byatt. If 'female identity is a process', we must recognise that the moment when web turns to fly-trap and mirror to monster is also part of that process; the hope is that it forms a 'provoking occasion' for new daydreams, a new construction of past, present and future.[23]

The Game and *The Waterfall* are novels of the 1960s; they are, moreover, sophisticated productions. Jane Eyre, however, has played her part in provoking that same movement from identification to self-consciousness in more popular fiction. Despite feminist relish for Jane as rebel, most modern reproductions of *Jane Eyre* have tended to domesticate her story, to emphasise its closure and to focus on her childhood experience not as 'mad cat' but as victim. Moreover, in spite of an apparent growth of feminist consciousness, critics and commentators outside academia still focus on the content of the story rather than its process. Fay Weldon's 1988 stage play, for instance, was meant to dramatise not just Jane's story but Jane's making of her story, and the female reviewer for the *Irish Sunday Tribune* saw that Charlotte, Emily and Anne were there on stage to 'tell us how the book might have been written'. The *Daily Telegraph* reviewer, by contrast, thought that 'the device of the peripheral family observing the action ... is an irrelevant intrusion'.[24]

Recognition of the writing process, on the other hand, appears in unexpected places. In 1990 *Good Housekeeping Magazine* launched a competition to rewrite the end of *Jane Eyre*, recognising its force as a catalyst for new writing rather than as a role model. In 1988 the sixteen-year-old winner of a Brontë Society writing competition enacts the negotiation between identification and writing as her essay, 'A Brontë childhood', begins in the first person as Charlotte Brontë, but shifts to the third person:

> Charlotte put down her pen ... She thought of all the dreams and aspirations they had had, and of her governess sisters and broken brother. As she thought a new emotion swept her tiny body, and fired by a new wave of hope she resolved to urge herself and sisters and brother to follow their common passion: the written word.[25]

The shift in narrative position here can be seen to mimic the move described by Maggie Berg from the mirror phase of literary identification, in which this writer writes 'as' Charlotte, and the 'self-consciousness' from which she recognises the distance between them, bridged by the writing process.

Sheila Greenwald's novel for teenage girls, *It All Began With Jane Eyre*, is built around this movement from identification to writing. The young narrator, Franny Dillman, tells how, because her life was less interesting than fiction, she tried to fit the people in her life into roles provided first by *Jane Eyre*, and later by modern stories, scandalising her family by imagining passion, incest and abortion among her relations. Eventually a literary friend persuades her to read *Jane Eyre* not just for its story but for its author's commentary: 'It is vain', Franny reads at last, 'to say human beings ought to be satisfied with tranquility: they must have action; and they will make it if they cannot find it.' Forced to confront the reasons for what she has done, she also realises that writing is a kind of action; the last line of the novel repeats the first as she sits down to write, 'My mother thinks it all began with *Jane Eyre* ...'. Sheila Greenwald's novel is not subtle, but it suggests that the processes familiar to feminist academics as 'writing the self' or 'searching for subjectivity', are proceeding on a broad front. The Franny Dillman who writes her own story occupies the same position as the critic Pat Macpherson, who affirms that 'in identifying with Jane Eyre as the subject, the narrator, the moral agent of her own experience, I practised how to become the nervy heroine, rather than the confused victim, of my own experience'.[26]

Interestingly, even a Mills and Boon novel which misreads Jane Eyre as conformist rather than rebel nevertheless shows its heroine in this active negotiation with the earlier text. In *Devil Within*, by Catherine George, the heroine conceives Jane Eyre to be a timid Victorian spinster:

> The fictional Mr Rochester in *Jane Eyre* was a pussycat compared with the dour, unfriendly man who had met her today without a word of

welcome. Not that she was any Jane Eyre, either, decided Claudia – it would take more than a bit of boorish behaviour to put her off life in this idyllic spot.[27]

Claudia's self-construction involves rejection of what, to her, is the Jane Eyre image of sexual propriety: 'her attitude had been one of antediluvian rectitude, like some Victorian prunes-and-prisms spinster drawing her skirts aside from contact with man's baser instincts' (p. 171). If one reads for the outcome of the story, *Devil Within* is reactionary in feminist terms, ending with Claudia 'deeply satisfied' with the prospect of marrying 'one of those chauvinists who consider woman's place is in the home' (p. 191). There is no doubt, however, that Claudia does go through the process described by Maurianne Adams and Pat Macpherson, of matching herself against a partially accurate mirror image. For Claudia, liberation and change are constituted by a less 'Victorian' attitude to sex, and although sophisticated feminists may feel that the permissiveness of the 1970s was a dead-end for women, there is still a measure of self-assertion to be read in her recognition of advance from an earlier model of male–female relations: 'It was hard to recognise the grim, dour Mr Rochester in this elated male creature who was occupying her bed in such flagrant nudity' (p. 190).

In 'The death of the author', Roland Barthes has written that:

> a text is made of multiple writings ... entering into mutual relations of dialogue, parody, contestation, but there is one place where this multiplicity is focused and that place is the reader, not, as was hitherto said, the author.[28]

It is not stupidity which prompts Catherine George, like Rachel Ferguson, to read *Jane Eyre* as a threat from the past, but the need to assert difference. *Jane Eyre* is a fascinating text because it compels generations of readers, in different historical circumstances, to measure themselves against Jane in confronting afresh the question, 'What will you give in return for love?' The answer will depend, not on the author, but on the reader, and the compulsion to work through afresh the struggle of Jane Eyre leads the reader to something more like Jane's own process of self-narration than a simple process of mirroring. Whatever the outcome of these endlessly repeated struggles, this process whereby readers become writers of their own lives is, as Pat Macpherson puts it, 'the psychosocial stuff of which identity is made'.[29]

Author's Note

This chapter is a condensed version of material which appears scattered through several chapters in Patsy Stoneman, *Brontë Transformations:*

The Cultural Dissemination of Jane Eyre and Wuthering Heights (Hemel Hempstead: Harvester Wheatsheaf, 1996).

Notes

1   See Elizabeth Gaskell, *The Life of Charlotte Brontë* ([1857] Harmondsworth: Penguin, 1975), p. 308.

2   Valerie Grosvenor Myer, *Charlotte Brontë: Truculent Spirit* (London: Vision Press, 1987), p. 108. See also Elaine Showalter, 'Looking forward: American feminists, Victorian sages', *Victorian Newsletter*, 65, (Spring, 1984), pp. 6–10, on the influence of Victorian novels as modern feminist role models.

3   Playbill/poster for *young jane eyre*, Children's Theatre Company, 2400 Third Avenue, South Minneapolis, MN 55404 (8 Jan – 27 Feb, 1988).

4   O. C. Ogunyemi, *Signs*, 11, 1, (Autumn, 1985) p. 66; see Patricia Duncker, *Sisters and Strangers: An Introduction to Contemporary Feminist Fiction* (Oxford: Blackwell, 1992), pp. 24–7; Maya Angelou, Virago publicity leaflet for *Reading Women Writers*, a learning resource produced by the National Extension College (September, 1991); Tsitsi Dangarembga, *Nervous Conditions* (London: Women's Press, 1988), pp. 93, 92; Hideko Maki, MS note to Japanese programme for *Jane Eyre*, directed by Miss Kazue Kontaibo, 1978 (in Brontë Parsonage Museum Library, Haworth); Barbara T. Christian, 'Response to "Black Women's texts"', *NWSA Journal*, Vol. 1 (1) (1988), pp. 32–3.

5   Arlyn Diamond and Lee R. Edwards (eds), *The Authority of Experience: Essays in Feminist Criticism* (Amherst: University of Massachusetts Press, 1977), p. 68; Cheri Register, 'American feminist literary criticism: a bibliographical introduction', in Josephine Donovan (ed.), *Feminist Literary Criticism: Explorations in Theory* (Lexington: University Press of Kentucky, 1975), p. 20; Maurianne Adams in *The Authority of Experience*, p. 145; Toril Moi, *Sexual/Textual Politics* (London: Methuen, 1985), p. 8.

6   Adams in Diamond and Edwards (eds) *The Authority*, pp. 140–1, 137; Pat Macpherson, *Reflecting on Jane Eyre* (London: Routledge, 1989), p. xii; Christian, 'Response', pp. 34–5.

7   Maggie Berg, *Jane Eyre: Portrait of a Life* (Boston: Twayne, 1987), pp. 37–8, 24.

8   Umberto Eco, 'Casablanca: cult movies and intertextual collage' (1984), in David Lodge (ed.) *Modern Criticism and Theory* (London: Longman, 1988), p. 447.

9   A. S. Byatt, *The Game* ([1967] Harmondsworth: Penguin, 1987); Margaret Drabble, *The Waterfall* ([1969] Harmondsworth: Penguin, 1971); John Hannay, *The Intertextuality of Fate: A Study of Margaret Drabble* (Missouri: University of Missouri Press, 1986) pp. 1–2; Antonia Byatt, 'Introduction' to Rachel Ferguson, *The Brontës Went to Woolworths* ([1931] London: Virago, 1988), p. iii.

10 Charlotte Brontë, *Jane Eyre* ed. Margaret Smith ([1847]) Oxford: The Clarendon Press, 1973) Ch. 12; Julia Kavanagh, *Nathalie: a Tale*, 3 Vols (London: Henry Colburn, 1850), Vol. II, p. 138.

11 Sigmund Freud, 'Creative writers and day-dreaming' (1908) in James Strachey (ed.), *The Pelican Freud Library*, Vol. 14 (Harmondsworth: Penguin, 1985), pp. 134–5; Florence Nightingale, 'Cassandra' (1859), in Ray Strachey, *The Cause* ([1928] London: Virago, 1978) p. 397; Marxist-Feminist Literature Collective, 'Women's writing: *Jane Eyre, Shirley, Villette, Aurora Leigh*', in Francis Barker et al. (eds), *The Sociology of Literature: 1848* (Colchester: University of Essex, 1978), p. 188.

12 Brontë, *Jane Eyre* p. 110.

13 Elizabeth Barrett Browning, *Poems* (including *Sonnets from the Portuguese*) (London, 1850), No. XXVI.

14 Brontë *Jane Eyre*, p. 110; Virginia Woolf, *Three Guineas* (1938; Harmondsworth: Penguin, 1977), p. 86.

15   Judith Kegan Gardiner, 'On female identity and writing by women', *Critical Inquiry 8*, (Winter, 1981) pp. 354, 356, Note 18; John Hannay, *The Intertextuality of Fate*, pp. 1–2.

16   Sigmund Freud, 'Creative writers', p. 135.

17   Linda Anderson, 'At the threshold of the self: women and autobiography', in Moira Monteith (ed.), *Women's Writing: A Challenge to Theory* (Brighton: The Harvester Press, 1986), pp. 54–5.

18   Freud, 'Creative writers', p. 135; Anika Lemaire, *Jacques Lacan*, trans. David Macey (London: Routledge, 1970), p. 87.

19   Gardiner, 'On female identity' pp. 356, 349; A. S. Byatt, *The Game*, pp. 24, 219, 230, 235, 238.

20   Fay Weldon (adaptor) *Jane Eyre*, directed by Helena Kaut-Howson, first presented at Birmingham Repertory Theatre in 1986; Susan Stanford Friedman, 'Women's autobiographical selves: theory and practice', in Shari Benstock (ed.), *The Private Self: Theory and Practice of Women's Autobiographical Writings* (London: Routledge, 1988), p. 44; Georges Gusdorf, 'Conditions and limits of autobiography' (1956), quoted in Friedman, pp. 34, 38; Gardiner, 'On female identity', p. 347; Drabble, *The Waterfall*, pp. 114, 130; Byatt, *The Game*, p. 97.

21   Carol Gilligan, *In A Different Voice: Psychological Theory and Women's Development* (Cambridge, Mass. and London: Harvard University Press, 1982); Byatt, *The Game*, p. 230; see Joanne V. Creighton, 'Sisterly Symbiosis: Margaret Drabble's *The Waterfall* and A.S. Byatt's *The Game*', *Mosaic* 20:1 (Winter 1987): 15–29.

22   Sandra Gilbert and Susan Gubar, *The Madwoman in the Attic: the Woman Writer and the Nineteenth-Century Literary Imagination* (London and New Haven: Yale University Press, 1979), p. 39; Drabble, *The Waterfall*, pp. 84, 233.

23   Elizabeth Gaskell, *The Life of Charlotte Brontë*, pp. 173–4; Stevie Davies, *Emily Brontë* (Hemel Hempstead: Harvester, 1988), pp. 89–90; Nancy Friday, *My Mother My Self* ([1977] London: Fontana, 1979), p. 67; Byatt, *The Game*, p. 230; Gardiner, 'On female identity', p. 349.

24   Mary O'Donnell, 'Difference between passion and page 3', *Sunday Tribune* 9 Dec 1990; Peter Mortimer, 'Theatre north: no plain Jane', *Daily Telegraph* (20 April 1988).

25   Catherine Tillotson, 'A Brontë childhood', Brontë Parsonage Museum Haworth National Essay Competition for Schoolchildren, 1988, printed by The Brontë Society.

26   Sheila Greenwald, *It All Began With Jane Eyre* (New York: Dell Publishing, 1980), pp. 47, 122–3; Macpherson, *Reflecting*, p. xiii.

27   Catherine George, *Devil Within* (Richmond, Surrey: Mills and Boon, 1984), pp. 37, 171, 191, 190.

28   Roland Barthes, 'The death of the author', in David Lodge (ed.), *Modern Criticism and Theory* (London: Longman, 1988), p. 171.

29   Macpherson, *Reflecting*, p. xii.

4

Gina Wisker

If Looks Could Kill: Contemporary Women's Vampire Fictions

Vampires were supposed to menace women, but to me at least, they promised protection against a destiny of girdles, spike heels, and approval.[1]

In this opening quotation Nina Auerbach defines the talisman offered her by the vampire metaphor: its protection against conventional representations and constraints of femininity, conformity and domestic bliss: the 'happy ever after' of romantic fictional promises for 'real life'. In so doing she begins to define for us the project of contemporary women's horror and vampire fictions and their creative mutation of romantic fictional formulae. In reappropriating, and newly valuing, culturally constructed demonic representations of women – the perpetual, undead *femme fatale* of male sexualised terror, the epitome of which is the female vampire – contemporary women's vampire and horror fictions rescript romance. What results in the work of Anne Rice, Sherry Gottlieb and others is transgressive of social norms as well as fictional genres. It redirects romantic fictional trajectories, building on the one hand on the promise of eternal undying love, and on the other exposing the self-seeking, predatory energies informing much conventional romance. Vampiric couplings can be the end to any seemingly romantic alliance. They are often same-sex couplings, never driven by the need to procreate (which cannot be their result) and above all they emphasise the eroticism of sexualised (if not actually sexual in the genital sense) exchanges, an eroticism given extra spice by its almost inevitably fatal last act.

The sexuality of the vampire and vampire narratives is uppermost:

The vampire is everything we love about sex and the night and the dark dream-side of ourselves: adventure on the edge of pain, the thrill to be had from breaking taboos.[2]

Differently constructed by different cultures at different times, the vampire is the most radical, imaginatively challenging and creatively transgressive figure in contemporary fictions by women writers. Fictional vampires confront and overcome taboos and the sexual and political constraints they express. In particular, by intervening on the narrative trajectory of romantic fictions and reconfiguring the body of woman, and of the Mother, they set up a different economy of sexual and social exchange. Contemporary women's vampire fictions foreground the relationship between blood, sexuality and the body and revalue the figure of the monstrous Other by emphasising erotic exchange, women's power and sexuality.

This chapter considers conventional romantic fiction formulae and the interventions offered by conventional and unconventional vampire fictions. In so doing it initially highlights the cultural construction of *the deadly woman*, the *femme fatale*, and more specifically, the vampiric woman and her parallel, the 'femivore' who is a romantic partner (true or false) in romantic fictions. In vampire fictions he is likely to be a male vampire, seductive, powerful, and highly attractive to potential female victims. The comparisons between conventional romantic and vampire fictions expose their similar investment in upholding a sexual status quo and rewarding ideals of eternal union. Contemporary women's vampire fictions intervene in both conventional vampire and romantic fictions. Rescripting romantic fictions they return power to women and undermine patriarchal reductionism.

Vampire Fictions and the Trajectory and Formulae of Romantic Fictions

A couple is one who loves plus one who lets love. Couples make up the townspeople world. If you're not part of a couple, you don't exist and no one will speak to you outcast. Go to hell outcast.[3]

Romantic fictions are compelling vehicles for the construction and reinforcement of 'couple' relationships seen here by Acker as vehicles for enforcing a blinkered reductive conformity which in itself leads to binary oppositions of black/white, right/wrong, male/female, social insider/outsider and all the destructive rigid duties this positivistic approach encourages. Vampire fictions and the figure of the vampire are a direct assault on such conformity, but while conventional vampire fictions openly trouble and terrify, they eventually restore order: the weak and the victim are sacrificed, normality continues. Not so contemporary women's vampire fictions which refuse the romantic and conventional vampire formulae, providing genuine alternatives. Crossing the boundaries of these binaries is one of all vampire fiction's great transgressive strengths. Vampire fictions reverse and undermine value systems exposing their limitations. They seize and build on that which is feared and abjected.[4] The outcast of conventional fictions might literally go to hell to seek their radical alternative relationships, their challenges to the status quo.

Conventional vampire fictions are comparable in their narrative trajectory to romantic fictions. Like conventional romantic fictions, their impetus is to encourage normalised heterosexual unions which replicate the economic and gendered (im)balances of society. In many romantic fictions, stereotypically attractive women of usually inferior economic status seek tall, dark, handsome men with wealth and status to awaken and educate them sexually and to provide domestic comfort in a future beyond the narrative. After a series of hurdles (another suitor, lies, his previous sufferings, the economic gap between them and so on) they find eternal union and bliss as twin halves of a whole person. In this economy the vampire lover is often seen to intervene dangerously on the normal union by seducing the woman on the eve of her wedding, as in *Dracula* (1897).[5] He is a threat to conventional romance, but he also adopts guises, posing as a version of the powerful, attractive, invading male. One danger which the vampire embrace proffers is that of unleashing the powers of the erotic: essentially highly disturbing and challenging to conventional order. The threat posed by the vampire either bears fruit and the sexually voracious demonic vampiric female awoken by her vampire lover has to be punished by death, *or* she is rescued upon the death of the vampire (in some versions of the myth) and restored to her future husband.

The male vampire might be a disturbing demon, a femivore, but the female vampire is a real nightmare product born of fears of deception, uncertainty, loss of sexual power, property ownership and inheritance.[6] She is the ultimate *femme fatale*, like Medusa and the sirens: a combination of attraction and destruction/castration whose sexualised love bite reinforces a fear and disgust of women's sexuality and power. She must be decapitated/staked/coffined and that revelation of terrifying deadly attraction locked safely away for social order to reign.

In a radically transgressive act, contemporary women writers reconfigure the female vampire and intervene on the narrative trajectory of both romantic fictions and conventional vampire fictions, exposing their rather similar underlying ideologies.

Formulae Vampire Fictions and Romantic Love

Contemporary women's vampire fiction follows the trajectory of popular romantic fiction, but with a difference. These texts both expose and embody romantic fiction's paradoxes: often they reward the fantasies and take the clichés seriously. If someone 'offers their heart on a plate', they literally do so (see Judith Katz, 1996) while 'taking you away from all this' leads to a union and an existence which denies the bounds of space and time (see Sarah Smith, 1994 and Anne Rice, 1976, 1985, 1988, 1992).[7]

In romantic fictions tall, dark, handsome, often rather sexually threatening or overwhelming men are tamed. Many male vampires with the same general characteristics are exposed as femivores who attract, mislead, then devour their swooning adorers. This undercuts romantic closure: it leads to death. It also, of course, in true Gothic form, dissolves boundaries and unites opposites. Eros and Thanatos are linked, and same-sex partners.[8] Some contemporary women vampire fiction writers, however, linger on the enjoyable eroticism of the fatal bite/kiss as in Sherry Gottlieb's *Love Bite* (1994), or separate the physical attractiveness of the vampire from sexual partnering (see Anne Rice 1976, 1985, 1988, 1992).[9] Feeding/being fed upon is one response to being overwhelmed by the vampire's attraction, and another is joining the eternal vampire ranks; a *volte face* which genuinely offers eternal union and so rewards the fictions and fantasies of romance.

Women vampires, like the highly sexed women of popular romantic fiction (generally 'the rival'), are connotative of terrifying sexual power. In contemporary women's vampire fictions these *femmes fatales*, Medusa and siren figures are seized as powerful, interesting and trangressive; rewarded in their transgression rather than punished.

Vampire fictions enable a liberated exploration and dramatisation of erotic potential. Anne Rice's fictions, in particular, emphasise the erotic swoon of the vampire embrace, rewarding rather than refusing to denounce it (unlike *Dracula*). Contemporary women's vampire fiction retains the eroticism of the conventional vampire figure but frequently casts a woman in the vampire role.

Anne Rice's vampire novels, Sarah Smith's short story, 'When the red storm comes', Sherry Gottlieb's crime/romance/vampire fiction *Love Bite* and Angela Carter's 'Lady of the house of love' (1981) will be discussed to explore ways in which contemporary versions of the vampire narrative replay the formulae and expose the contradictions, fatal attractions and failures of romantic fiction.[10]

Femmes Fatales and Sexualised Terrors

A commonplace figure of terror in conventional popular romantic and vampire fictions is the sexually powerful woman, always figured as deceptive and evil.

> Her head was serpent, but ah, bitter-sweet!
> She had a woman's mouth with all its pearls complete ...

Her throat was serpent, but the words she spake
Came, as though bubbling honey, for Love's sake.[11]

Love can be fatal, Keats seems to warn, despite the powerfully seductive attraction of the loved one. She is not what she seems; she cannot fulfil the male desires and fantasies from which she has been drawn, and her deceptiveness is terrifying.

Literature and film are riddled with images of women who, drawn from male sexual fantasy, turn, serpent's fangs and all, and devour/destroy their hapless lovers. They are the stuff of sado-masochistic fancy and the thrill their male audiences/readership/creators experience is directly related to the fascination of the compelling, lethal beauty they project, and the violence and destruction which their evil, seductive lures instigate. Female readers and viewers might have some difficulty with this.

Much mainstream contemporary literature and film replicates these versions of women, though the cultural context has changed. Much contemporary feminist fiction deconstructs the *femme fatale* figure. Other contemporary feminist fiction, and particularly women's vampire fiction, however, reclaims her and her sister, the 'monster woman': it turns the tables and revels in her power. The chief figure which enables this reinterpretation of representations of women's sexual power is that of the female vampire. Reclaiming the figure of the female vampire and changing the economy of vampire fictions enables a direct confrontation with gendered configurations of power. Rescripting the romantic fictional formulae upon which the conventional vampire myth is built enables contemporary women writers of vampire fictions to expose and disempower not merely these often repressive restrictive formulae but, more important, their informing ideologies.

What is terrifying and threatening to men is culturally inflected, notes Angela Carter:

Desire does not so much transcend its object as ignore it completely in favour of a fantastic recreation of it. Which is the force by which the *femme* gets credited with fatality. Because she is perceived not as herself but as the projection of those libidinous cravings which, since they are forbidden, must always prove fatal.[12]

Femmes fatales and monster women in various guises can therefore be seen as the product of a widespread male fantasy and guilt malady, projected as female collusion. What the characters/caricatures of the *femme fatale* and her variants (Medusa, the vampire, the mermaid, the siren, the witch) have in common is their sexuality, and the male fears they represent. Some are devouring Mother figures: their nurturing qualities overwhelming, their strength seen as something which will symbolically 'drown' the male. Some turn into hags, their beauty dissolving in a conflagration brought on by greed, pride and excess sexual desire.[13] This is often the fate of the female vampire when punished for her disruptive sexuality.

Julia Kristeva has explored male fear of women, and particularly of powerful, sexually aware women as potential and/or real castrators:

> Woman is dangerous because it is her 'wish' to castrate man; it is the virgin's hostility, arising from penis envy, that man should justifiably fear. Freud does not consider the other possibility that it is man who constructs woman as a castrator and that he has displaced his anxiety on to woman.[14]

Medusa's defiant sexual power renders her terrible. Fatal, writhing snakes remind us of Eve's choice of knowledge over passivity. In Freud's interpretation of the myth the goddess turns all men who look on her to stone, parodies an erection, and destroys them:

> an interpretation suggests itself easily in the case of the horrifying decapitated head of the Medusa ... a representation of woman as a being who frightens and repels because she is castrated ... (it) takes the place of a representation of the female genitals, or rather ... it isolates their horrifying effects from their pleasure-giving ones.[15]

Medusa is hideous, with a boar's tusks and writhing snakey hair. She is the *vagina dentata*, a 'womb gullet' represented 'by the terrible face with its gnashing teeth'.[16] This terrifying threat must be removed; woman is more than deceptive snake, she is a destroyer. She also disgusts because of her difference, represented as the 'abject', that which must be rejected as waste, not self, so that the self can be recognised.

> The medusa's entire visage is alive with images of toothed vaginas, poised and waiting to strike. No wonder her male victims were rooted to the spot with fear.[17]

Both Medusa and female vampires connote a deep-seated terror of female sexuality and its power. This equation of sex and death is overwhelmingly threatening, and so, in myth, the greatest macho move is to behead the monster, vanquish the threat female sexuality represents. Perseus is legendary for overcoming male fear by turning Medusa's gaze against herself and decapitating her. In conventional fictions, female vampires, heterosexual or lesbian, must be staked, coffined, punished and banished.

As Barbara Creed has suggested in *The Monstrous Feminine*:

The female vampire is conventionally represented as abject because she disrupts identity and order ... driven by her lust for blood, she does not respect the dictates of the laws which set down the rules of proper sexual conduct. Like the male, the female vampire also represents abjection because she crosses the boundary between the living and the dead, the human and the animal. (p. 61)

The female Dracula or vampire figure is masculinised because she penetrates her victim. She becomes an active predatory seducer. Vampires also disgust, being equated with blood and leakage: 'any secretion or discharge, anything that leaks out of the feminine or masculine body defiles' as Kristeva reminds us.[18]

A host of contemporary films equate the image of the sexually beguiling female with devouring. Common among these are vampire films representing women as simultaneously monstrous and sexually attractive. In this context *The Hunger* (1983) is the prime example of a film text which began to reverse the entirely demonised image of vampires and align them with the exciting sexual transgression we find, for example, in Poppy Z. Brite's work (1992, 1993, 1994, 1996).[19] More conventionally, the vampire lovers reflect a commonplace of romantic fictions and present an (often misleading) promise of eternal undying unity in their love. Sexual sophisticates Catherine Deneuve and David Bowie, armed with necklet razors rather than teeth, maintain their everlasting life by feeding off victims picked up in trendy nightclubs. In a couple of episodes of *The X Files* nightclub pickups end in fatal sexual excess. The vampire lover switches gender to attract either men or women.

Vampire films (*The Vampire Lovers*, 1971; *Vampyres*, 1974; *The Hunger*, 1983; *Bram Stoker's Dracula*, 1993) present us with close-up shots of women's open mouths, pointed fangs and bloodied lips – a terrifying and graphic image of the *vagina dentata*. Sexual intercourse and death are visually associated in the image of the bloodied lips and teeth. So Lucy, bent over a child victim in Coppola's *Bram Stoker's Dracula* is an image combining both the devouring Mother and the sexual siren, whose kiss will seal up her lover forever in his role as 'partner vampire' or merely misled, seduced victim. The highly eroticised image of Lucy attracts as it repels: woman's sexuality is deadly, it seems. In several vampire films (e.g. *The Loves of Count Iorga, Vampire*, 1970) lesbianism flourishes, producing another spin on the terrible and the taboo: same-sex passion. Films which depict women as predatory and lustful often equate this with same-sex passion in order to demonise women's sexual powers. Such demonising always depends on a mixture of desire and disgust, and necessarily discriminates against women's freedoms. Lisa Tuttle exposes the deep-seated problem in her discussions on the gendering of horror:

And how to understand the awesome depths of loathing some men feel for the ordinary (female) human body? We all understand the language of fear, but men and women are raised speaking different dialects of that language.[20]

Repression, such as that explored then exorcised in conventional horror, is dangerous, argues David Punter:

> to channel sexual activity into the narrow confines of conventionality is repressive and, in the end, highly dangerous ... It is our repressions which kill us, because they conjure up forces within which are far stronger than our fragile conventionality can withstand.[21]

However, in feminist reappropriations of the vampire/Medusa/castratrix figure of male terror the monstrous is embraced and found empowering to women. Indeed, her actions are sometimes a product of her mistreatment by fearful males. In this version of the monstrous, if sensible of what she does, she represents an often gruesome celebration: this is what happens when men's worst fears of demonic female violence are dramatised. However, these tales do not merely reinforce stereotypical terrors. More frequently, they challenge these stereotypes, embracing and reinterpreting demonising myths and turning the tables of sexual power and control.

Blood replaces milk in the exchange between vampires and their lovers while the abjection of the lover/Mother is revalued in contemporary women's vampire texts; whether the more mainstream work of Anne Rice, the lesbian vampire fictions of Jewelle Gomez and Jody Scott, or the erotic work of Poppy Brite. Intermingling bodily fluids, particularly blood, sets up a radically different relationship within contemporary women's vampire fictions in which patriarchy and the Law of the Father are fundamentally challenged in both form and content. Celebration of a monstrous vampiric body is a deliberate feminist act of carnival. This revaluation of the monstrous woman is a direct challenge to patriarchal controls. Contemporary revelations of the vampire woman are a prime example of this revaluation.

Bakhtin's work on carnival and the grotesque is useful in understanding this new economy of contemporary women's vampire fictions where violations of taboos – milk/blood, life/death, same-sex partnerships, bodily invasion and shape shifting – are a feminist/queer challenge: liberating, radical and carnivalesque.[22] Vampire texts become politicised and erotic, straining social prohibitions.[23] For vampires the celebration involves the ultimate carnal act: the devouring of the victim/lover's blood. It violates the ultimate taboo against cannibalism while offering a kind of eternal life for the chosen ones. In so doing such texts confirm their closeness to romantic fiction, yet the couplings offered in contemporary vampire fictions are essentially transgressive, involving bodily invasion, usurpations of ownership in established partnerships, married or not; relationships between mothers and sons, and same sex relationships. They elaborate upon the fantasy and desire inherent in romantic fiction and instead of using it to express and exorcise socially disruptive forces, settling the safe partners down in wedded bliss, it unleashes the radical evolutionary energies of desire which questions social norms. As Kathy Acker in *Blood and Guts in High School* argues: 'Every position of desire, no matter how small, is capable of putting to question the established order of a society.'[24]

Femivores: Tall Dark Handsome Strangers and Fatal Attractions

The figure of the male vampire has been associated with dangerous sexual pleasures since Stoker transposed the legend of an essentially brutal and potentially cannibalistic tyrant (Vlad the Impaler) into the dashing Count Dracula whose elegance and mystique cast a seductive spell over even his waking victims: men and women (as Jonathan Harker almost fatally discovered). Dracula is thus the prototype for the femivore, whose attractiveness proves fatal to his admirers.

When Roger C. Schlobin, following Sherri S. Tepper's novel *The Bones*, explores the figure of the femivore he is describing the fatally seductive appeal of the male vampire in terms of the formulae of romantic fiction.[25] This 'drop dead gorgeous' figure literally devours the women he has seduced. The promise of eternal love as the prize for true romance is only realised for the vampire's chosen few. Those others who fall for this handsome, male stereotype realise no romantic ideal. Their erotic swoon is followed by a literal 'bleeding dry': the fate of domestic imprisonment, unwritten code of much pulp romantic fiction, is developed to horrific ends. Women are food for more than his demanding ego. Sherri S. Tepper labels him 'the femivore', describing his powers as manifestly seductive:

[He] was simply too good-looking by far, improbably good-looking. He broadcast a kind of fatal fascination. Like Count Dracula. The kind of man who eats women for breakfast and lunch and dinner. (p. 221–2)

As Schlobin also elaborates:

The femivore's essential nature is that he infatuates and seduces women and leaves them bereft of spiritual and often physical life. He sucks them dry, dooming them to perpetual states of waiting. (p. 1)

Count Dracula is therefore a classic protagonist of romantic fiction: the frock-coated seducer, the dangerous Other in love triangles who invades space reserved for the conventional hero, almost wooing the betrothed from her intended partnership. As such, then, his good looks spell danger: his erotic powers are disruptive, and the relationships with such a creature, best configured as 'more than' and not quite a man (eternal and godlike but behaving like a devouring animal) lead to social upheaval. We know Victorian readers might recognise their own hidden erotic urges in the response of Mina and Lucy to the invading foreign count, who would only be seen as safe when staked and destroyed. Giving in, however unconsciously, to their sexual urges, the women under Dracula's spell become sexually voracious in a manner totally at odds with the everyday moralities of the Victorian period, and are thus demonised. The 'moral' of the novel may therefore be seen as an indictment against female sexual exploration and pleasure, a response in part to the 'new woman' fiction, and women's very early attempts at assertion of their equality in society, education, the professions and domestic life.

Conventional vampire fictions demonise women's sexuality. They also replicate the trajectory of romantic fiction which upheld the fabric of conventional society. One powerful exception to this is the transgressive romantic fiction *Wuthering Heights* which, in acting out the promise/metaphor of 'undying love' troubles the genre's normal closure.[26] This brings *Wuthering Heights* much closer to contemporary vampire narratives in which the fantastic, disruptive, transgressive powers of love/desire/the erotic are embodied and rewarded. For Cathy, the disruptive powers of the dark demonic outsider, Heathcliff, are enough to make her dissatisfied with her cosseted existence with conformist Edgar, and seek eternal love among the rocks, stones and trees (or heather) in romantic fashion, after death. Conventional vampire narratives condemn/demonise eternal love yet simultaneously exploit the fascination with such forces. In *Dracula*, it is a horrifying predatory existence condemned by everything normal in society and all God-fearing people. And in both conventional, socially conformist romantic and vampire fictions, the potential disruptive seducer is unmasked and dispatched. At the same time, although it is too disruptive to be rewarded, escaping time and place with the intrusive socially destructive stranger/demon lover of course ironically replicates conventional romantic fiction *fantasies*. Such a revolutionary questioning of romantic fiction's norms is found and rewarded in Sarah Smith's short vampire story.

Sarah Smith: 'When the Red Storm Comes'

Sarah Smith's short story utilises the tropes of romantic fiction and rewards the vampire hero's chosen partner with material and temporal transcendence as well as everlasting love.[27] Like Angela Carter's 'The lady of the house of love' the tale is set at the advent of the First World War. Sarah Smith works with some of the familiar settings and scenarios of nineteenth-century romantic fiction: lower-middle-class heroine, thwarted by restricted life, condemned to a pointless and dull existence within a household whether married or unmarried, and dashing, good-looking stranger. In the archetypal *Pride and Prejudice*, such a hero would have to be rejected (Wickham) as dangerous and unstable, and a more stolid, monied, landed hero, redolent with upper-class values would win the day, nevertheless enabling the lively heroine to have her romantic cake and eat it even within matrimony.[28] Sarah Smith sides with the less stolid, drifting, dangerous, good-looking man and in doing so both challenges and rewards romantic fiction formulae. With a vampire you can achieve eternal, erotically charged love and escape material pressures. The vampiric coupling also critiques cultural constrictions and rigid social behaviours such as those associated with wartime; the First World War is the favourite example of such mass pointless carnage born of rigid thinking and senseless boundary disputes (see Virginia Woolf's indictment in *Three Guineas*).[29] War is thus rejected in 'When the red storm comes' where it is clearly seen as a greater waste of hopes and life than vampiric couplings. The young heroine seems condemned to a life of cutwork when in Portsmouth, in 1905, she meets a dashing young foreigner, Count Ferenc Zohary who, spotting her copy of *Dracula*, seduces her with both his love-making and his offer of eternal power, a power which will enable her to rise above the coming carnage born of patriarchal rigidity and imperialistic boundary disputes. Under the vampiric tutelage of the Count, the heroine sees visions of individual destruction, and a sea heaving with bodies. His offer is to make her what she clearly potentially is: a vampire. He embodies her own desires to escape and transgress: to cross the boundaries between obedience, conformity and the marginalised but insightful vampire position. He also offers the erotic opportunity through crossing the living/dead boundary to actually achieve her own sexual desires:

> I could sit down beside them, drink tea, and listen to the orchestra for the rest of my life. For me there would be no vampires ... The blood, crusted at the base of his fingers, still welled from the slit he had made in his palm. It was bright, bright red. I bent down and touched my tongue to the wound. The blood was salty, intimate, strong, the taste of my own desire. (p. 159)

The choice is erotically fired. She chooses and becomes the Other, her desire, part of herself. Crossing the boundary between those dying in life and the undead, she can cross other seas, call up the storm of blood and war, rise above the pointless death. What could be seen as an encounter with the abject, with the vampire role, is embraced rather than abjected. This vampire fiction, following the trajectory of conventional romantic fictions, refuses the normalising entry into domestic bliss. Paradoxically, it rewards

the fictional, fantastic promises of eternal undying love, and the chance
to 'take you away from all this'.

Angela Carter: 'The Lady of the House of Love'

Carter's 'The lady of the house of love', featuring a female vampire,
critiques both traditional formulae of romantic fiction and the society which
upholds and uses them as transmitters of ideology.[30] In so doing she
refuses the assumptions of conventional romance formulae: her sleeping
beauty vampire lady is awoken to death, not life, with the kiss of her mortal
lover. Romantic fiction is exposed as a dangerous and potentially fatal
construction. There is no love or life beyond the grave. The society which
upholds such fictions itself is, as with Sarah Smith's short story, headed
towards the carnage of the First World War.

Descendant of the original vampire, Vlad the Impaler, the Lady is
entombed in a Gothic castle coated in dust and moth-ravaged velvet.
Her unnatural, ideal beauty occasionally lures benighted travellers to their
death but she is a reluctant vampire feasting on woodland creatures,
using her mandarin-length nails to gouge her prey, then retire. She is a
figure of provocative beauty: 'In a white lace negligée stained a little with
blood, she lies down in an open coffin' (p. 98).

Flowers and scents dominate. It is a heady atmosphere which overcomes
the potential victim:

> the flowers themselves were almost too luxuriant, their huge
> congregation of plush petals somehow obscene in their excess, their
> whirled, tightly budded cores outrageous in their implications. (p. 101)

The First World War soldier who passes by and stays the night is overcome
by the pungent scents, the vaginal formations of the flowers, the lady's
beauty and his culturally induced fantasies which figure all thin beautiful
women as whores: 'unnaturally' sensual. To him she has:

> an extraordinarily fleshy mouth, a mouth wide, wide full prominent
> lips of a vibrant purplish crimson, a morbid mouth. Even – but he put
> the thought away from him immediately – a whore's mouth. (p. 101)

Vulnerable, she is sensual yet mechanical, and most attractive because
of her compulsive automatic behaviour. These versions of her derive
from his social conditioning which inevitably views women as dolls and
whores. She is:

> like a great ingenious piece of clockwork. For she seemed inadequately
> powered by some slow energy of which she was not in control; as if she

had been wound up years ago, when she was born, and the mechanism was inexorably running down and would leave her lifeless. The idea that she might be an automaton ... deeply moved his heart. (p. 102)

Instead of feeding on him she falls in love. His conventional romantic role of seducer or hero is undercut by the brevity of his visit and his highly conditioned sensuous thoughts and sexual inaction. She, on the other hand, becomes a victim to romantic fictions and fantasies through the agency of the vampiric blood. Letting him chivalrously kiss the blood on her hand, she condemns herself to death. Although the abundant growth surrounding the castle reminds us of that romantic fictional stereotype, Sleeping Beauty, the irony surrounding her awakening undercuts all romantic fictions. One kiss from this young man renders the Lady mortal. He returns to barracks with just a rose to remember her by, unaware he has truly broken her heart. As with Sarah Smith's tale, the sacrifice of the First World War, predicated upon imperialistic greed, is seen as a logical relation to the reductive romantic fictions which underlie this tale. Carter offers no escape.

Fantasy and the Erotic Vampire Exchange

Whether engaging with directly politicised claims, the near (or completely) pornographic, and deploying techniques as various as stream of consciousness, opulent lyricism, or a graffiti-style 'realism', it can be argued that all modes of erotic writing confront the problems and potential for change of the material world. The realm of fantasy functions through a lens shaped by our imaginations and the fantasy writing which most completely engages with the erotic is that of vampire tales.

At the end of this century, as at the end of the nineteenth, vampirism has become an overwhelmingly popular metaphor for the erotic. In Rosemary Jackson's words vampirism is 'perhaps the highest symbolic representation of eroticism'.[31] Richard Dyer in 'Children of the Night' locates the attraction of the vampire as erotic metaphor in the private setting: both our beds and our innermost thoughts.[32] The equation of blood-draining with sexual ecstasy, the domination and swooning, the sensuality, the promise of eternal love and life, align the vampire motif with erotic depiction and imaginings.

Women's vampire narratives are redolent with the celebration of the body, blood, beauty, eternal youth, passion, and above all, the erotic. The metaphor of vampirism has been reappropriated: it features as compulsively attractive for the sexually-alive twentieth-century feminist perhaps facilitated by the so-called 'hyper-realism' of postmodern culture which encourages us to play with 'death' at a symbolic level. After all, eternal beauty, eternal love with, perhaps, several opposite or same-sex partners and a categorical answer to women's fears of being reified and disempowered are all embodied in the female vampire.

It is not merely a *feminist* erotic that vampiric narratives celebrate and embody of course, and Anne Rice's immensely popular *Interview with the Vampire* can be explored as a fine version of the feminist erotic at times, and the homo-erotic, at other times. Richard Dyer's essay concentrates on the latter. Vampirism here is a metaphor for social controls, fears of sexuality walking the night streets, and an expression of the taboo of eroticism. But, once again, Dyer locates the figure of the contemporary vampire in relation to conventional popular romantic fiction:

> The ideas in vampire fiction of what sexuality is like – privacy, secrecy, uncontrollability, active/passive – have a complex relationship to the place of sexuality within the social order. Until the 1960s – and, really still today – sexuality was approved within marriage. Vampirism takes place outside of marriage. Marriage is the social institution of the privacy of sexuality – the vampire violates it, tapping at new windows to get in, providing sexual scenes for the narrator to witness. Marriage contains female sexuality – hence the horror of the female vampire walking the streets at night in search of sex. Men are allowed to walk those streets for that purpose, hence the ambivalence of the male vampire, the fulfilment of the importunate nature of male sexuality, dangerous, horrible, but also taken to be what men, alas, are. Finally marriage restricts sexuality to heterosexuality – vampirism is the alternative, dreaded and desired in equal measure. (p. 54)

Dyer thus annexes vampirism as a metaphor for an empowering sexual deviance. The male vampire seeks female victims/partners, and often also males, while female vampires, the paradigmatic over-sexed demonic women, also traditionally seek both sexes. Carmilla is probably the first fictional lesbian vampire.[33] The lesbian/gay reading is but one of many contemporary readings of how vampirism is used to depict the thrill/fear, repulsion/attraction, temptation, fulfilment, and threat of potential danger inherent in eroticised sexual encounters.

Anne Rice's *Interview with the Vampire* rejects the images and language of disgust, repulsion and loathing to be found in Bram Stoker and other conventional vampire narratives, using instead the language of the erotic to describe the vampire Lestat's 'draining' of Louis, and Louis of Claudia: here the strongest and most chosen of the 'victims' are then turned, by this draining, into vampires themselves. Louis initially hates Lestat for this act which condemns him to feed on small animals and people. However, the first person description of this and other vampiric acts is languorous, intense, hypnotic, ecstatic. Louis, turning Claudia's woman friend Madeleine (a favourite vampiric name) into a vampire by their mutual request, enables them both to soar (literally in the film version) to amazing heights of passion and new life. It is a compellingly eroticised description:

She gasped as I broke the flesh, the warm current coming into me, her breasts crushed against me, her body arching up, helpless, from the couch. And I could see her eyes, even as I shut my own, see that taunting, provocative mouth. I was drawing on her, hard, lifting her, and I could feel her weakening, her hands dropping limp at her sides, 'Tight, tight' I whispered, 'look at it !'. Her heart was slowing, stopping and her head dropped back from me on the velvet, her eyes dull to the point of death ... I felt the gentle pressure of her mouth, and then her hands closing tight on the arm as she began to suck. I was rocking her, whispering to her trying desperately to break my swoon; then I felt her powerful pull. Every blood vessel felt it, I was threaded through and through with her pulling, my hand holding fast to the couch now, her heart beating fierce against my heart, her fingers digging deep into my arm, my outstretched palm. (p. 292)

In *The Vampire Lestat* Lestat's most erotic exchange is with his mother, Gabrielle, whom he rescues from death by making her his vampire companion. Their relationship challenges cultural taboos against incest. Psychoanalytically speaking, their exchange of bodily fluids, and eroticised vampire swoon, rescues the body of the Mother from a place of abjection and places her in the role, not of rejected Other, but of chosen companion. The exchange directly comments on the norms of romantic fiction, and, equally importantly, on the ideologies underpinning romantic fictions. It also rescripts the conventional representations of powerful sexualised women and of the Mother's body as terrifying: something to be rejected and destroyed.

In this way, the vampire narrative does more than merely tinker with that of romantic fiction. The disturbing power of the erotic and the re-evaluating of the Mother totally upset the economy of romantic fictions. Contemporary vampire narratives refuse the disgust and rejection of conventional vampire narratives: an exciting double rejection and transgression figuring vampire lovers as historically unconfined cultural voyeurs and critics, and eternal erotic companions.

Sherry Gottlieb: *Love Bite*

Sherry Gottlieb's *Love Bite* is a mixed-genre vampire/crime/romantic fiction which plays with the formulae of all three.[34] It also emphasises the erotic charge of the (venomed) vampire embrace, which effectively physically persuades the victim that this particular sexual encounter is worth death.

Love Bite is transgressive not merely because of the vampire, Rusty, at its centre, but because of its deliberate intervention in genre fictions. The novel incorporates police procedural and romance novel formulae, switching first-person narrative from the policeman, Jace, who tracks the serial murderer, to Rusty/Risha the vampire he tracks, and with whom he falls in love. A first-person narrator vampire, like Louis in Anne Rice's *Interview*, who recounts his tale to Daniel, thus ensures our identification with, and confusions over, the morality of his actions and decisions. But Rusty/Risha is not a moralising vampire of the same sort as Louis. Sherry Gottlieb's transgressions of the formulae of *both* crime and romantic fiction enable radical interventions in the values each genre conventionally espouses. Her complex generic manoeuvres align her with other feminists, such as crime writers Mary Wings and Barbara Wilson, and horror writers Melanie Tem and Suzy McKee Charnas. None of these returns the genre tale to a conventional closure: one which would reinforce a patriarchal status quo and authorise certain realistic and logical structures of belief and behaviour.

The novel is an erotic thriller. Jace seeks love but his personal tragedy, the inheritance of Huntingdon's chorea, makes him a major candidate for vampiric transformation. Rusty's venom causes a sexual 'high' before the victim dies. She, too, seeks a mate with whom to spend more than a lifetime, having lost Gregor Bathory (the name recalls Countess Elizabeth Bathory, contemporary of Vlad the Impaler). A photographer, her night-time 'LA City of Angels' photos expose the underside of the city to public acclaim, but she retains her anonymity and nocturnal routines, significantly unphotographable herself except with mirrorless special cameras. Rusty's technological skills make her safe. She is cunning. Her use of the hunting knife to gash throats and blur teeth marks on victims both labels her a serial killer to be caught *and* covers up the vampirism. The detectives home in relentlessly, logically, on the problem that the gash offers.

The narrative trajectory is that of a crime novel, the tracing and hunting down of the serial killer whose MO is bloodletting and removal on a massive scale. It is also a romantic fiction as Jace and Rusty each seek partners through small ad sections in dubious magazines. Rusty selects men as either partners, or feeders: the one embodying the predatory nature underlying romance, the other the promise of eternity. Gradually both enter each other's space and discover their mutual attraction. Rusty is a contemporary creation. Her feeding habits are morally directed. She largely feeds on the detritus of the city – tramps and runaways – though the odd crimplene-wearing nerd also falls victim to her fashion-sensitive choices. Both seek the resolution of life problems through romantic union with another. The desires of each transgress the norms of the genres in which they are described, even as the genres interlock and transgress their own formulae.

As a romantic fiction *Love Bite* concentrates on the search for love and meaning in life by one aware of mortality, and another terrified at a lone eternity. Rusty's relationship with Jace is a cool-headed logical recognition of what each has to offer. There is no punishment; the lovers will last happily ever after, self-aware, erotically fulfilled, and presumably continuing, without retributions, to feed from the unsuspecting hordes around them in conventional society. A hybrid fiction, *Love Bite* completes the narrative trajectory of a romantic fiction while its interdiscursivity (tropes from crime and thriller genres, and the horror genre of vampire tales) radically disrupts the kind of closure offered by conventional and conformist texts: the crimes are unpunished, the love does indeed live on outside society, or rather *beside* it, beyond the grave.

Contemporary women's vampire fictions may be seen to rescript popular romantic fiction by utilising the conventional narrative as promise of 'love eternal', to fantasise 'real' love eternal, beyond the grave. Such tales are transgressive and celebratory hybrids: romantic fictions for an age which seeks to demythologise many lingering and repressive hang-ups – and their formulae and mythologies, moving forward into the unconventional and disruptive, are creative and liberatingly new.

Notes

1   Nina Auerbach, *Our Vampires, Ourselves* (London: University of Chicago Press, 1995), p. 4.
2   Poppy Z. Brite (ed.), *Love in Vein 1* (New York: Harper Prism, 1994), p. vii.
3   Kathy Acker, *Blood and Guts in High School* (London: Picador, 1984) p. 94.
4   'The abject' is defined as that which is not you, which has to be rejected and exited from the body in order that the identity of the self be recognised. In the growing child the body of the Mother is abjected as the child begins to recognise itself, and at the same time faeces are also ejected and seen as not the self. The body of the Mother, and by implication other women, people who are not the self, particularly of different race, of colour, or seen as alien in some way, become Otherised and abjected and are treated with disgust and repugnance. See Julia Kristeva, *The Powers of Horror*, trans. Leon S. Roudiez (New York: Columbia University Press, 1972).
5   Bram Stoker, *Dracula* ([1897] Harmondsworth: Penguin, 1979).
6   Roger C. Schlobin, 'The femivore: an undiscovered archetype', *Journal of the Fantastic in the Arts* (Spring 1989) p. 252.
7   Judith Katz, 'Anita, Polish vampire, holds forth at the Jewish Café of the Dead', in Victoria A. Brownsmith (ed.) *Nite Bites* (Washington: Seal Press, 1996); Sarah Smith, 'When the red storm comes', in Michele Slung (ed.), *Shudder Again* (Harmondsworth: Penguin ROC, 1994); Anne Rice, *The Vampire Chronicles: Interview with the Vampire* ([1976] St Ives: Futura, 1977); *The Vampire Lestat* (St Ives: Futura, 1985); *Queen of the Damned* ([1988] London: Warner, 1994); *Tale of the Body Thief* (Harmondsworth: Penguin, 1992). All page references to the works of Sarah Smith and Anne Rice will be given after quotations in the text.
8   Victoria A. Brownsmith, 'Twelfth night', in Brownsmith, *Nite Bites*, Jewelle Gomez, *The Gilda Stories* (London: Sheba, 1992); Paulina Palmer, *Lesbian Gothic Fiction: Transgressive Narratives* (London: Cassell, 1998).
9   Sherry Gottlieb, *Love Bite* (New York: Warner, 1994); Anne Rice, see note 7.
10 Angela Carter, 'The lady of the house of love', in *The Bloody Chamber and Other Stories* (Harmondsworth: Penguin, 1981).
11 John Keats, 'Lamia' in *John Keats: The Complete Poems* (Harmondsworth: Penguin, 1977).
12 Angela Carter, 'Scream and dream', in *Nothing Sacred* (London: Virago, 1986), p. 120.

13 H. Rider Haggard, *She* ([1887] London: Magnet, 1989).
14 Julia Kristeva, *Powers of Horror: An Essay on Abjection*, trans. Leon S. Roudiez (New York: Columbia University Press, 1972).
15 Sigmund Freud, 'Medusa's head', in *The Standard Edition* of the *Complete Psychological Works of Sigmund Freud*, trans. James Strachey (London: Hogarth, 1953–66), Vol. 18, p. 273–4.
16 See Bram Dijkstra, *Idols of Perversity: Fantasies of Feminine Evil in Fin de Siècle Culture* (New York: Oxford University Press, 1986).
17 Barbara Creed, *The Monstrous Feminine: Film, Feminism, Psychoanalysis* (London: Routledge, 1993), p. 121. Further page references to this volume are given after quotations in the text.
18 Julia Kristeva, *Powers of Horror*, p. 102.
19 Poppy Z. Brite, *Lost Souls* (Harmondsworth: Penguin, 1992); *Swamp Foetus* (Harmondsworth: Penguin, 1994); *Drawing Blood* (Harmondsworth: Penguin, 1993), *Love in Vein I* (New York: Harper Prism, 1994); *Love in Vein II* (New York: Harper Prism, 1996).
20 Lisa Tuttle, *Skin of the Soul* (London: The Women's Press, 1990), p. 5.
21 David Punter, *The Literature of Terror* (London: Longman, 1980), p. 410.
22 See Mikhail Bakhtin, *Rabelais and his World* trans. Hélène Iswolsky (Bloomington: Indiana Press, 1984).
23 See Stallybrass and White's interpretation of carnival as *carne levare* – taking away of meat after holiday excess, leading to images of cannibalism. Peter Stallybrass and Allon White, *The Politics and Poetics of Transgression* (Ithaca, New York: Cornell University Press, 1986).
24 Acker, *Blood and Guts in High School*, p. 94.
25 Roger C. Schlobin, 'The Femivore'; Sherri S. Tepper, *The Bones* (New York: Tor, 1987). Page references to both these texts are given after quotations in the text.
26 Emily Brontë, *Wuthering Heights* ([1847] Harmondsworth: Penguin, 1967).
27 Sarah Smith, 'When the red storm comes'. Page references are given after quotations in the text.
28 Jane Austen, *Pride and Prejudice* ([1813] Harmondsworth: Penguin, 1972).
29 Virginia Woolf, *Three Guineas* ([1938] Harmondsworth: Penguin, 1979).
30 Angela Carter, 'The lady of the house of love'. Page references are given after quotations in the text.
31 Rosemary Jackson, *Fantasy: The Literature of Subversion* (London: Methuen, 1981), p. 120.
32 Richard Dyer, 'Children of the night: vampirism as homosexuality/homosexuality as vampirism', in Susannah Radstone (ed.), *Sweet Dreams: Sexuality, Gender and Popular Fiction* (London: Lawrence and Wishart, 1988), p. 54. Page references to this essay are given after quotations in the text.
33 J. Sheridan le Fanu, 'Carmilla', in Adele Olivia Gladwell and James Havoc (eds), *Blood and Roses* ([1872] London: Creation Press, 1992).
34 Sherry Gottlieb, *Love Bite*.

Filmography

Bram Stoker's Dracula (dir. Francis Ford Coppola, 1993).
The Hunger (dir. Tony Scott, 1983).
The Loves of Count Iorga, Vampire (dir. Bob Kelljan 1970).
The Vampire Lovers (dir. Roy Ward Baker, 1971).
Vampyres (dir. Joseph Larraz, 1974).
The X Files (Fox Television).

5

Flora Alexander

Prisons, Traps and Escape Routes: Feminist Critiques of Romance

Love, perhaps even more than childbearing, is the pivot of women's oppression today.[1]

Whether or not they wish to be identified as 'feminist', Fay Weldon, Angela Carter, Margaret Atwood, Margaret Drabble and Aritha van Herk all write fiction which challenges traditional views of women as passive and dependent. Each of these writers plays on the conventions of popular romance and demonstrates the deceptiveness of the way in which it portrays women's relations with men.

Analysts of the romance and its readership have pointed to factors that explain the enthusiasm with which it is read. Janice A. Radway suggests that their permeable ego-boundaries, explained in Nancy Chodorow's theories about the construction of feminine identity produce in women a great need for the balance and completion provided by other individuals.[2] She considers that, because of the inability of males to behave as relational partners in the way desired by women, the romance may function as a representation of female needs accompanied by a satisfactory resolution. The fantasy of romance thus fulfils desires which are basic to women's psychological construction.[3] Tania Modleski sees the reading of romance as a fairly sophisticated process in which the reader has a fuller awareness than the heroine, and which offers a means by which women can work through psychic conflicts generated by the unequal distribution of power in family relationships.[4]

By contrast, Weldon, Carter, Atwood, Drabble and van Herk see the romance in its various forms – Harlequin, Gothic, and the tragic romance – as distorting, damaging, or limiting, and they revise its formulae critically or satirically. The ways in which the ideology of romance damages women, by giving them false expectations that the key to lasting happiness is the 'right' husband, are exposed by Weldon in her short stories, and by Carter in her early novel, *The Magic Toyshop* (1967). The romantic stereotypes of masculine dominance and feminine submissiveness are shown by Drabble in *The Waterfall* (1969), and by Atwood in *Lady Oracle* (1976) and *Bodily Harm* (1981), to encourage women in a self-indulgent dependency, and even to induce an element of masochism in female acceptance of male power. The position of the woman who writes the romantic fiction which distorts women's judgement is satirised by Weldon in *The Life and Loves of a She-Devil* (1983) and Atwood in *Lady Oracle*. In all of these critiques, the predominant effect is to represent the ideology of romance as something that pervades our cultural climate, and from which we have little hope of liberating ourselves. More positive revisions of romance come from Aritha van Herk in *No Fixed Address* (1986) and in Carter's later novel *Nights at the Circus* (1983). In each of these texts the codes of romance are subverted in such a way as to produce an assertion of woman's autonomy and power.

An essential premiss of popular romance is the belief that a woman is not complete without a man, and that happiness depends on some kind of fate bringing partners together. This component of the ideology of romantic love, in the form of lovers seeking a lost part of themselves, has had wide currency from medieval romance through to the popular fiction of the late twentieth century.[5] Fay Weldon satirises this tradition, producing out of conventional materials narratives which violate the expectation of lasting happiness promised by romance. In stories from her collection *Polaris and Other Stories* (1985), Weldon looks beyond the union of lovers to what comes later, and produces a feminist critique of the way that women, deceived by the notion of being reunited with a lost half of the self, or meeting a predestined mate, enter into relationships in which in due course they are betrayed.[6] The lovers who are the central figures in 'Birthday' (1981) are born on the same day of the same year. Their stars decree that they are partners: Mark thinks of Molly as 'his heavenly twin, his earthly mate'.[7] They appear to be made for each other, but the idea that they are joined together by destiny or celestial influence is called into question by the narrator's observation that Molly 'labours' to 'create' an atmosphere of romance.[8] Weldon's strategy is to organise her narrative around significant differences between the lives of the two partners, and thus to undermine the concept of the perfect match. The divergence between them is derived from conventional notions of masculinity and femininity: Molly is more home-loving than Mark, which the narrator notes, with ironic effect, 'is as it should be'. The different expectations of life which men and women may have are signalled by the detail that Molly's moon is in Capricorn, which is a sorrowful sign, whereas Mark's is in Taurus which is 'just plain sexy'. The married life of the predestined couple takes a course predictable to the reader, although not to the gullible wife. As a couple they share a financial problem, but Molly's resulting life of hard domestic work is contrasted with the comfortable career Mark enjoys in advertising. This allows him, while claiming stress and exhaustion, to enjoy expensive meals, and also an affair with Stella from Market Research. The narrative dwells increasingly on distinctions between their two lives, and progresses towards the moment on the couple's fortieth birthday when a video, brought by Mark's colleagues as part of the celebrations, reveals the deceptions of twelve years. The text discloses that the ideology of love has been a tool for deceit, while at the same time allowing the reader to conclude that Molly has been foolish to be taken in by it.

In 'Who?' (1985), Weldon presents the relationship of a pair of adulterous lovers, Howard and Elaine, who exemplify the concept of love at first sight. Their lives are transformed in the first few moments of meeting, and the dialogue defines this notion of love explicitly:

'We were destined,' said Elaine.
'Two halves of a whole,' said Howard, 'that somehow got split.'[9]

Their relationship is contrasted with ordinary relationships by the distinction Howard makes between merely 'loving' his wife Alice and being 'in love with' Elaine, and through the imagery of light and flame which they use to characterise their love, while their previous lives and the lives led by Howard's wife and their children are seen in terms of shadows and dimness.[10] But overtones of Antony and Cleopatra ironise the narrator's account of Howard and Elaine: 'Nor did custom diminish their attraction for one another', and 'he thought all was well lost for love of Elaine'.[11] The plot demonstrates the fragility of their love when, after a period of coping with the practical hardships and difficulties caused by their illicit relationship, Howard, always poor at recalling names, fails to recognise the name of Elaine when she telephones him. Weldon introduces into the story an authoritative voice, that of Elaine's mother, who explains to Howard that 'the reason you can't remember names is because you don't believe in anyone's reality, only your own'.[12] In these stories Weldon produces dramatic reversals of conventional plotting, and creates a narrative voice which conspicuously refrains from criticising the selfish male characters. The reader is prompted to see women's folly in adopting the positions which romance offers them, but at the same time the stories emphasise, by the use of simple and repetitive language, how deeply our culture is permeated with this particular set of expectations.

Angela Carter in *The Magic Toyshop* makes a similar point about the disparity between the expectations fostered by romantic love and the actual conditions of women's lives, using a different mode, the rewriting of fairy-tale. Her method is to write lavishly within the discourse of romance, and at the same time to undermine this discourse with words which destabilise the romance mode. The collision between romantic fantasy and actual experience is introduced in the opening scene, in which the dominant concerns are with female objectification and male power. Melanie's fantasies are focused on marriage, the culmination of the romance plot. The centrality of marriage in women's thoughts is confirmed by Mrs Rundle, the housekeeper, who has adopted the married title 'as a present to herself', and, in a counterpoint to Melanie's fantasies, sits 'dreamily inventing the habits and behaviour of the husband she had never enjoyed'.[13] The opening scene in which Melanie explores her changing body before a mirror – assessing herself by standards drawn from the work of the (male) painters, Cranach, Titian, Renoir, Toulouse-Lautrec – produces an insistent reminder of a regime in which the male gazes at the female. Melanie's conviction of the need to remain slender so as not to endanger her marriage prospects, and her anticipation of a honeymoon in Venice or Cannes, and of the rituals of the wedding night, are brought into sharply critical perspective by the language of consumption: 'She gift-wrapped herself for a phantom bridegroom.'[14] The escapade in which Melanie tries on her mother's wedding gown is presented with rich detail of satin, tulle, roses and lily of the valley, but the picture is disrupted by the accompanying image of her trapped in the veil, 'a mackerel in a net'.[15] Through the episode in which Melanie goes out in the night wearing the dress, climbs an apple tree, and then finds that the door has closed behind her, so that to get back into the house she must climb in painfully through the window, lacerating herself and tearing the dress to shreds, Carter offers a review of the structuring of female sexuality by the ideology of romantic love. The glamour associated with marriage leads into an experience of pain and terror.

Carter is deeply interested in power in sexual relationships, and Elaine Jordan has noted how Melanie's narcissism is 'ready-made to collude with the scenarios her Uncle Philip, the cultural puppet-master, wants to play out', which are to constitute a major element in the plot.[16] Melanie is a Sleeping Beauty, awakening in a bedroom papered with red roses and luxuriant foliage, but fairy-tale expectations of awakening to love are denied, and she faces instead a sordid confrontation with her uncle. His puppet show, in which Melanie is compelled to play Leda raped by the swan, is a plan for actual vicarious rape, since he intends that his young brother-in-law, Finn, should be aroused by the performance to violate the girl. Although Finn's decency preserves Melanie from harm, and the narrative enacts the defeat and death of the tyrannical male, Carter systematically denies the romantic expectations set up for Melanie in the first chapter. Melanie and Finn grow into a mutual affection, but only after she has overcome her initial distaste at his dirtiness and odd appearance and reconciled herself to his difference from the bridegroom of her fantasies. Their union is indicated in strongly anti-romantic episodes, such as a scene in which Melanie takes both Finn and her small sister Victoria into her bed for warmth and comfort, so that they appear as a family unit rather than a romantic couple. The 'new found land' of love that Melanie anticipated at the beginning of the story is achieved in the final pages, but it is marked by dull ordinariness, not by glamour and comfort.

Margaret Atwood's critique of romance in *Bodily Harm* situates the personal life in a wider public arena, and exposes the disjunction between the deluding simplicities of romance and the complexity of experience. Like Weldon and Carter, she shows that romantic thinking blinds women to reality, and in this variation on the political thriller-romance the woman's blindness creates danger. Using as her central figure Rennie Wilford, a 'lifestyle' journalist who strays into a world of political intrigue on a Caribbean island, Atwood plays on the gap between facile ideas that love can provide security, the realities of politically motivated imprisonment and murder, and Rennie's own potentially fatal illness. The narrative method, moving constantly between present and past, allows the reader to observe Rennie's 'vacation romance' which occupies the present of the novel, in relation to a recently ended relationship with her lover, Jake, and another recent romantic attachment to Daniel, the doctor who operated on her breast cancer. Daniel is constructed out of the conventional materials of romantic fiction. He has the erotic charm of power and knowledge. It is important to her that 'he knows what she's like inside', and 'She longed to be sick again so that Daniel would have to take care of her.'[17] She fantasises that she is only one of a whole line-up of his patients who are in love with him, and her overstatement betrays the nature of her delusion: 'We can't help it, he's the only man in the world who knows the truth, he's looked into each one of us and seen death.'[18] In Rennie, Atwood creates a figure who, unlike many heroines, is sufficiently sophisticated to be aware of the traps set for women by romance. While she indulges in the comfort of loving Daniel, she also understands that it is based on fantasy. She regards falling in love with her doctor as banal and ridiculous, and reflects that she has imprinted on him like a duckling. She looks at herself in terms of the journalistic cliches which are her professional currency, thinking, even while she is having lunch with him, 'Romance makes a Comeback',[19] while her friend Jocasta mocks her attachment as 'steamy dreams' and 'purple passion'.[20] Rennie is also astute enough to see that Daniel can only sustain the relationship with her as long as she continues her affair with Jake: 'Any damage to Jake and Daniel would be off and running.'[21] But all her awareness does not protect her from succumbing to the hazards of dependency. The layer of overt discussion of romance inserted into the text works to destroy its credibility. Rennie's own self-conscious reflections on the prospect of an affair with Paul, the mysterious American she meets on St Agathe, draw attention to the unsoundness of her position. She is conscious that her readers will be looking for 'gaiety and the possibility of romance' from her, and as she allows it to happen she is conscious that 'she's fallen right into the biggest cliche in the book, a no-hooks, no-strings vacation romance with a mysterious stranger'.[22] Unlike Carter's Melanie, an innocent exposed to a series of disappointments and unpleasant surprises as she emerges from a world of comfortable illusion into a kind of reality completely beyond her previous awareness, Rennie is an experienced and knowledgeable woman, and Atwood's treatment of her thought processes makes very clear that she is largely responsible for her own fate. She disregards Paul's advice to leave the island, and assumes complacently that, being a tourist, she can always go somewhere else when she wants to. The third-person narration, focalised through Rennie's own consciousness, makes the point explicitly that 'She should know better.'[23] Rennie does achieve clarification in the end, as her romantic notions collide with dangerous political intrigue and the experience of imprisonment. Her holiday expectations of sexual excitement are effectively disposed of when she recognises that Lora, her fellow-prisoner, has obtained chewing-gum for them both by selling sexual favours to the prison guards. At this point Atwood introduces a reminder of the durability of the tradition of romance, as Rennie's recognition of the facts is expressed graphically in the terminology of medieval narrative: 'The truth about knights comes suddenly clear; the maidens were only an excuse. The dragon was the real business. So much for vacation romances, she thinks.'[24] Atwood's novel is shaped by a sober insistence on clearing away comforting and misleading illusions. It is also negative in the impression it delivers about possibilities for women. While *The Magic Toyshop* insists that the world of romance is a lie, Atwood makes a further point. If Rennie, with all her shrewdness, still cannot resist the enticement of romance, the woman reader of *Bodily Harm*, interpellated by the voice that conveys Rennie's insights, may have to recognise that she also, despite her understanding of how the ideology works, has difficulty in disengaging herself from it.

Another familiar element of romance, the figure of the powerful, brutal hero, is exposed to criticism in Margaret Atwood's treatment of the sado-masochistic streak in Rennie's relationship with Jake. Their playful violence and his rape fantasies are made to seem less and less acceptable as the narrative demonstrates their connection to other terrifying manifestations of misogyny. The opening episode, in which an intruder into Rennie's flat leaves a coiled rope on the bed, establishes implications of sexual violence. Later, when Rennie asks Jake for his reaction to a specimen of pornography displayed to her by the police (in her professional role as a journalist), which includes a rat's head emerging from a woman's vagina, his response is, 'You think I'm some sort of pervert? You think all men are like that?' The brevity of the following sentence, 'Rennie said no', implies that her negative reply is less than honest.[25] The suggestion of a continuum which links Jake's actions with perversion and violence does conclusive damage to the stereotype of the brutal hero who shows tenderness to the 'right' woman.

The dynamic that exists between the dependent woman and the strong, menacing romance hero is also explored in Margaret Drabble's *The Waterfall*, a critique of the tragic romance.[26] Drabble's subject is an extra-marital love affair, given extra potency by the fact that Jane Gray's lover is the husband of her cousin Lucy, and by the origins of their love in the days when James is helping to care for her following the birth of her child. Jane is a first-person narrator, but within the first-person narrative there is an alternative account, presented as Jane's story written by herself in the terminology of romance. In this version Jane is extremely passive and unusually vulnerable to the emotional upheaval of sexual passion: 'She wondered if it would kill her, the thin clear air of so much happiness.'[27] The sense of menace associated with the romantic hero is emphasised in Jane's repeated perception of James as 'dangerous' or possessing an 'ominous strain'.[28] Her third-person narrating voice displays awareness of the damaging nature of her passion, and her inability to resist it: it is 'habitual addictive pain'.[29] Her passivity and insecurity are defined in an analogy with Tennyson's Mariana at the moated grange, waiting for the lover who does not come, and her dependency is further exposed by her stealing things from James and gazing at them as if they were magic relics.

The first-person narrative is presented as more authoritative than the third-person one. Jane speaking in the first person disputes her third-person record as 'a pack of lies'.[30] The first-person voice draws attention to the omissions from the third-person account: the guilt, the anxiety, even the rottenness of her adulterous passion. Her dysfunction is given plausible psychological and sociological explanations, including a family history which has led her to wish to emulate, perhaps even to *be* her cousin Lucy, James's wife. Although the Jane who narrates in the first person still has a contradictory voice, she sees more clearly than the other version of herself. She intervenes repeatedly into the third-person narrative which she has herself created, commenting on its inadequacies. She recognises her own obsessiveness, her over-simplification, pointing for example to how she has edited out her feelings for her baby, because she could not find a place in a narrative of passion for such an emotion. She sees the incongruity of her situation, articulating the absurdity that she, a married woman and the mother of two children, should sigh with the same romantic feeling out of which Charlotte Brontë wrote *Villette*. Words like 'bondage' – a reference to Havelock Ellis – and 'madness' define her condition. She places her emotional turmoil in context by recognising that love is nothing new, but a classic malady shared by both sexes, in which she suffers in the same way as her predecessors, the heroines of nineteenth-century fiction like Maggie Tulliver, who also had a cousin named Lucy.

Drabble's critique of romance is clearly articulated in the ending of the novel, in which the first-person account is allocated an authoritative position. The concluding pages contain a series of moves which undermine romance conventions. Jane mocks her exaggerated presentation of herself in extremity at the beginning of the story: 'Poor Jane'.[31] Speaking with the insight acquired from her experience, she points to the way in which ideology constructed her as a subject for romance, identifying how she had been led by cultural representations to believe in the power of passion, and suggesting that if she had not expected such events they would not have occurred. Drabble ironises conventional expectations of tragic or dramatic endings, making Jane reflect that this story, unlike the traditional romance, does not have a real conclusion. Neither she nor James died, the affair petered out, and the former lovers still have occasional contact. Metafictionally, Drabble makes Jane foreground the artifice by telling how she had thought of ending the narrative with impotence, 'the little, twentieth century death'.[32] What she chooses instead is at least as damaging to the codes of romance. The erstwhile lovers make a low-key visit to Goredale Scar, during which, absurdly, Jane spills talcum powder in their bedroom so that it contaminates a glass of whisky which James later drinks. Instead of a love potion they share a drink which 'tasted dreadful, ancient, musty, of dust and death'.[33] The Tristan motif is further ironised when Jane reveals that but for the accident she might have continued taking the contraceptive pills which had induced thrombosis in her leg, and which might have killed her – a deeply unglamorous contemporary version of dying for love. *The Waterfall* depicts a woman working through experience until she comes at the end of the narrative to a position in which romance is seen as a source of illusion, and a dangerous encouragement to passivity and self-destruction. The metafiction highlights the constructed nature of romance, and the splitting of Jane's narrative into first- and third-person voices allows in the third-person voice a very clear exposure of how it feels to have internalised the ideology, and in the first person voice a degree of recognition of how its procedures work. As in *Bodily Harm*, understanding romance does not enable the woman to free herself from it, and even in the closing pages of the novel, the rational, first-person Jane still uses emotionally charged language, speaking of how she loves James's face, and repeating the word 'lovely', both of James's appearance, and of the visit with him to the Yorkshire beauty spot. Drabble shows romance as something which her heroine can perceive as damaging, but from which she cannot extricate herself completely.

Weldon and Atwood have both satirised the romance in novels which focus on women who make their living as practitioners of the genre, in each case stressing the damage done by its distortion of gender relationships. Weldon's fable, *The Life and Loves of a She-Devil*, is a savage elaboration on the theme of 'Birthday' and 'Who?': that ideas about romantic love are harmful lies. The plot deals with the complex and ingenious revenge taken by Ruth, a large and unglamorous woman, after her accountant husband leaves her to live with his pretty client, the romantic novelist Mary Fisher. Their affair begins in the typical cliched language of romance, with a look exchanged 'across a crowded room', after which the future is 'full of wonderful and dangerous mystery'.[34] The insubstantiality of love is demonstrated when the new relationship proves unable to stand up to the stresses placed on it by Ruth's revenge, as she destroys her husband's business and also contrives that he and Mary must share their idyllic life in a high tower by the sea with his children and Mary's mother. The text demonstrates twice over the unreliability of romance, by exposing the lies in Mary's life and also the essential flaw in her work. The process of production of romantic fiction is shown to depend on protection from ordinary experience, so that Mary's work suffers when she is compelled to engage with real problems and relationships. When she writes a novel which departs from the old driving simplicity, and allows an element of gritty realism to break in, her publishers judge that it will not be a success. She loses touch with the formula, because romance has to be removed from the everyday world. And, as the voice of Ruth asserts, 'Her lies are worse because now she knows they are lies.'[35] Weldon's critique of the influence of romance on women is completed with a final, deeply disconcerting turn in the plot. Ruth, after taking her calculated revenge on Mary and Bobbo for their adultery, uses her immense resourcefulness and willpower to arrange extensive cosmetic surgery, from which she emerges dainty and beautiful, transformed into a version of Mary Fisher. Thus she acquires the power which society allows to the pretty, feminine woman, and regains Bobbo. By showing Ruth finally conforming to the conventions and the stereotype which initially harmed her, the novel provides a bleak acknowledgement of the difficulty of effecting change in these matters.

Margaret Atwood's more playful *Lady Oracle* (1976) is a comic study of romance, with a central focus on the misleading ideas generated by the 'costume Gothics' written by the novel's heroine, Joan Foster. Joan's consciousness offers a defence of what she does, in terms of the useful function which romance performs for its readers:

Escape wasn't a luxury for them. It was a necessity. In hundreds of thousands of houses these hidden selves rose at night from the mundane beds of their owners to go forth on adventures so complicated and enticing that they couldn't be confessed to anyone, least of all to the husbands who lay snoring their enchanted snores and dabbling with nothing more recondite than a Playboy Bunny.[36]

Joan is presented as consumer as well as producer of romance, submerging herself in a Harlequin written by Paul, her former lover, which allows her to share briefly the simplicity of love between nurse and handsome doctor, in 'an impossible white paradise where love was as final as death'.[37] Atwood's focus, like Weldon's and Drabble's, is on romance as an ideology which damages women by distorting their view of the world. Joan stands in a line of descent from Catherine Morland in *Northanger Abbey*, unable to distinguish between fiction and the world she lives in.[38] Thus she imagines herself pursued by men, as in the absurd closing episode in which she assumes that a man who comes in search of her, identifying himself as a reporter, cannot be anything so innocent, and so knocks him out with a Cinzano bottle. Atwood uses Joan's writing to demonstrate that the conventions of 'Gothics' are based on illusion. Joan's novels depend on a systematic division of characters into heroines and villains, and Atwood incorporates into the text a sustained sequence of parodies of the genre. Initially these fragments are characterised simply by the cliched language of romance: the hero has 'a dry mocking laugh' and his wife 'smouldering eyes', but the extracts become more and more highly coloured, until eventually Joan reaches a stage where the writing becomes impossible for her.[39] Joan reflects, 'Felicia [the heroine's enemy] smelled, these days, of wilted hyacinths ... Sympathy for Felicia was out of the question, it was against the rules, it would foul up the plot completely.'[40] Joan is driven to resist the binary opposition between good woman and bad woman, and thus she undermines the whole basis of the Gothic romance, in which virtuous heroines are finally rescued from evil to find happiness. She finds that the conventions cannot be upheld: the boundaries between good and evil collapse, and the whole enterprise of producing such an over-simplified text is dissolved in ridicule.

With differing emphases, the texts I have discussed so far are preoccupied with the idea that romance distorts women's views of the world, leading them to have false expectations, encouraging them in passivity, or rendering them unable to reach an accurate interpretation of the behaviour of other people. A contrasting feminist stance can be identified in work of the 1980s by Aritha van Herk and Angela Carter, both of whom have produced richly comic texts that deal positively with women's sexuality. Van Herk's *No Fixed Address* (1986) parodies romance to assert female strength and independence, and Carter's *Nights at the Circus* (1983) modifies romance to present a celebration of love between a strong woman and a new man. Writing from the Canadian west, and locating herself uneasily in an overwhelmingly male tradition, van Herk makes a gesture towards explaining her assertive position when she says:

> I come from the west, kingdom of the male virgin ... To be female and not-virgin, making stories in the kingdom of the male virgin, is dangerous ... Try being a writer there. Try being a woman there.[41]

Like Drabble in *The Waterfall*, she employs metafictional strategies to destabilise the romance, but in this case the product is a comic celebration of female sexual energy, which defies the stereotype of the sexually inexperienced heroine. Her sexually voracious Arachne Manteia is named after two predatory females, and the spider component of her identity is playfully used in her lustful awareness of 'beautiful fuzzy-legged men'.[42] In her perception, the roads she travels 'spider over the prairie', and they function in the text as a figure for her desire.[43] Arachne's status as an emblem of female desire and autonomous sexuality is indicated by her refusal of a stable relationship with her lover, Thomas, and her series of casual sexual encounters with miscellaneous men: a Mountie, a poet, an accountant. Aggressively 'not-virgin', she rejects the notion of the predestined partner satirised by Weldon in 'Birthday'. Her own voice in dialogue with her friend Thena defines the nature of her lust: 'I just get this itch.'[44] The narrator's voice confirms the degree of Arachne's deviance from the pattern of feminine purity and passivity, in terms which turn upside down the gendered expectations that men are promiscuous while women want love and fidelity. She 'has learned to get her pleasure fast, catch what she can, has trained her body to pleasure itself. The man can be anyone as long as he's half decent.'[45] The point is emphasised with an anti-romantic scientific metaphor:

> Women are cherished for being soft and pliable, for their grace. Arachne instead displaces mass. Thomas thinks of her in scientific terms: 'like mercury, you are never prepared for the weight.'[46]

Arachne's refusal of the traditional benefits of marriage subverts the convention that a heroine from a humble background wins, along with love, a social position and financial security. Her career as a representative in ladies' underwear presents a comical challenge to familiar expectations about male sales representatives as sexual adventurers. Romance is reduced to a comical cliche by the description of her stock of panties, in colours 'suffused with romance'.[47] The journeying which structures the narrative is sustained by an extensive elaboration on maps as a metaphor for desire, beginning with Arachne's response to the map which Thomas has left behind in the bus she was driving, 'a beautifully drawn and coloured map of southern British Columbia. Twisting roads around the names of hesitant towns. Under the gray light in the bus, the elegant lines convert those curves into longing.' The connection between the map and their attraction to each other is clinched by her perception that 'he loves the map'.[48] In the presentation of their first drive together, van Herk plays on the endless deferral of desire: 'It's too far to try for Calgary tonight', Thomas says. 'Neither wants to think of arriving', and moves into parody as Arachne 'caresses the bakelite wheel', and 'along the Similkameen they travel a black plunger of secret elation'.[49]

The text parodies the form of an investigation into the history and philosophy of women's clothing, and is presented in three sections, all identically titled 'Notebook on a missing person'. The Notebooks move progressively away from realism, and refuse conclusion. Arachne's end, after she kidnaps an old man for erotic purposes and drives off to escape the law, is to turn into a pure embodiment of women's desire. Her journey into Vancouver Island, and thereafter northwards into the Yukon, to the end of the road and beyond, is a comical progress marked by an endless trail of Ladies Comfort panties in scarlet, peach and sunshine yellow. At the same time it is presented as a mythic movement through the land of the dead, and she must ultimately drive off the map, because the object she is pursuing cannot be realised in the world of actual contemporary experience.

In *Nights at the Circus* (1983) Angela Carter deals radically with sexuality and, like van Herk, produces a comic female picaresque text which celebrates female autonomy. But where van Herk's rewriting of tradition is anarchic, Carter's is Utopian, and she ends with a new vision, albeit a tentative one, rather than the postmodern flourish with which Arachne disappears from Canadian territory. Writing as a socialist and a feminist, Carter creates a text set in the closing moments of the nineteenth century, which envisages new possibilities for women in relationships both heterosexual and lesbian. Voices anticipate, in the words of Ma Nelson the brothel-keeper, 'the New Age in which no women will be bound down to the ground'.[50]

Several structural features of romance are parodied in *Nights at the Circus*. Lizzie's metafictional warning to her stepdaughter advertises Carter's burlesquing method:

> Don't you know the customary endings of the old comedies of separated lovers, misfortune overcome, adventures among outlawed and savage tribes? True lovers' reunions always end in a marriage.[51]

The traditional motif of the hunt of love is reversed. In the opening episode the narrator remarks about Walser, in his pursuit of an interview with the famous acrobat, that 'His quarry had him effectively trapped.'[52] Later, when they have been separated in the wastes of Siberia, Fevvers, disregarding Lizzie's warning, goes in search of Walser, and romance vocabulary is used ironically to relate how her spirits lift at the sight of his footprint. 'And she would see, once again, the wonder in the eyes of the beloved and become whole. Already she felt more blonde.'[53] Carter also plays with the traditional romance device of placing the heroine in a situation where she must solve a set of puzzling circumstances. Here Fevvers is the one in control of mysteries, and Walser is placed in the role of searcher for enlightenment. Fevvers reveals as much, in the end, as she pleases, but remains authoritative and enigmatic. In 'Envoi' she discloses unromantically that she and Lizzie have been using Walser to send back to England secret revolutionary information, and also confesses that at their first meeting they played a trick on him, by manipulating time. She retains the power of knowledge in her handling of Walser's final question about her status as 'fully-feathered intacta'. The narrative ends with her pervasive laughter, released over the world, laughter provoked because 'I fooled you.'[54]

Carter's is a carnivalistic text, and in it she deploys illusions and mimicry, so that although the voice of intense emotion is present it is balanced within a polyphony of different voices. Strong feeling is expressed lyrically in the imagery of mercury, a strange and beautiful substance, which represents the desire that exists between the lovers: 'his molten heart spilled out of his bosom and flowed towards her, just as one drop of mercury flows towards another drop of mercury'.[55] But the pleasure and idealism of love are placed in a context of misunderstanding – Fevvers thinks at this point that Walser has taken Mignon as his mistress – and is succeeded by a scene of comic humiliation in which she scrubs off his clown's paint. In the same episode, the romantic feeling is heightened by Mignon's singing of Byron's song, 'We'll go no more a-roving', but the feeling is ironised by the fact that Mignon does not understand the words she sings, and by the situation in which she learned the song, from a homosexual English stableboy who befriended her. The discourse of love is further relativised by a range of alternative languages spoken in the text. Fevvers herself, for example, speaks in terminologies of politics, economics and philosophy as much as those of love.[56]

Carter's presentation of Fevvers is an outrageous burlesque of conventional notions of femininity. Although she is first introduced as 'the blonde' and she dyes her wings pink, the details of her person violate grotesquely the usual criteria for female attractiveness. She is large and clumsy, coarse in her manners and materialistic in her habits, and has the voice of a 'celestial fishwife'.[57] She has economic power, sufficient to support herself and Lizzie in reasonable comfort. She shatters decorum by introducing discussion of sexual matters at an early stage of her acquaintance with the hero, Walser, and in a knowing tone, pointing out to him, 'though I blush to admit it, intacta as I am', that she is not suited to lying on her back for purposes of sexual connection.[58]

In *Nights at the Circus* there is, alongside the triumph of the strong, confident young woman, a more general revision of power relations and affirmation of female autonomy. Women are shown freeing themselves from bonds. The brutal Ape-man learns gentleness. The text accommodates homosexual as well as heterosexual love. Mignon finds contentment in a lesbian relationship with the Princess of Abyssinia, keeper of the tigers, which releases the Princess from her accustomed silence. The harmony of their union is conveyed powerfully through musical imagery, when in the wastes of Siberia they happen to find a grand piano, the Princess tunes the instrument, Mignon sings, and the resulting delight extends to Siberian tigers who come to listen, 'laid low by pleasure'.[59]

Weldon, Carter and Drabble writing in England, and Atwood and van Herk both writing with a strong consciousness of themselves as Canadian women, share an understanding that romance has been built on a set of assumptions which are limiting and damaging to women. Weldon, in *The Life and Loves of a She-Devil*, offers an especially bleak view of the possibilities of contesting this ideology, since even Ruth, extraordinarily clever and resourceful though she is, is incapable of stepping outside the pressures to conform to romantic stereotypes. Atwood similarly depicts intelligent women, in both *Lady Oracle* and *Bodily Harm*, failing to learn lessons that ought to be obvious. In her handling of character she remains always aware of the multiple and contradictory nature of the self, and in her vision of the possibilities open to women there is a recognition that Joan and Rennie carry with them needs that drive them to unwise choices. Drabble's Jane in *The Waterfall* has a voice which differs in timbre from the voices of Atwood's women, being less shrewd and witty, and more sober and philosophical. Jane's discourse is shaped by a strong sense of traditional culture, and even as she strives to define the distortions contained in romance, she betrays that she too is unable to move completely beyond its reach. Van Herk and Carter move the subject into a different territory. Neither of them attempts to contain her story within the contemporary world, and thus they gain freedom to invent. Arachne survives for a time in the towns and on the roads of Western Canada, but ultimately must move on into the wilderness, because the freedoms van Herk envisages are not at present attainable. Carter's Fevvers is shown looking forward to a new world which, a century later, has not yet come to pass. Nevertheless the nature of the discussion of romance is changed in important ways by the energy of Arachne and the confident laughter of Fevvers.

Notes

1   Shulamith Firestone, *The Dialectic of Sex* (1971), quoted in Juliet Mitchell (ed.), *Women: The Longest Revolution. Essays in Feminism, Literature, and Psychoanalysis* (London: Virago, 1984), p. 142.
2   Nancy Chodorow, *The Reproduction of Mothering. Psychoanalysis and the Sociology of Gender* (Berkeley and Los Angeles: University of California Press, 1978).
3   Janice A. Radway, *Reading the Romance. Women, Patriarchy, and Popular Literature* (London: Verso, 1987), pp. 93–6.
4   Tania Modleski, *Loving with a Vengeance: Mass-Produced Fantasies for Women* (London: Methuen, 1984).
5   Juliet Mitchell discusses the history of romantic love in Western society in *Women: The Longest Revolution*, Part 1, 'Feminism and the question of women', pp. 103–14.
6   Fay Weldon, *Polaris and Other Stories* (London: Coronet, 1985).
7   Ibid., p. 147.
8   Ibid., pp. 148–9.
9   Fay Weldon, 'Who?', in *Polaris*, p. 174.
10   Ibid., p. 176.
11   Ibid., p. 178.
12   Ibid., p. 178.

13   Angela Carter, *The Magic Toyshop* ([1967] London: Virago, 1992), p. 3.
14   Ibid., p. 2.
15   Ibid., p. 15.
16   Elaine Jordan, 'Enthralment: Angela Carter's speculative fictions', in Linda Anderson (ed.), *Plotting Change: Contemporary Women's Fiction* (London: Edward Arnold, 1990), pp. 18–42, p. 28.
17   Margaret Atwood, *Bodily Harm* (London: Cape, 1982), p. 81, p. 83.
18   Ibid., p. 142.
19   Ibid., p. 142.
20   Ibid., p. 153.
21   Ibid., p. 154.
22   Ibid., p. 43.
23   Ibid., p. 258.
24   Ibid., pp. 211–12.
25   Ibid., p. 212.
26   *The Waterfall* is discussed as a tragic romance in John Hannay, *The Intertextuality of Fate: A Study of Margaret Drabble* (Columbia: University of Missouri Press, 1986), pp. 18–47.
27   Margaret Drabble, *The Waterfall* (London: Penguin, 1969) p. 72.
28   Ibid., p. 12; p. 28.
29   Ibid., p. 134.
30   Ibid., p. 84.
31   Ibid., p. 226.
32   Ibid., p. 238.
33   Ibid., p. 238.
34   Fay Weldon, *The Life and Loves of a She-Devil* (London: Hodder and Stoughton, 1983), p. 37.
35   Ibid., p. 192.
36   Margaret Atwood, *Lady Oracle* (London: Virago, 1976), pp. 34–5.
37   Ibid., pp. 318–19.
38   Jane Austen, *Northanger Abbey* ([1818] Oxford: OUP, 1980).
39   Atwood, *Lady Oracle*, p. 31.
40   Ibid., pp. 318–19.
41   Aritha van Herk, 'Women writers and the prairie: spies in an indifferent landscape', *Kunapipi* 6, 2 (1984), p. 15.
42   Aritha van Herk, *No Fixed Address* (London: Virago, 1989), p. 49.
43   Ibid., p. 163.
44   Ibid., p. 174.
45   Ibid., p. 70.
46   Ibid., p. 113.
47   Ibid., p. 169.
48   Ibid., pp. 89–90.
49   Ibid., pp. 96–101.
50   Angela Carter, *Nights at the Circus* (London: Chatto and Windus, 1984), p. 25.
51   Ibid., p. 280.
52   Ibid., p. 9.
53   Ibid., p. 285.
54   Ibid., pp. 294–5.
55   Ibid., p. 142.
56   Ch. 10, pp. 279–91, offers examples of the range of discourses employed by Fevvers. For an example of polyphonic and carnivalesque texts and reading strategies see also Lynne Pearce, *Reading Dialogics* (London: Edward Arnold, 1994).
57   Ibid., p. 43.
58   Ibid., p. 82.
59   Ibid., p. 249.

6

Maroula Joannou

Essentially Virtuous? Anita Brookner's *Hotel du Lac* as Generic Subversion

In *The Name of the Rose*, Umberto Eco describes a postmodern response to a romantic predicament; that of a man who is in love but cannot say 'I love you madly', because he knows that she knows (and that these words have already been written by Barbara Cartland).[1] However, he can say, 'as Barbara Cartland would put it, I love you madly'. Eco explains the usefulness of such an enabling strategem. Having stated clearly that it is no longer possible to speak innocently, the man will nevertheless have succeeded in saying what he wanted to say to the object of his devotion: that he loves her, but that he loves her in an age of lost innocence.

Anita Brookner writes romantic fiction without resort to the carnivalesque, the humorous, the macabre, the parodic, or the other familiar devices adopted by authors to make romance palatable to a knowing twentieth-century audience that has lost its innocence. Read alongside the gun-toting fantasies of Pam Houston or the time-travelling/gender-bending inventiveness of Jeannette Winterson, Brookner appears sedately traditional; anachronistically expending energy on affairs of the heart which are designed to come to nothing, rather than on the narrative transgression that more often characterises the twentieth-century novelist revisiting the romance. Moreover, the old-fashioned belief in the redemptive power of romantic love that characterises her work, and distances her from many of her contemporaries, would appear, on the basis of interviews which Brookner has given, to be subscribed to not only by the author herself but also by the heroines of her first four novels: *A Start in Life* (1981), *Providence* (1982), *Look at Me* (1983) and *Hotel du Lac* which won the Booker prize in 1984.[2] As Edith Hope, the romantic novelist at the centre of *Hotel du Lac*, declaims, 'I cannot think or act or speak or write or even dream with any kind of energy in the absence of love. I feel excluded from the living world. I become cold, fish-like, immobile. I implode.' (p. 98). In a letter to her lover which is never posted, at the end of the novel, the unrepentant Edith refutes any suggestion that 'I wrote my stories with that mixture of satire and detachment that is thought to become the modern writer in this field.' On the contrary, she asserts that 'I believed every word that I wrote. And I still do.' In a 1988 interview with John Haffenden Anita Brookner described *Hotel du Lac* as 'a love story, pure and simple: Love triumphed over temptation'.[3]

Anita Brookner has proved to be among the most resistant of contemporary women writers to feminist appropriation or analysis. Like another contemporary Booker prize-winning novelist, A. S. Byatt, Brookner has consistently refused to acknowledge that the gendered nature of writing matters and has distanced herself from feminism: 'You'd have to be crouching in your burrow to see my novels in a feminist way.'[4] The range of concerns in her early writing is narrow and, for the most part, excludes wider social issues. She is a miniaturist working on a small canvas, and like Jane Austen, with whom she is sometimes compared, refuses in her early writing to stray far beyond the world she knows. Anita Brookner excels at the scrupulous analysis of the passionate inner lives of women and at delineating distinctly feminine internal worlds which are fraught with anxieties. The narrowness of her focus on intimate feminine experience is pinpointed in Joan Smith's novel, *A Masculine Ending*, in which a character remarks, 'I can't see any point in her books at all. You might as well watch a documentary about depressed women on Channel 4.'[5]

Between them *Hotel du Lac, Providence, Look at Me* and *A Start in Life* provide a smattering of European exiles and displaced persons, but her characters are usually middle class in taste and aspirations and heterosexual in their sexual inclinations. There is little probing into working-class character or the alternatives to the dominant modes of (hetero)sexual expression in Anita Brookner's early fiction. She is at her best with formal dialogue; the intelligent conversation that would not be out of place in a nineteenth-century novel, the studied manners of the middle strata of English society among whom her early novels are set. Her appeal is to those who prefer the pre-modern to the postmodern and the non-experimental in their choice of reading matter. As John Skinner has put it in the only full-length study of Brookner published in England to date, her novels 'have been castigated (and only occasionally commended) for their "minimalism"; they have also been more unreservedly attacked for their formulaic quality, their weak sentimentality and – more ominously – their close proximity to the conventions of Harlequin romance'.[6]

On the surface, Brookner would seem to be an unpromising subject for feminist inquiry. Why, then, have feminist readers including myself derived the pleasure from Anita Brookner's fiction that we have? The purpose of this chapter is to establish the case for *Hotel du Lac* as an example of generic subversion and to show how Anita Brookner's novels generate patterns of significance for the woman reader which may not have been consciously intended by the author but which do not require her authorisation to be accepted as interpretations of the text. I want to draw attention to the largely unrecognised feminist potential of Brookner's work, including the importance of her revisions of women's traditions of writing; her questioning of dominant cultural myths – primarily the myths of Cinderella and of the hare and the tortoise – the internalisation of which have proved particularly damaging to women. Anita Brookner's subject matter is often the suffering of sensitive, isolated, intelligent women. As Flora Alexander has pointed out, 'everything in *Hotel du Lac* has some bearing on how women live their lives, and the nature of their relationships with men'.[7] It is the focus on women's intimate experience in Brookner's early writing – not until *Lewis Percy* (1989), her ninth novel, does she centre squarely on the consciousness of a male protagonist – that has largely been responsible for 'an emphatic male hostility towards a certain kind of "woman's novel"' and her dismissal by critics as 'the fictional specialist in migraines, flushes and female malaises'.[8]

But it is precisely because of its focus on women's day-to-day experience that her fiction is of interest to the women who, as Anita Brookner acknowledges, constitute the vast majority of her readers. I do not wish to suggest in any naive way that woman-centred novels are necessarily feminist novels or that *Hotel du Lac* is straightforwardly subversive – the novel perpetuates some aspects of the English romantic tradition at the same time as it subverts others – but I do wish to argue that *Hotel du Lac* generates as many tensions, contradictions and conflicts for women as any that it may resolve. In *Hotel du Lac* Anita Brookner provides the woman reader with critiques of relationships between women, and of women's behaviour in relationships with men, of their behaviour as mothers, and in the other roles that women perform within the family. Moreover, the interaction of the characters in *Hotel du Lac* provides important insights into the relational character of women's identity and creativity and a variety of contrasting perspectives on the worlds in which women live. As Margaret Diane Stetz has put it, 'in continually emphasizing the importance of social and emotional ties between women as the primary influences upon and stimuli to women's writing, Brookner shapes a philosophy of creativity quite compatible with that of the group she disowns. Thus, she becomes an author who, if not politically feminist, is nonetheless aesthetically feminist.'[9]

As mentioned, the central character in *Hotel du Lac* is Edith Hope, a writer of romantic fiction in the Barbara Cartland/Mills and Boon tradition. The newest romance on which she is working is '*Beyond the Visiting Moon*', a title that somewhat incongruously evokes the grand passion of Shakespeare's Antony and Cleopatra. In the secluded Swiss hotel where she has gone to 'forget the unfortunate lapse which led to this brief exile, in this unpopulated place, at this slowly darkening time of year' (p. 8), Edith converses with her literary agent who cautions that the market for romantic fiction is beginning to change: 'It's sex for the young woman executive now, the Cosmopolitan reader, the girl with the executive briefcase' (p. 26). Edith's riposte is that her readers, for whom she has respect, are 'essentially virtuous' (p. 28). Moreover, they still want 'to believe that they are going to be discovered, looking their best, behind closed doors, just when they thought that all was lost, by a man who has battled across continents abandoning whatever he may have in his in-tray to reclaim them' (p. 27). What Edith Hope (re)presents here, albeit in an updated form, is the medieval narrative of the damsel in distress awaiting rescue by the knight on a white charger. As she observes, her readers 'prefer the old myths' (p. 27).

The romance plot is a key locus of many of the most deeply rooted shared assumptions of our culture. However dismissive, critical or ambivalent feminists may feel towards it, as Lynne Pearce and Jackie Stacey have put it, romance still remains 'one of the most compelling discourses by which any of us is inscribed'.[10] In *Hotel du Lac* Brookner subverts the genre she so competently deploys in order to explore the social determinants of relationships between the sexes; to probe the relationship between gender and identity; and to show how the past still casts a long shadow over the present. As in Mills and Boon novels, *Hotel du Lac* traces the troubled path to the reunion of the heroine and the missing hero. The heroine is a serious author writing popular romantic fiction; a genre which always has an overwhelmingly female readership. Edith Hope is independent, highly educated, fastidious, career-orientated, competent and passionate, but with some inhibition. She is also a model of rectitude, 'a householder, a ratepayer, a good plain cook, and a deliverer of typescripts well before the deadline' (p. 8). *Hotel du Lac* evokes the formulaic elements of romantic fiction: the wealthy, married man; the sensitive adoring woman worshipping from a distance. It also provides the elements that are not usually present in Mills and Boon: subtlety of plot, self-reflexiveness, complexity of character, preciseness of observation and sensitivity to language. The heroine, although career-orientated and independent, knows that she will find her emotional and sexual fulfilment in marriage. Edith admits that she is a 'domestic animal' (p. 100) who longs for the comforts of stability and ordered routine.

When Mr Neville suggests that what she needs is marriage Edith does not demur. In common with Mills and Boon it is not the plot in *Hotel du Lac* which is important, but the states of mind of the heroine. Readers are encouraged to identify with the heroine and to imagine themselves in her place; to participate in her experience so that they are predisposed to see things from her point of view. The novel alternates between detached third-person narration and first-person narration in the intimate, confessional mode used in Edith's letters to David, who is characterised in his absence by the identifying traits by which Edith chooses to remember him: a large appetite, a boyish charm and a cultivated interest in antiques.

Edith is no longer young and there is a distinct sense of time running out. The security and social status that Mr Neville offers her are therefore attractive. At her stage in life the blandishments of 'pleasant companionship, comfort, proper holidays' represent a 'reasonable prospect' (p. 118). By seeming to uphold the desirability of passion, of hope deferred, if not hope fulfilled, to the alternative of its abandonment, Brookner addresses the nature of woman's sexuality and the social constrictions of socialisation into feminine behaviour patterns. Mr Neville's proposal of marriage – he is not addressed by his first name at this point – is reminiscent of two famous set-pieces of nineteenth-century literature: Mr Collins' proposal to Elizabeth in *Pride and Prejudice* and St John Rivers' to Jane Eyre, in its insensitivity to the heroine's romantic, emotional and sexual needs. The proposal is predicated on a fundamental misreading of Edith's character. Mr Neville pays her the compliment of believing that she will never indulge in the 'sort of gossipy indiscretions that so discredit a man' (p. 167), that she will never shame or ridicule him, or hurt his feelings. It is, of course, precisely such indiscreet behaviour, the jilting of her dull but kindly and attentive suitor on their wedding day, that has precipitated Edith's exile in Switzerland. Mr Neville's exterior of dessicated calculation – 'a heartless man', 'furiously intelligent' (p. 97) – is in reality the protective carapace of the cuckold. His 'wife ran away with a man ten years her junior and despite everyone's predictions she is still radiantly happy' (p. 93).

As Byron expressed the discrepancy, man's love is 'of man's life a thing apart', and it is 'women's whole existence'.[11] As Edith listened to him expounding his shrewdly acquisitive and self-interested personal philosophy, and his attempts to persuade her that life is lived better without emotional investment, she had observed that 'as a devil's advocate Mr. Neville was faultless. And yet, she knew there was a flaw in his reasoning, just as there was a flaw in his ability to feel' (p. 97). To Mr Neville Edith is simply another acquisition which will enhance his status like the collection of rose dishes that has pride of place in his fine Regency house. Mr Neville coldly suggests that the fate that awaits Edith if she rejects his marriage of convenience is the discovery that she has a 'lot in common with all the other discontented women' and the prospect of spending the rest of her life talking to 'aggrieved women about your womb' (p. 100). The alternative to this travesty of feminist solidarity is the old-fashioned and faintly ridiculous model of genteel spinsterhood traditionally befitting a woman of Edith's disposition: 'You are a lady, Edith. They are rather out of fashion these days. As my wife you will do very well. Unmarried, I'm afraid you will still look a bit of a fool' (p. 165).

The conflict of need exposed within these important passages of the novel is that of a woman torn in opposite directions between emotional dissidence and social conformity. *Hotel du Lac*, then, is a study of the altercation between pragmatic resignation and romantic idealism, the one represented by Mr Neville, the other by Edith Hope, although Edith is practised at reining in her romantic longings, her propensity for romantic excesses being tempered by common sense: 'It is high time I forgot my hopes, the hopes I was born with and faced reality' (p. 118). But despite the disappointments to which Brookner's intelligent, disingenuous heroines are invariably subjected they manage to retain their belief in the holiness of the heart's affection. As Barbara Hardy puts it, 'Edith's final affirmation of integrity makes a tiny contribution to the great moral tradition of the romantic story.'[12]

As Patricia Waugh has noted, Anita Brookner's fiction is marked by its 'perception of the relational basis of identity and its portrayal of her woman characters' obsessive need for and fear of connection'.[13] Their beings are grounded in insecurity and their desires for commitment and stability often go back to inadequate parenting and unfulfilled emotional needs in childhood. As Edith observes 'the charming tableau' of Iris and Jennifer Pusey 'entwined, their arms locked about each other' (p. 44) she becomes painfully aware that 'there was love there, love between mother and daughter, and physical contact, and collusion about being pretty, none of which she herself had ever known' (p. 48). Earlier, she had remembered her mother's unkindness, the memory of which helped to explain why she was still continually on her guard against more hurtful behaviour from women. She then reasons, 'but women are not all like Mother, and it was really stupid of me to imagine that they are' (p. 88). For Patricia Waugh 'all Brookner's novels explore the infantilizing effects of family life on women'.[14] And the heroines express their ego-identity problems, their journey to mature female personhood, in the quest for the older man who will substitute for the missing father and take away the memory of childhood pain.

A fundamental objective of feminist approaches to the literary text is to analyse how gender relationships are constituted within it and how existing gender relationships may be altered. The questioning of an overly romanticised view of personal relationships has always been consonant with feminist critiques which have resisted men's propensity to place woman upon a pedestal, arguing that such idealisation is not natural but part of the gendered ordering of society. Although it is quintessentially a romantic novel in its structures of feeling, a substantial section of *Hotel du Lac* is dedicated to questioning the nature of romantic love. However, the deconstruction of the ideology of romantic love that feminists might welcome in the novel is associated exclusively with the world-weariness and cynicism of Mr Neville, who argues unconvincingly that 'there is no such thing as complete harmony between two people, however much they profess to love one another. The light touch is more effective than the deepest passion' (p. 95). But Mr Neville's views are clearly at variance with the accumulated wisdom of Western societies (*amor vincit omnia*) that has made love the only acceptable basis for marriage. The anti-romantic disquisitions in *Hotel du Lac* are, therefore, likely to meet with resistance from many of Brookner's non-feminist readers who, in common with her feminist readers, do not read passsively but will also bring their own preconceptions about the importance of romantic love to the text, and collaborate in the making of its meanings.

In one of her conversations with Mr Neville Edith muses that 'people divide writers into two categories. Those who are preternaturally wise, and those who are preternaturally naive as if they had no real experience to go on. I belong to the latter category' (p. 94). Despite Mr Neville's attempts to relieve her of her illusions Edith is the embodiment of hope over experience which bears out the appropriateness of her family name. He also attempts to persuade Edith that 'whatever they told you about unselfishness being good and wickedness being bad was entirely inaccurate. People feel at home with low moral standards, it is scruples that put them off' (p. 96). But despite her disappointments Edith never allows herself to become cynical, although 'the most potent myth of all', the ultimate victory of the tortoise over the hare, is the one which she is able to take apart with an uncharacteristic display of wit: the fable of the hare and the tortoise is, of course, a useful metaphor for the female pursuit of the male, 'in my books it is the mouse-like unassuming girl who gets the hero, while the scornful temptress with whom he has had a stormy affair retreats baffled from the fray, never to return' (p. 27). But despite her adroitness in providing wish fulfilment for her readers Edith is all too aware of the distinction between fact and fiction: 'In real life, of course, it is the hare who wins. Every time. Look around you. And in any case it is my contention that Aesop was writing for the tortoise market' (pp. 27–8).

As Daphne Watson has pointed out, Anita Brookner's work is steeped in European traditions of high art which make no allowance for an unread readership and her perceived audience is very different from the 'simple-sentence lovers of the Mills and Boon preferred mode of expression' whose predelictions Edith Hope understands so well.[15] Brookner has publicly stated that the ideal to which she aspires is that of Enlightenment rationalism.[16] The heroine of *Hotel du Lac* values herself as a rational person, 'I always was a reasonable woman' (p. 118), and much of the novel is spent reasoning about her situation, although her final decision to remain in her position as the mistress of a married man is determined by emotional rather than rational considerations. Yet Brookner's reliance on Enlightenment rationalism is profoundly contradictory for, as feminist philosophers have pointed out, Enlightenment philosophers did not include women among those thought capable of emancipating themselves through the appeal to reason. As Jane Flax puts it, the motto of the Enlightenment, '"Sapere aude – have courage to use your own reason" rests in part upon a deeply gender rooted sense of self and self-deception'.[17] Brookner is a highly literate writer whose work is steeped in the Romantic tradition of European literature and art to which her novels make frequent reference. In *Providence*, for example, Kitty Maule is an academic who specialises in the Romantic tradition 'which still affects us today although we may not recognise it' (p. 177). Kitty explores the nature of Romanticism with her students: 'It is characteristic of the Romantic to reason endlessly in unbearable situations and yet to remain bound by such situations' (*Providence*, p. 134). Moreover, 'romantic love can lead to disastrous fidelities. Or indeed ultimately to chastity' (p. 133). Romanticism is also important in *A Start in Life* where there are clear parallels between the careers of Balzac's *Eugenie Grandet* in the eponymous novel and another academic, Ruth Weiss, who at one point in the novel can no longer identify with her favourite literary heroine: 'She felt she was in control of her life, that it was no longer at the mercy of others, that she could not be disposed of against her will or ignorance of her fate' (*A Start in Life*, p. 139). But, in fact, the conflict between passion and social conformity in the two women is strong and both eventually become disillusioned and sacrifice their romantic aspirations in loveless marriages.

In an interview with Shusha Guppy (see note 16), Brookner has drawn a distinction between romance novels 'which are formula novels' and the 'true Romantic novel' which 'is about delayed happiness and the pilgrimage you go through to get that imagined happiness'. Romantic writers are 'characterised by absolute longing – perhaps for something that is not there and cannot be there. And they go along with all the hurt and embarassment of identifying the real thing and wanting it.'[18] But there are significant aspects of the romantic tradition to which it is clear that Brookner feels deep ambivalence; notably 'that we are deceived into believing that virtue is rewarded, that good will win in the end, and that Cinderella will always get the Prince'.[19] It is these aspects of romanticism that Brookner interrogates by the use of the Cinderella story in reverse in her fiction.

Ruth Weiss, who thinks that 'the most beautiful words a girl could hear' are '"Cinderella shall go to the ball"' (*A Start in Life*, p. 8), is a prime example of such feminine self-delusion. *Hotel du Lac* demonstrates the destructiveness of this fantasy at the same time as it argues for its potency. In reality, the belief in culturally condoned myths has disastrous emotional consequences for women. *A Start in Life* begins with the sentence 'Ruth Weiss had been ruined by literature.' Suffering is shown to be the corollary of romantic love. And the Western cultural heritage that values romantic attraction above all else is seen to be heavily weighted against women. Two of Brookner's honest and principled heroines, Frances Hinton in *Look at Me* and Kitty Maule in *Providence*, forfeit the man of their dreams to more selfish and attractive rivals. Edith Hope's dream of domestic contentment with her loved one can never come true since David Simmonds has a wife, and Ruth Weiss is left alone at the end of *A Start in Life* contemplating the ball to which the would-be Cinderella was never invited.

At the end of *Hotel du Lac* Edith decides to return to her lover in England. The decision is prompted by one of the moments of truth that is common in Anita Brookner's fiction; an epiphany or revelation after which things can never be the same. In *Hotel du Lac* this is Edith's glimpse of the duplicitous Mr Neville's departure from Jennifer Pusey's bedroom. Edith amends the wording of a telegram informing David of her decision from 'coming home' to 'returning'. Brookner has explained the significance of this change. '"Coming home" would be coming back to domestic propriety: "home" implies husband, children, order, regular meals, but "Returning" is her more honest view of the situation.'[20] To that extent Brookner suggests that Edith does break through to a clearer vision and recognises the need to accept compromise and disappointment as unavoidable aspects of adult existence.

Anita Brookner is fascinated with the thought processes of the woman-as-writer and the woman-as-reader. Each of the heroines of her first four novels is a writer in some form or another and for all of them there is a clear link between the act of writing and the expression of gendered identity. As her heroines struggle to make sense of their own desires they are trying to establish a hold on the self that remains elusive by committing their actions and thought processes to the written word. For Frances Hinton in *Look at Me*, for example, writing is a means of gaining attention: 'If my looks, and my manner were of greater assistance to me I could deliver this message in person. "Look at me"; I would say. "Look at me".' (p. 20). In the end, literature proves to be less painful than life for Frances: 'In future I would become subsumed into my head and into my writing hand' (p. 179). But Brookner is not only concerned with the reasons why women write: 'writing novels preserves you in a state of innocence – a lot passes you by – simply because your attention is otherwise diverted. The moral examination, self-examination, pre-empts every other perception: you don't even notice what's going on under your nose'; she is also interested in the reasons why women choose to read romances.[21] As Janice Radway has put it, reading the romance might be seen 'as a collectively elaborated female ritual through which women explore the consequences of their common social condition as the appendages of men and attempt to imagine a more perfect state where all the needs they so intensely feel and accept as given would be adequately addressed.'[22]

Anita Brookner's early fiction offers several examples of older women for whom the reading of romantic fiction is a compensatory activity, a refuge from the disappointments of life. Ruth's mother in *A Start in Life* is addicted to popular romantic fiction of the Catherine Cookson type and consumes six tales a week of governesses being swept off their feet by the dashing son of the household. *Hotel du Lac* provides two devotees of romantic fiction for whom reading also functions as a palliative. First, there is Edith's mother, who 'comforted herself, that harsh, disappointed woman by reading love stories, simple romances with happy endings' leaving her daughter to speculate 'perhaps that is why I write them' (p. 104); second, there is the overblown Iris Pusey who bears a striking resemblance to Barbara Cartland. Mrs Pusey's 'indeterminate age' is revealed to the unsuspecting guests to be seventy-nine, and her scarlet nails, opulent jewellery, radiantly ash blonde hair, and general air of baroque splendour provide the glamour that contrasts with Edith's quiet good taste.

For Iris Pusey the romantic fiction written in Edith's revealing pseudonym of Vanessa Wilde is an antidote to a distasteful world of greed, sensationalism and easily available sex: '"Love means marriage to me," pursued Mrs Pusey. "Romance and courtship go together. A woman should be able to make a man worship her"' (pp. 74–5). But to Edith the pampered Mrs Pusey is an abomination of self-centredness; the type of manipulative, parasitic woman that she has come to despise most: these are the 'ultra-feminine ... the complacent consumers of men with their complicated but unwritten rules of what is due to them. Treats. Indulgences. Privileges. The right to make illogical fusses. The cult of themselves' (p. 146). For Edith Hope fiction is 'the time honoured resource of the ill at ease'. Her preferred reading matter is not romantic fiction but 'that sly old fox, Colette' (p. 67).

At the same time as Brookner has expressed her personal preference for the company of men and her dislike of feminism, her writing is saturated with references to women's traditions of writing. The question that pursues Brookner in her writing, no less than it obsesses Edith Hope in *Hotel du Lac*, is 'the question of what behaviour most becomes a woman, the question around which she had written most of her novels' (p. 40). It is also a question that connects her novels thematically to the eighteenth- and nineteenth-century conduct book. The ideal woman, according to Brookner in an interview given to *The Paris Review*, 'lives according to a set of principles and is somehow very rare and always has been'.[23] Brookner insists on high levels of ethical awareness from the heroines of her novels. Ruth Weiss in *A Start in Life*, for example, not only strives to live by exacting moral precepts but writes her doctoral thesis on vice and virtue in Balzac's novels. Frances Hinton, the heroine of the earlier *Look at Me*, talks of her own 'good behaviour, moral stuffiness, and general lack of experience in the wilder and more interesting areas of human conduct' (p. 75). However, sexual propriety and personal morality are not conflated and this separation provides for some of the interesting tensions and contradictions in Brookner's fiction. While these punctilious heroines aspire to honesty and scrupulous behaviour in their personal lives, Edith Hope and Ruth Weiss are both engaged in love affairs with married men.

The second tradition of women's writing to which Brookner's work connects is the novel of sensibility. Beginning from her statement that the women writers she admires in the English tradition are Rosamond Lehmann, Elizabeth Taylor and Storm Jameson, Olga Kenyon has situated Brookner within a tradition of twentieth-century women novelists to which can be added Rose Macaulay, Jean Rhys, Barbara Pym and Elizabeth Bowen.[24] Kenyon has argued that these authors are 'gifted at linking character and background, representing the restrictive effects of environment on a girl's psyche'. Moreover, they are able to 'represent the social frustration and intimate thought-processes of gifted, undervalued women'. In their novels of sensibility this group of women writers 'understand the suffering of women morally alone, the vulnerability of the ingenuously affectionate in a scheming, conventional society'.

Hotel du Lac has unmistakable echoes of Elizabeth Bowen's The Hotel in its setting and shrewdness of observation, and of Rosamond Lehmann's The Weather in the Streets in its emotional intensity. In an obituary in the Spectator Brookner gives details of her deepening friendship with Rosamond Lehmann in the latter's declining years: 'I dedicated Hotel du Lac to her because I hoped it might be the kind of novel she would find to her taste.' Brookner pays fulsome tribute to Rosamond Lehmann as 'a novelist in the grand tradition, and more than this, an innovator, the first writer to filter her stories through a woman's feeling and perceptions. She succeeds in giving a unique account of the world seen through feminine eyes.'[25]

The third way in which women's traditions of writing are invoked in Hotel du Lac is in Anita Brookner's homage to Virginia Woolf, the epitome of twentieth-century women's writing in the feminine tradition. From the beginning we are told that Edith Hope bears a strong 'physical resemblance to Virginia Woolf' (p. 8). Mr Neville flippantly addresses Edith as Mrs Woolf when he formally introduces himself. Later in their acquaintance he volunteers that 'whoever told you that you looked like Virginia Woolf did you a grave disservice, although I suppose you thought that it was a compliment' (p. 158). Virginia Woolf acts as an unseen but benign presence in Hotel du Lac. It is her influence which forces Edith to moderate her behaviour, to admit to her prejudices against women, and to modify her earlier harshness. In one telling incident Edith finds herself alone in her hotel room where she 'thought with shame of her small injustices, of her unworthy thoughts to those excellent women who had befriended her ... She bent her head, overcome by a sense of unworthiness. I have taken the name of Virginia Woolf in vain, she thought' (p. 88).

In an important study of writing by twentieth-century authors Rachel Blau Duplessis has commented on the importance of the displacement, erosion, or removal of the conventional marriage plot from the centre of the novel in the work of many twentieth-century women writers. Blau Duplessis has termed this project 'writing beyond the ending', 'taking ending as a metaphor for conventional narrative, for a regimen of resolutions, and for the social, sexual and ideological affirmation these make'.[26] What joins these otherwise disparate writers according to

Duplessis is their common desire to scrutinise the ideological character of the romance plot and related conventions in narrative and to change fiction so that it makes alternative statements about gender and its institutions.[27] Anita Brookner's romantic fiction clearly participates in the general collapse of these narrative paradigms. Romance is presented not as a source of joy but as a source of protracted anguish for her heroines. Edith's emotional legacy is a miscellany of twentieth-century insecurities which inevitably end in disillusionment as she refuses to relinquish her romantic dream but realises that 'that none of it can ever come true for me' (p. 181).

In what senses, then, is *Hotel du Lac* subversive? It is significant that Brookner's romantic novels provide the reader with neither a happy ending nor the conventional resolution in marriage that is the traditional outcome of the Mills and Boon romance. Instead, they substitute many examples of love misplaced, unrequited, or misunderstood that would appear to underline the truth that pure and absolute love is often dependent for its very existence upon a wilful ignorance of the true nature of the world. As Elizabeth Bowen once commented, 'it is not only our fate but our business to lose innocence, and once we have lost that it is futile to attempt a picnic in Eden'.[28]

The relationship of women to society in Brookner's early writing is in many ways ambivalent. It is one which at once expresses and denies illicit sexual desires. And because happiness remains elusive for her heroines it is also one which reproduces and reinforces a strong sense of female resentment. As Brookner has admitted, there is a strongly auto-biographical element in her fiction: 'One has to use one's own life: one has no other material.'[29] Although Edith Hope appears to be a highly assured and successful woman, appearances are deceptive. In reality, Edith, like Brookner herself, remains exceptionally vulnerable. The heroine's surface composure conceals the deep unhappiness that results from aspirations that cannot be met within the institutions of marriage and family in which those needs are created and expressed, and from an existence in which there is no community of female friends to which to turn for support. The sense of isolation to which Anita Brookner has confessed – 'I feel I'm walking about with the mark of Cain on my forehead. I feel I could get into *The Guinness Book of Records* as the world's loneliest, most miserable woman' – is also shared by her heroine in *Hotel du Lac*.[30]

Since no external impediment is placed in the way of the continuation of her career as a writer, Edith is not faced with the choice between marriage and her profession. Indeed, Mr Neville even suggests that the married name of Edith Neville would be a good name for a writer. But Anita Brookner resists the feminist implications of her own writing by showing all the alternatives to marriage as second-best options for women and holding the absence of a central and permanent relationship with a man as responsible for her heroines' states of isolation, lovelessness and unfulfilment. *Hotel du Lac* does not deny the importance of personal autonomy for women. Quite the opposite, the success of the heroine in her chosen profession is a measure of how seriously she takes herself. But the novel does construct a specific kind of female self: the self in relation to others, as well as a notion of psychic wholeness which is guaranteed only by the heroine's connection to the object of her desire. In this respect Anita Brookner's writing perpetuates rather than subverts the old-established traditions of English romantic fiction.

Notes

1   Umberto Eco, Postscript to *The Name of the Rose* (New York: Harcourt Brace Jovanovich, 1984), pp. 67–8.
2   Anita Brookner, *A Start in Life* (London: Jonathan Cape, 1981); *Providence* (London: Jonathan Cape, 1982); *Look at Me* (London: Jonathan Cape, 1983); *Hotel du Lac* (London: Jonathan Cape, 1984).
3   John Haffenden, 'Playing straight: interview with Anita Brookner', *The Literary Review* (September, 1984), pp. 25–31, 29.
4   Ibid., p. 28.
5   Joan Smith, *A Masculine Ending* (London: Faber and Faber, 1987), p. 125.
6   John Skinner, *The Fictions of Anita Brookner: Illusions of Romance* (Basingstoke: Macmillan, 1992), p. 1.
7   Flora Alexander, *Contemporary Women Novelists* (London: Edward Arnold, 1989), p. 33.
8   Anita Brookner, *Lewis Percy* (London: Jonathan Cape, 1989); Skinner, *Anita Brookner*, p. 1; Peter Kemp, 'The mouse that whinged', Review of *Lewis Percy, Sunday Times* (27 August 1989), G6, quoted in Skinner, p. 128.
9   Margaret Diane Stetz in Suzanne W. Jones (ed.), *Writing the Woman Artist: Essays on Poetics, Politics and Portraiture* (Philadelphia: The University of Pennysylvania Press, 1991), pp. 96–112, 102.
10 Lynne Pearce and Jackie Stacey (eds), *Romance Revisited* (London: Lawrence and Wishart, 1994), p. 32.
11 Byron, *Don Juan*, ([1819] London: Penguin, 1986) c.l. cxxiii.
12 Barbara Hardy, 'A Cinderella's loneliness', *Times Literary Supplement* (14 September 1984), pp. 10–19.
13 Patricia Waugh, *Feminist Fictions: Revisiting the Postmodern* (London: Routledge, 1989), p. 126.
14 Ibid., p. 145.
15 Daphne Watson, *Their Own Worst Enemies: Women Writers of Women's Fiction* (London: Pluto Press, 1995), p. 14.
16 Shusha Guppy, interview with Anita Brookner, *The Paris Review*, Fall, 1987, pp. 325–42, 331.
17 Jane Flax, 'Postmodernism and gender relations in feminist theory', in Linda Nicholson (ed.), *Feminism/Postmodernism* (London: Routledge, 1990), pp. 39–62, 43.
18 Shusha Guppy interview, pp. 335–6.
19 Ibid., p. 328.
20 John Haffenden interview, p. 29.
21 Ibid.
22 Janice Radway, *Reading the Romance: Women, Patriarchy and Popular Literature* (Chapel Hill: The University of North Carolina Press, 1984), p. 112.
23 Shusha Guppy interview, p. 336.

24   Olga Kenyon, *Women Writers Today* (Brighton: The Harvester Press, 1988), p. 49.
25   Anita Brookner, 'Rosamond Lehmann', *Spectator* (17 March 1990), pp. 20–1, 21.
26   Rachel Blau Duplessis, *Writing Beyond the Ending: Narrative Strategies of Twentieth-Century Women Writers* (Bloomington: The Indiana University Press, 1985), p. 21.
27   Ibid., p. x.
28   Elizabeth Bowen, *Collected Impressions* (London: Longmans Green 1950), p. 265.
29   John Haffenden interview, pp. 69–70.
30   Ibid., p. 36.

7

Lynne Pearce

Another Time, Another Place: The Chronotope of Romantic Love in Contemporary Feminist Fiction

> In the literary artistic chronotope, spatial and temporal indicators are fused into one carefully thought out, concrete whole. Time, as it were, thickens, takes on flesh, becomes artistically visible; likewise, space becomes charged and responsive to movements of time, plot and history.[1]

The above quotation is perhaps Mikhail Bakhtin's most suggestive statement on the complex inter-relatedness of time and space as it is represented in the literary text. Meaning literally 'time-space' (chronos-topos), the chronotope, considered until recently a rather incidental element in Bakhtin's theoretical universe, offers readers a means of focusing on the 'intrinsic connectedness of temporal and spatial relations' and revealing their ideological function.[2] In an article entitled 'Chronotopes for women under capital', for example, Mary O'Connor has pointed to the 'defamiliarization' of domestic time-space in the work of contemporary women writers.[3] She argues that through an emphasis on the 'presentness' of domestic existence, authors like Alice Munro and Bharati Mukerjee have graphically captured the claustrophobia experienced by their female protagonists. These are texts in which time slows down and 'thickens' (to invoke Bakhtin's term) to such an extent that it becomes synonymous with the spatial confines of the women's lives. Thus, what at first appears to be a purely formalist interest in narrative poetics yields a complex political comment on the texts concerned.

In this chapter I want to cross the same bridge between the formal and the ideological by looking at the representation of romantic love in contemporary feminist fiction. This investigation derives directly from my own earlier work with Bakhtin's theory. My book, *Reading Dialogics* (1994) has a chapter entitled 'Gendering the chronotope' in which I perform readings of Jeanette Winterson's *Sexing the Cherry* (1989) and Toni Morrison's *Beloved* (1987) and in which I argue that we must recognise the gendered specificity of all spatio-temporal relations.[4] This is to correct the blatant gender-blindness evident in Bakhtin's own presentation of the chronotope. My reading of Winterson's text also reveals the existence of a 'romantic love chronotope': a spatio-temporal continuum which exists apart from the 'historical' lives of the characters, but into which all are liable to be swept as into a black hole. This chronotope of romantic love differs from all the other chronotopes represented in Winterson's profoundly *polychronotopic* novel in that it is, in terms of Bakhtin's own vocabulary, 'empty time': a spatio-temporal corridor running 'outside' or 'beyond' the diachronic processes of the material world.[5] Bakhtin writes about this condition of chronotopic suspension in his analysis of the 'adventure chronotope' in early mythological literature.[6] In such texts, he argues, time effectively 'stands still': the 'empty time' between the beginning and end of the action (usually represented by the meeting and marriage of two lovers) is effectively immune from the effects of the passing years. It is, indeed, a black hole in which all the usual rules of time and space which govern our everyday, 'historical' existence are suspended.

The radical ('magical') dislocation of time/space associated in the popular imagination with the moment of falling in love (what Roland Barthes names *'ravissement'*), is captured in Winterson's text by her central character's inability to 'fix' it within the diachronic sequence of his life.[7] On his travels through the New World, Jordan chances upon the 'City of the Twelve Dancing Princesses' where he encounters a woman, Fortunata, whose rediscovery becomes his holy grail. Their eventual union is so dislocated from the rest of his adventures, however, that even as he describes it he is unable to say whether it belongs to the past or to the future. He observes:

> The scene I have just described to you may be in the future or in the past. Either I have found Fortunata or I will find her. I cannot be sure. Either I am remembering her, or I am still imagining her. But she is somewhere in the grid of time, a co-ordinate, as I am.[8]

When he finally does rediscover Fortunata, moreover, Jordan has no sense of whether it is 'years' or 'days' since he first set eyes on her. Although, according to the life story she subsequently relates, Fortunata should now be an old woman, she appears to Jordan – in true Sleeping

Beauty fashion – magically unchanged: 'Then I saw a young woman, darting in a figure of eight in between the lights and turning her hands through it as a potter turns clay on the wheel.'[9]

What my more recent research has uncovered, however, is that Winterson's text, predicated upon a faithful reinscription of Bakhtin's 'adventure chronotope', is very much the exception in contemporary feminists' representations of romantic love. What I have found, and what I shall be arguing here, is that feminist novelists, from Patricia Highsmith (1950s) to Margaret Elphinstone (1990s), and ranging across a broad selection of genres (romance, fantasy, science-fiction and crime) are resistant to the notion that the chronotope of love is 'empty' (in the sense that the protagonists' former/other/'on-going' lives are forgotten or suspended.[10] While the experience of love represents the same transportation to 'another time'/'another place' as it does in classic and/or fairy-tale romance, and while (as I shall be arguing) this identification with a 'new world' is integral to the *politics* of romantic desire, connections with the 'old world' are rarely suspended. Instead, the transportation effected by the *ravissement* positions the lover in such a way that she is able to see her other life clearly and for the first time. This is to say that while she is physically/psychically removed from its sphere, she carries it with her as a memory or burden (as symbolically represented by the piano in Jane Campion's film of the same name).[11] This might, of course, be interpreted as evidence of a deep core of anti-romantic sentiment in contemporary women's writing (women no longer allow themselves to be 'swept off their feet'), but I prefer to see it as a radicalising dimension *within* a discourse which still upholds the emotional/political necessity of romantic desire. While our love/desire for another remains essential to our growth and self-development, we should embark on love's journey with our eyes open rather than shut. Even as we cross the border to the 'new world', so should we keep looking back at the old, and measuring the distance between. And we must also bear the full cost of this journey within us: its purpose is clearly to enable us to grow and change, not to escape. It is for this reason that the romance chronotopes of contemporary feminist fiction cannot be 'empty': the lovers will alter and age just as quickly there (perhaps more quickly!) as they would in their other (co-existent) lives.

The analysis of the representation of the romantic love chronotope in contemporary feminist fiction which follows is broad ranging. Rather than perform close analyses of one or two texts I have preferred, in this instance, to emphasise the similarities between the texts and genres by cross-referencing between a number of texts from the 1950s to the present. This said, most of the those I have selected are British, and the majority were published in the 1980s. The criterion for this selection was largely personal (the texts which happened to come my way), but I was interested in representing a variety of genres: science-fiction and crime (two of the most popular genres amongst today's feminist readers) seemed, for example, to espouse plot conventions which would put interesting new pressures on the tempo-spatial experience of romantic love. Meanwhile, I begin my own chronotopic wanderings with an examination of the way in which in contemporary feminist fiction, even as in classic or popular romance, the moment of *ravissement* is pre-empted by, or necessitates, a journey to 'another place'.

Stranger in Paradise: The Demise of Classic Romance

The exotic locations of popular romantic fiction (Mills and Boon/Harlequin) are commonly seen as part of their escapist appeal, although few commentators have thought to question what this displacement represents other than a 'setting' for the love affair. While it is true that in 'formula' romance the changes in location (and/or historical setting in the case of 'historical romance') are often the only distinguishing factors between texts, the scenery is clearly more than a backdrop to the action. Indeed, I would argue that in many instances it is the *lifestyle* implicit in the location, rather than the hero himself, that the heroine desires. In classic romance (and its popular rewrites) the location and the hero are, of course, intertwined in a nexus of wealth and status. He is an aristocrat who owns an estate or its modern equivalent, the business empire; or he is an heroic wanderer/exile whose journeys take him to the most remote and dangerous corners of the globe. It is the freedom and autonomy represented by these 'masculine' chronotopes, I would suggest, that the heroine is principally desirous of: which is why the spaces/places of romantic fiction are described in such complete and fetishistic detail. As she enters her lover's house/kingdom, the heroine is able to vicariously inhabit his 'time'. This habitation has nothing to do, of course, with her relationship to the space/place at the end of the story. The closure of the classic romance sees the heroine (now permanently instated as 'wife') as distanced as before from the masculine chronotope inhabited by her husband, but during the period of the romance itself she will have become fully (if temporarily) identified with its pleasures. Hence we must see the wild moors, gothic buildings, expansive seas and exotic sunsets of romantic fiction not as mere conventions, but as symbols of (another) life redolent with freedom, excitement and the possibility of change.

It is the sad fact that within most popular romantic fiction, however, change and transformation are the prerogative of the (male) hero.[12] He is 'tamed' by the heroine to reveal another (caring, morally responsible) aspect of his character which has been erstwhile repressed, while she merely 'discovers' her lost self through her love for him. This is to say, the unformed, 'orphan' identity she inhabits at the beginning of the narrative never grows or develops except in the direction of her vicarious identification with her lover. As we have already noted, however, to identify with is not to become: the classic romance heroine does not become (like) her lover, but his wife. In chronotopic terms she has entered paradise, but as a stranger. Having no cultural/economic rights to his home/kingdom she must remain forever in exile.

How, then, have feminist writers reconceived the spatio-temporal displacement intrinsic to romantic fiction? Certainly they have not dispensed with the convention itself.

A Stake in Paradise: The Feminist Alternative

The majority of texts I am dealing with here begin, in classic romance style, with a hero/ine whose 'social identity is thrown into question', and whose romance begins with a journey to a new location.[13] We have already observed, for example, how Jordan, the hero of Jeanette Winterson's *Sexing the Cherry* undertakes a fantastical voyage to the 'New World' (it is the mid-seventeenth century) and in the City of the Twelve Dancing Princesses discovers its first lady, Fortunata. Implicit in the fairy-tale conventions by which Winterson abides is the *extremity* of the displacement. Falling in love 'properly' requires transportation to a world in which the protagonist is forced to 'fold up the maps and put away the globe' because nothing in that world corresponds with his/her existing coordinates of time and space.[14] The same convention is observed by Ellen Galford whose novel *The Fires of Bride* (1986) opens with its narrator (a newspaper reporter) being despatched to Cailleach, 'the outermost island of the Utter Utter Hebrides'.[15]

> I have arrived. Dear goddess, what now?
> I am used to loneliness in my line of work. A wintry week in Peterhead, surveying fishing-industry fatalities and fending off oil-related sales reps in the hotel bar. A fortnight in the suburbs of Aberdeen, doing an under-cover shock-horror probe on battered middle-class housewives (they never screened it) ...
> But there is nothing quite so lonely as to sit in the bar of the Cailleach Inn, listening to a jumble of conversation between people who have known each other all their lives. And joining in none of it (as if I could – it's half in Gaelic). Outside the battering rain, carried on a dirty wind from the mainland, makes escape impossible.
> Meanwhile I memorise the maps and study the (skimpy and badly printed) local guidebook, trying to get a fix on the place in time and space.[16]

Of course, according to the convention that I have just invoked, it is absolutely necessary that the romantic hero/ine begins their adventure *without* a fix on time and space. Sorting out this puzzle is part of the process of getting to know the 'new world', and is quickly synonymous with the process of 'falling in love' with its romantic representative. In Galford's novel, for example, the heroine, Maria Milleney (who is a character separate from the narrator, Liz) is very obviously prepared for her romance with the local GP, Catriona MacEochan, by her desire to 'know' Cailleach:

> You'd think she was made of iron filings, so strongly does the magnetic North attract her. Whenever she has escaped from anything, she does so by working her way to the top of the map ...
>
> Now, though, she's heading North in a big way. She has bought an Ordnance Survey map, a pair of hiking boots, and an elderly second-hand *Guide to the Outer Isles*.[17]

What is significant about Galford's text, however, and a point to which I shall return, is the fact that Maria Milleney's love affair with Cailleach is, from the beginning and throughout, *in excess* of her desire for Catriona. In this text, unlike those of classics or popular romance, the desirability of the location/lifestyle is kept separate from the person who is its representative. And by this means the lover can work towards an identification with her 'landscape of desire' which is not vicarious.

One of the reasons for Maria Milleney's journey to the 'Utter Utter Hebrides' is 'the definitive ending to a terminally ill love affair' and former failed romances are, of course, one of the most common reasons hero/ines 'absent' themselves from home.[18] In these scenarios the strangeness of the new location represents an emotional/cultural challenge to the protagonists that helps them loosen their hold on their old obsession. This is very manifestly the case in one of the most popular lesbian romances of recent years, Jane Rule's *Desert of the Heart* (1964).[19] In this text the heat of the Nevada desert, combined with the extreme cultural displacement effected in Evelyn's move from a West Coast university to the gambling town of Reno, are so totally consuming (and initially threatening) that the heroine is freed from the illusory 'reality' of her former existence:

> The street fingered out from the main crossroad for just three short blocks of faded bungalows and no trees. At the end was the desert, sudden, flat, dull miles of it until it heaved itself upward and became the mountains. An irrational fear, as alien to Evelyn's nature as heat lightning seems to a summer sky, struck through her body. For a moment she could not move. Then she turned slowly, refusing in herself the desire to run, and walked back to the house.[20]

This is not to say (in line with my previous comments) that the heroine enters an 'empty time' in which her 'other life' disappears from view, but rather that it is defamiliarised to such an extent that she is able to question its authenticity.

This provision for interrogating a past life is also the experience of Walser, the American reporter-hero of Angela Carter's *Nights at the Circus* (1986), whose exile in Siberia is the only displacement extreme enough to cut the cords to his former life which have hitherto prevented his reconstruction as a subject fit for Fevvers' love:

> As Walser slowly began to recover his wits among the forest dwellers, those wits proved of as little use to him as one crazy eye would have been to a company of the sightless. When he was visited by memories of the world outside of the village, as sometimes happened, he thought that he was raving. All his previous experiences were rendered null and void.[21]

It is also highly significant that in Carter's text it is the hero more than the heroine who is in need of an educative displacement. In an ironic reversal of the classic romance plot, Carter has Walser as the unformed *ingenue* whose desire for Fevvers and transportation to a 'temporal dimension which did not take history into account' combine to 'hatch' him anew.[22]

In all the texts mentioned thus far, the journey to the new world prefigures the romantic encounter *per se*. In other texts/genres, however, the journey is *intrinsic* to the romance. In Patricia Highsmith's *Carol* the two female protagonists (nineteen-year-old Therese and the older wife and mother, Carol) are only able to confront their sexual desire for one another once they have left their home city of New York and begun a long motor trip across America. In 'Forms of chronotope in the novel', Bakhtin alludes to the 'chronotope of the road' as a common ingredient across literary genres, and twentieth-century culture has most certainly celebrated this particular temporal-spatial displacement through a new species of picaresque novel and the 'road movie'.[23] In Highsmith's novel it is clearly both the anonymity and provisionality of travel that enable the protagonists finally to 'risk' their desire. Significantly, the consummation of the relationship occurs in a time/space so anonymous and displaced that it is only afterwards that the lovers discover its name (Waterloo), upon which Therese observes: 'There's a couple of Waterloos in every state.'[24]

The road is also the principal chronotopic trajectory for the majority of feminist detectives. As they move from clue to clue, from crime to crime, and from novel to novel, the heroines of feminist crime fiction enjoy a lifestyle so picaresque that it is unhelpful to think of them in relation to fixed pasts or presents. Their romances, too (which are an intrinsic ingredient of most crime fiction, feminist or otherwise) tend to mimic the transitoriness of their lives, and lovers are turned over almost as frequently as crimes. Sometimes, as in Val McDermid's 'Lindsay Gordon' series, a love affair might stretch across a number of novels, but the conventions of the genre demand that the lover always has a predecessor (who is being mourned) and a successor.[25] The romance of feminist crime fiction is the romance of serial monogamy and, since the action invariably takes the heroine on some kind of journey, it is also the romance of the road. This is clearly a rather different deployment of the chronotope of the road from Highsmith's novel (where it represents a primary displacement similar to the journeys of the other romances we have considered), but for the hero/heroine scared of commitment (another convention of the crime genre) it symbolises a similar kind of liberation. This is not to say, however, that the road romance is a reinscription of the 'empty time' of Bakhtin's adventure chronotope. The sense of the road stretching behind them might give these heroines a new perspective on the past (it diminishes), but it is not forgotten. In these texts, just as in the others I have mentioned, the purpose of the romantic journey is to gain critical perspective on the other time/place, not to escape it.

From these examples and the other texts I will subsequently cite, it may be seen that contemporary feminist writers have just as much investment in the convention of sending their protagonists on a journey as have the authors of classic and popular romantic fiction. A spatial dislocation is necessary to break the bonds which have until then tied the hero/heroine to the 'old world', but *unlike* popular romance the purpose of the displacement is clearly not only one of 'preparing' the protagonist for a (new) romance. Indeed, in the case of the previous citations, the primary purpose of the removal would seem to be to enable the heroine to realise the parameters of her (previously repressed) desires (to figuratively 'broaden her horizons'), to be able to reflect (critically) upon the narrowness of her former life/circumstances, and to prepare for a deconstruction/reconstruction of the self (that will not be resolved by a simple identification with the impending lover/Other). Indeed, in every respect the new location heralds possible transformations *in excess* of a romantic attachment. We feel that through their journeys these protagonists are going to 'realise' themselves in new and creative ways. These novels of romance are thus more properly novels of education and development (*bildungsroman*). As such they are novels in which romance precipitates confrontation, not escape.

The View from the Bridge

> The river is drowning its hands.
> You are not here this evening.
> I am crossing the same bridge alone.
> Underneath it is dark and fast, the river,

I can't see myself. Lights hang on trees
by the banks – glowing and forbidden.
Dropping like fruit into the dark water,
only to rise again.

No matter how many times we try to sink
our past – old bundles of clothes in the river –
the body surfaces

suddenly, covered in wreaths.[26]

This extract from Jackie Kay's poem, 'The crossing', describes the way in
which our new romances are always haunted by the old. As for the
heroine of Jane Campion's film, *The Piano*, the speaker of Kay's poem
cannot escape a burden ('body') of past memories which keep resurfacing.
In chronotopic terms, what is suggestive about Kay's poem is the way in
which this past is viewed spatially through the metaphor of the (static)
bridge and the (flowing) river. Following Bakhtin's configuration, this is
a perfect instance of the way in which time and space can become
expressions of one another. From the bridge (a place of crossing from the
old world to the new), the speaker looks down/back upon her former life,
the river, only to realise that it is still part of her present as it passes *under*
the bridge on which she stands (the present).

This confrontation of past selves/relationships through a chronotopic
displacement in the present is also, as I have been suggesting, a feature
of much contemporary feminist fiction. 'Falling in love' provides the
protagonists of these novels with a metaphorical bridge, or crossing,
from which they can review their former (ongoing) lives.

One of the most original and explicit utilisations of the 'crossing'
chronotope in recent fiction is Margaret Elphinstone's novel, *A Sparrow's
Flight* (1989). In this remarkable text, set in a future many centuries
beyond our own, but seeming more like 'the past' because the 'time
before' was laid waste by a nuclear disaster, two travellers (Naomi and
Thomas) undertake a month-long journey across the Scottish borders,
during which they come to terms with their past lives through their
growing involvement with one another. While this is certainly not a
romance in the classic sense (Thomas's homosexuality prevents the
possibility of a sexual closure to the narrative), their meeting is most
certainly a catalyst for change and transformation. In a subtle reworking
of the romance formula, moreover, the journey of both characters to
Thomas's home in the so-called 'empty lands' (formerly the Lake District,
the country most poisoned by the nuclear catastrophe) provides a
chronotopic displacement similar to that of the 'road' novels/films discussed
earlier. Naomi's spatio-temporal disorientation as they cross the
borderlands is similar to Evelyn's when she arrives in Reno:

Naomi looked. More hills, disappearing into twilight. She was in the heart of it now, a vast country traversed by this road of his she couldn't even see. It was like a place in a dream. All she wanted now was to sleep and for the dream to stay with her. She had no more words, so she merely nodded, and let him lead on.[27]

Where this chronotopic displacement breaks with the traditional romance conventions is in the fact that both protagonists undertake the journey together (though this is also, as we have seen, a feature of Highsmith's *Carol*), and that for Thomas the journey is not only a journey *away* (from his recent life on 'the Island') but also a journey *home*. What I want to suggest as part of my argument here, however, is that in this double movement (away/home) Elphinstone is merely making explicit what is the hidden subplot of all romance: that our journey towards another place/person is simultaneously a trajectory of return. There are, of course, plenty of psychoanalytic discourses to explain this: in Freudian, Lacanian and object-relations theories all romantic desire is understood as an attempt to fill the gap caused by the loss of the original 'love object' (mother/father), but Elphinstone's text (like Kay's poem) also encourages us to think of the reflex in terms of subsequent adult relationships that need to be revisited. What is striking about *A Sparrow's Flight* in this respect is the way in which the 'romantic' journey is manifestly *not* one of escape. Although Naomi and Thomas travel through the 'empty lands' they never come to occupy the 'empty space' of Bakhtin's adventure chronotope: the past is ever with them (indeed it is the painful 'object' of Thomas's journey), and becomes more visible (like the body resurfacing in Kay's poem) the further they go. About her lost child Naomi thus observes: 'I dream about him so much on this journey. More than I have for years. It reminds me, somehow. When I'm awake I don't think about it, but in my dreams it all comes back, and I can't stop it.'[28]

In chronotopic terms, moreover, this continual criss-crossing between past and present, new world and old, is graphically encoded in the symbol of the border. As they make the hundred-mile journey from north to south and east to west, Naomi and Thomas are constantly presented with views both ahead and behind. In this spiralling journey they may, perhaps, be thought of as the metaphorical equivalent of the Border Reivers (Scottish and English clans) who, for a long and violent period of history, made raids into one another's territory. What Naomi and Thomas are, of course, raiding, is not property but the topography of past and future.

Another fantasy text in which a romantic encounter in the present is very explicitly an attempt to re-evaluate a former life is Marge Piercy's science-fiction novel, *Body of Glass*.[29] As for Thomas in Elphinstone's novel, Shira's (the central protagonist) adventure is precipitated by a journey home, while her romantic and sexual involvement with the Cyborg, Yod, offers a 'bridge' or 'crossing' from which she is able to get a new perspective on her relationship with her former lover, Gadi. As would be expected in a science-fiction story of the twenty-first century, the radical displacement of time and space as we know it is intrinsic to the defamiliarisation of relationships offered by this text.

The fact that Shira, the central heroine, has never been able to escape her early involvement with Gadi is symbolically supported by the fact that she is still linked to him through the sophisticated system of communication and computer technology that engenders and sustains a complex network of 'virtual' relationships. Any moment of the day or night she is able to access his whereabouts in the present, or rerun episodes from their 'past' relationship. Indeed, past and present have been so collapsed by the new technology that attempts to 'escape' one's former existence (as in classic romance) are impossible. Thus imprisoned by the virtual evidence of her past life, it is significant that Shira is able to break free of Gadi's enduring hold on her only through Yod's displacement of him in 'the Base' (the 'deepest' level of the computer system to which the protagonists have access). Physical gestures of escape/displacement (such as excursions into the 'raw': the world outside the 'wrap' protecting all cities from the toxic atmosphere) are ineffectual. The chronotopes of the twenty-first century are defined by laws of time and space other than Einstein's. By connecting with Shira in the Base in the way that he does, however, Yod fills Shira's 'available mental space' so completely that Gadi is temporarily erased.[30] The sexual consummation which follows this 'mental' connection between the lovers is insignificant by comparison. Yod fully recognises this when he tells her: 'But you are what I want. This isn't crazy but good. I want to know all of you, I want to enter every part of you, as I enter the Base and explore it.'[31] For the lovers in this text, then, the establishment of a romantic connection requires much more than a spatial relocation. Not for them the magical, 'empty time' in which one's past life drops away; rather a 'war of chronotopes' in which one time-space seeks to assert itself as more vitual than another.

Conclusion: Across the Border

In the last section we have seen how falling in love (*ravissement*) is a liminal chronotopic experience (bridge/border/crossing) which, far from being an escape, provides its actors with a new time-space from which to confront their former (other) lives. I would like to conclude by considering, briefly, what sorts of changes/transformations this enables the lovers of contemporary feminist fiction to make: how the perception and materialisation of their desires/frustrations enables them to reconstruct a new and better existence.

In Carter's *Nights at the Circus*, the central transformation, as we have already observed, is Walser's. Through his radical spatial/temporal displacements (Fevvers' dressing room, where the clock stands still; the circus; Siberia) and through his slowly emerging desire for Fevvers he is reconstructed as the newest of 'new men'. Until this moment in his life he has been, we are informed, something of a *tabula rasa*. It is not, as is the case with the heroine of classic romance, that his life has been 'narrow or 'limited' (he has travelled widely throughout the world), but that it has been empty. This, indeed, suggests a nicely ironic inversion of Bakhtin's 'adventure chronotope' in which the 'empty time' is the time outside/before the romance. Instead of the hero/ine ceasing to age/grow/develop when he or she falls in love, it is the moment Walser begins.

Meanwhile, as she comes to recognise her desire for Walser, Fevvers starts to deconstruct/reconstruct also. During the journey through Siberia, in which she breaks her wing and sees her blond hair turning brown, Fevvers comes to terms with the limits of her self-invention and realises that her life is as provisional as Walser's. Desire for one another, and for the approval of one another ('She felt her outlines waver; she felt herself trapped forever in the reflection of Walser's eyes'), makes both characters realise that human identity is contingent and profoundly dialogic.[32] Romantic love, in this case, is most certainly a quest for the self rather than for the other.

In some of the other texts mentioned here, such as Galford's *The Fires of Bride* and Elphinstone's *A Sparrow's Flight*, we have observed that the space/place of romance (or the journey towards it) is the expression of a desire in excess of the love relationship itself. This conforms, in my opinion (and as I indicated at the beginning of the chapter) with the covert subtext of much romantic fiction: what the heroines most desire are the spaces/places of romance rather than the man who presently 'owns' them. In contemporary feminist fiction, however, this displacement of romantic desire is made explicit. Although Maria Milleney, the heroine of Galford's *The Fires of Bride*, is clearly burned by her affair with Catriona, this human infatuation becomes incidental alongside her passionate involvement with the island of Cailleach (its landscape, its history, its community), and it is Cailleach rather than Catriona that gives Maria back her creativity. The ability to work, rather than the reciprocating love of another human being, is thus the closure of this particular feminist romance, and it is interesting to observe that a credible professional identity is also what Therese achieves through her relationship with Carol in Highsmith's novel.

In *A Sparrow's Flight*, meanwhile, the 'sought-for-object' of the romantic quest is rather less easily named, although we recognise that once again it is not love itself.[33] Naomi and Thomas do not discover each other so much as themselves *through* one another. The purpose of travelling to another time/place has been to explore the possibility of living in another world, without losing sight of the old.

In a short story entitled 'Fair Ellen and the wanderer returned', Janice Galloway turns Bakhtin's 'adventure chronotope' on its head.[34] In an unflinching rewrite of the classic fairy-tale romances which have the hero go out into the world for ten years to prove his manhood before returning to claim the woman who has waited patiently for him, the 'wanderer' of Galloway's text returns to find Ellen aged, worn down, broken, and married to another:

> You have come back as you promised and I'm grateful. But you have come back too late.
> She let him stare. It took time till the dullness began filming on his face, seeping slow into his features. She let it take time, then spoke again, knowing he was ready to hear now.
> You have come back too late. I am married.[35]

What Galloway's text is saying, of course, is that time – even for lovers – does not stand still. During her lover's absence, Ellen has been obliged to care for two sick parents until their deaths, and now for a sick husband. She has suffered untold economic hardship and privation. She has aged dramatically. And on his heroic quests through the world the hero has aged also. His brown face is covered with lines and his hair is grey. During all the time that he believed time to be suspended, it has been moving forward – relentlessly. The romantic chronotope, whatever its magic, is never empty.

This sober postscript is not, however, the whole story. As I have already suggested, contemporary feminist fiction's insistence that we reject the tempo-spatial 'escapism' of classic romance is *not* to deny the importance of romantic love *per se*. Rather, as we have seen, desire for another (and the alternative space/place they inhabit) can be the means by which individuals negotiate a new life for themselves. The journey across the border is, at best, a journey of change and self-actualisation. Past lives and former relationships are not left behind, but perceived with a (liberating) critical distance. From our place in the new world, we can finally 'fix' the times and spaces of the old. Falling in love requires a careful use of map and compass.

Notes

1   Mikhail Bakhtin, *The Dialogic Imagination: Four Essays by M.M. Bakhtin* ed. Michael Holquist, trans. Caryl Emerson and Michael Holquist (Austin, Texas: University of Texas Press, 1981).
2   Ibid., p. 84.
3   Mary O'Connor, 'Chronotopes for women under capital: an investigation into the relation of women to objects', *Critical Studies* 2, 1–2, pp. 137–51.

4   Lynne Pearce, *Reading Dialogics* (London: Edward Arnold, 1994). See also Jeanette
    Winterson, *Sexing the Cherry* (London: Bloomsbury, 1989).
5   Polychronotopic is the term I invoke to describe texts in which multiple chronotopes
    exist side by side. See *Reading Dialogics*, p. 175.
6   Bakhtin, *The Dialogic Imagination*, p. 91.
7   See Roland Barthes, *A Lover's Discourse: Fragments*, trans. Richard Howard
    (Harmondsworth: Penguin, 1977).
8   Winterson, *Sexing the Cherry*, p. 104.
9   Ibid., p. 103.
10 See Patricia Highsmith, *Carol* (first published as *The Price of Salt* in 1952) (London:
    Bloomsbury, 1991); and Margaret Elphinstone, *A Sparrow's Flight* (Edinburgh: Polygon
    Press, 1989).
11 *The Piano* (dir. Jane Campion, 1993). See also Jane Campion and Kate Pullinger, *The
    Piano: A Novel* (London: Bloomsbury, 1994). I also deal with this text in some detail
    in my book, *Feminism and the Politics of Reading* (London: Edward Arnold, 1997).
12 See Janice Radway, *Reading the Romance: Women, Patriarchy and Popular Literature*
    (Chapel Hill: University of North Carolina Press, 1984), for discussion of these 'trans-
    formations'.
13 'Social identity thrown into question': this is an allusion to Vladimir Propp's analysis
    of the folktale which proposed that all such texts are structured around 31 'functions'
    (events) including this, the catalyst of the subsequent action. See Vladimir Propp,
    Morphology of the Folktale ([1928] Austin, Texas: University of Texas Press, 1986).
14 Winterson, *Sexing the Cherry*, p. 88.
15 Ellen Galford, *The Fires of Bride* (London: The Women's Press, 1986), p. 5.
16 Ibid., p. 7.
17 Ibid., p. 19.
18 Ibid., p. 19.
19 Jane Rule, *Desert of the Heart* ([1964] London: Pandora Press, 1986). See also the film
    Desert Hearts (dir. Donna Deitch, 1985).
20 Rule, *Desert of the Heart*, p. 19.
21 Angela Carter, *Nights at the Circus* (London: Virago, 1986), p. 252.
22 Ibid., p. 265.
23 See Bakhtin, *The Dialogic Imagination*, p. 248.
24 Highsmith, *Carol*, p. 166.
25 Val McDermid has written four novels in this series: *Report for Murder* (London:
    Women's Press, 1987); *Common Murder* (London: Women's Press, 1989); *Final Edition*
    (London: Women's Press, 1991); *Union Jack* (London: Women's Press, 1993).
26 Jackie Kay, *Other Lovers* (London: Bloodaxe Books, 1993), p. 36.
27 Elphinstone, *A Sparrow's Flight*, p. 38.
28 Ibid., p. 238.
29 Marge Piercy, *Body of Glass* (Harmondsworth: Penguin, 1991).
30 Ibid., p. 226.
31 Ibid., p. 225.
32 Carter, *Nights at the Circus*, p. 290; 'Profoundly dialogic': here I am invoking dialogism
    in the everyday sense of 'interactive', although my chapter on 'Dialogism and the subject'
    in *Reading Dialogics* (Ibid., pp. 149–72) does suggest ways in which Bakhtin's literary
    and linguistic models may be used to rethink subjective and inter-subjective relations.
33 'Sought-for-object': another reference to Vladimir Propp's typology of the folktale (see
    note 13). The 'Princess' or 'Sought-for-Object' (which might not be human) is one of
    the seven 'spheres of action' he identifies in his structural analysis of these texts.
34 Janice Galloway, 'Fair Ellen and the wanderer returned', in *Blood* (London: Minerva,
    1991).
35 Janice Galloway, 'Fair Ellen', p. 72.

8

Judy Simons

Rewriting the Love Story: The Reader as Writer in Daphne du Maurier's *Rebecca*

In its interrogation of the classic romance, English fiction invariably engages with the conceptual frameworks of gender. Heroines such as Jane Eyre correspondingly renegotiate existing models of the feminine whilst complying with a fictive denouement that can absorb the problematics of a too-tidy solution. While post-feminist readers might wish to quarrel with the apparently humdrum prospect of domestic harmony with which Brontë's novel concludes, the dangers of imposing a twentieth-century ideological awareness, together with its attendant politically attuned sensibilities, on a text which is firmly grounded in its historical moment must be avoided. As Gillian Beer has argued, critical practice needs to 'recognise the *difference* of past writing and past concerns instead of converting them into our current categories ... The encounter with the otherness of earlier literature can allow us to recognise and challenge our own assumptions, and those of the society in which we live.'[1] *Jane Eyre* (1847) is sufficiently revolutionary in its reworking of the narrative formulae of its age without requiring Charlotte Brontë to manifest any additional percipience in foretelling the feminist future. Daphne du Maurier's *Rebecca* (1938) shows how the altered consciousness of the twentieth-century ideological climate facilitates radical variants of the basic *Jane Eyre* scenario so as to elicit the concealed subtexts detected by modern critics. Moreover, *Rebecca* does not abandon but exploits and redeploys the romantic conventions which sustain the readerly pleasure that traditional love stories evoke. Its familiar devices construct a narrative line which is immensely reassuring to readers because, in Janice Radway's words, 'the romantic writer's typical discourse leads the reader to make abductions and inferences that are always immediately confirmed. As she assembles the plot, therefore, the reader learns, in addition to what happens next, that *she* knows how to make sense of texts and human action.'[2]

Daphne du Maurier's *Rebecca* recasts the ingredients of *Jane Eyre*, and by implication those of earlier romantic, sentimental and Gothic fictions, so as to uncover and develop the subliminal intent of key elements in those narratives which carry further levels of meaning for a latter-day cultural consciousness. It reworks the Cinderella fairy-tale of the unloved and invisible ingenue who gains supreme social mobility when she is rescued from her position of servitude and neglect by the handsome prince, lord of all he surveys. In addition, the novel provides a version of the reformed rake syndrome, the Richardsonian formula that underlies *Jane Eyre* and that in *Wuthering Heights* (1847) seduces Isabella Linton into believing that she can successfully domesticate the wild and unregenerate Heathcliff. In *Rebecca*, the dark secret which haunts the hero and which is finally uncovered by the heroine is more extreme than the revelation of the existence of a mad first wife, for although attempted bigamy has disappeared from the list of the husband's crimes, it has been replaced by wife-murder, an act which (somewhat uncharacteristically) is greeted by the heroine with relief. The shock value is compounded by an unrestricted recital of the depravity and sexual profligacy which mark the first wife, only hinted at in Brontë's original, but which in both cases incite the husband's hatred and unleash his violence. The grand country house of which he is the master, and which appears initially to be the epitome of establishment power, becomes instead a symbol of degeneracy which must be destroyed by fire before any semblance of harmony can be restored. In a feminist reading, the identification of man and his estate is unmistakable.

Original critics of the novel were quick to notice the Brontë inheritance which du Maurier had embraced. '*Rebecca* is a Charlotte Brontë story *minus* Charlotte Brontë but *plus* a number of things which the latter would not have paused for', wrote Kate O'Brien, reviewing the book for the *Spectator* on its first appearance. 'Miss Du Maurier's plot is undoubtedly the kind of thing which the three girls of Haworth Parsonage would have liked to thrash out as they paced the dining-room arm-in-arm after Papa had gone to bed.'[3] American reviewers also recognised the similarities between the two while playing down the romantic aspects in favour of the sensationalist plot: 'For this is a melodrama, unashamed, glorying in its own quality, such as we have hardly had since that other dependant, Jane Eyre, found that her house too had a first wife.'[4] And when Penguin reprinted the novel in 1962, along with six other du Maurier works, their promotional material 'placed *Rebecca* firmly within a tradition of writing of particular importance to the *adult woman* reader: "There are said to be three books that every woman reads: *Jane Eyre, Gone With the Wind*, and *Rebecca*. And who can say how many men have read them all?".'[5] This automatic coupling of Charlotte Brontë and Daphne du Maurier with the idea of the female consumer is a helpful reminder of the pertinence of the whole subject of gender and writing to a pre-feminist literary consciousness, and the ways in which the middle-brow novel of the inter-war period drew on its predecessors in a continuing matriarchal tradition of authorship and reception. As Nicola Beauman has suggested, in the years 1914–39, women 'writers and readers formed a homogenous group', a specialised circle in which they were linked by mutual pre-assumptions and which relied on a reciprocal interchange of interests.[6] It is perhaps this interaction between a comforting sense of durability and the potential for regenerative contemporary renewal that makes the romance speak so directly and without condescension to successive generations of women readers. Rachel Brownstein has observed how that notoriously problematic phenomenon, 'the woman's novel', is distinguished by 'an idiosyncratically feminine emphasis or inflection – the sign of an ironic apprehension of conventional concepts of character and plot'.[7] This 'ironic apprehension' permeates *Rebecca* both in its revision of formulaic narrative mechanisms and in its construction of the narrator, who as an unnamed everywoman, is herself an archetypal reader of conventional love stories.

Like *Jane Eyre*, *Rebecca* takes an orphaned, plain, insignificant heroine and marries her to a man of property, whose imposing country mansion forms the locus of the romantic action. Maxim de Winter is a character firmly in the mould of the classical Byronic hero in his Brontë mutation: tall, dark and handsome, cultivated, restless, well-travelled, sexually experienced, and harbouring a sinister secret. The allusion to a lecherous past is an integral feature of his machismo, a vital constituent of that energy and vigour which when the heroine first meets him are diminished and which she plays a central role in reviving. As with Jane and Rochester, the primary dynamic between the heroine and Maxim is their unstated sexual ardour, with its corollary of female innocence and male domination. The source of the heroine's desirability for the worldly hero is her helplessness and simplicity, her very unlikeness to the prototypes of contemporary femininity who find Maxim an advantageous marriageable prospect and seek to ensnare him. The heroine, who significantly remains nameless throughout the novel and consequently open to the imposition of multi-dimensional identities, is thus defined through her alterity, her difference from the fashionable modern woman, who is sexually brash, elegant and self-confident. That difference forms a determining component of the text's investigation into the female psyche and the cultural constructions of femininity, through the oppositional yet symbiotic conjunction between the girl and her dead counterpart, Rebecca. It is a conjunction which becomes in effect the defining relationship of the novel, more powerful and certainly more charismatic than the heterosexual romance which provides the plot's structural pretext.

Both novels tell the story of a dislocated heroine who ultimately seeks to locate herself through marriage. Although *Jane Eyre* takes its heroine along the more traditional path up to the point of marriage, and the focus of *Rebecca* is on the girl's enlightenment after marriage, the central experience for both women is that of being an interloper in a house with a history that is concealed from them and which they have to unravel as part of a complex adventure of self-discovery. For the two heroines, their growth to sexual maturity is only fully realised through a recognition of alternative female identities, which they simultaneously internalise and resist. The wife of the first marriage, whether literally pacing the attic or rampaging through the young second wife's imagination, thus becomes an important signifier in the process of the heroine's self-construction, a rival and correlative measure. In their respective fictions, Bertha Mason and Rebecca constitute grotesque apparitions, who must be obliterated in order to restore the heroine's psychic health but whose propensities are nonetheless inherent in the maturing girl's own unformulated subjectivity.

Throughout *Rebecca* this sense of a dual identity unsettles the narrator, who is both drawn to her predecessor and fears what she represents. In her important cultural-materialist reading of the novel, Alison Light explains this dualism as intrinsic to the work's textual appeal and its contingent positioning of the woman reader, who finds in 'this narrative of wishful projection and identification, displacement and repulsion ... the story of all women, of what we go through in constructing and maintaining our femininity.[8] To the narrator, Rebecca is the incarnation of 'all the qualities that mean most in a woman', a comparator against which she can only see herself as deficient.[9] Her self-perception thus functions essentially on a model of difference, with Rebecca installed as the criterion of femininity. As the action unfolds, the girl's search for clues that will justify her imaginary configuration of Rebecca grows increasingly tenacious despite the fact that she dreads the confirmation her disclosures will bring. She both wants to eradicate Rebecca's presence with its troubling undercurrents and wants desperately to *be* Rebecca, treading in her footsteps, wearing her clothes and repeating her movements to the extent of transforming her facial gestures in unguarded moments. This transference functions so as to negate even further her own sense of self, for 'I had so identified myself with Rebecca that my own dull self did not exist' (p. 239).

The process of assimilation is analagous to the experience of reading romantic fiction, which, as cultural critics attest, invites the consumer into a fantasy and an identity which help to compensate for the tedium of domestic routine. In *Rebecca* this comes to a head in the closing pages of the novel, where the full implications of this sort of imaginative identification are made chillingly explicit. In an evocation of a key scene in *Jane Eyre*, the concluding nightmare finds the girl gazing at her reflection in a mirror only to recognise the enigmatic image of Rebecca reflected back.

I got up and went to the looking-glass. A face stared back at me that was not my own. It was pale, very lovely, framed in a cloud of dark hair. The eyes narrowed and smiled. The lips parted. The face in the glass stared back at me and laughed. And I saw then that Maxim was brushing her hair. He held her hair in his hands, and as he brushed it he wound it slowly into a long thick rope. It twisted like a snake, and he took hold of it with both hands and smiled at Rebecca and put it round his neck. (p. 396)

The ambiguous relationship between the heroine and her dark 'other', the dominant script of the novel, is here invested with a material reality. The incident complements the narrator's earlier fantasy in Rebecca's room, when she visualises Rebecca looking into the mirror to confront their two images interposed. The phallic inflection of the dream scenario merges tropes of masculinity and femininity to release an equivocal and disturbing sexuality that also resonates with presentiments of death. Indeed, death is a major factor in this text, which deals so centrally with shifting identities and a woman's tenuous hold on self. Throughout the novel, the narrator's attempts to absorb Rebecca's personality result in a pathological transfer of power, which feeds her own fascination with death and an almost suicidal wish. It is as if the dead and the living have exchanged roles as the girl's putative identity wanes in the face of Rebecca's increasingly powerful resurgence. Mrs Danvers tells the girl, '"She's the real Mrs de Winter, not you. It's you that is the shadow and the ghost. ... It's you that ought to be dead"' (p. 295) and the image of Rebecca's indestructible youth and beauty challenges the girl's sense of her own mutability just as it causes her to question her substantive reality.

In her sophisticated and highly theorised study of aesthetic representations of death, Elisabeth Bronfen analyses the significance of the revenant as a fictional double.

As harbingers of death the double incarnates the end of bodily existence, figures ephemerality and contradicts notions of wholeness and uniqueness due to the division of self it traces, even as the double also incarnates the notion of endless preservation of the body, the beginning of immaterial existence ... The logic these narratives unfold is that to attribute a fixed meaning to a woman, to solve the mystery of her duplicity is coterminous with killing her, so that her death can be read in part as a trope for the fatality with which any hermeneutic enterprise is inscribed.[10]

Bronfen's argument provides a useful paradigm against which to read *Rebecca*. In its delineation of a heroine whose love affair awakens in her the need for self-definition, the romantic novel maps the interaction between psychological and literary scripts of femininity. Not only does du Maurier's narrator form a sustained study in female anxiety but she illustrates some of the difficulties attendant on narrating the female story. In its fusion of the crime thriller and the romance, *Rebecca* enacts a collusion between the two literary genres, which merge to expose the indeterminacy that surrounds feminine identity in its cultural context.

The 'other woman', who as a revenant and alter ego menaces the young wife, essentially operates as a threat to the normative movement of romance towards harmonious marriage. Paradoxically, however, she is also an important stimulus in animating romantic desire, and critics have consistently interpreted her figurative diffusion in *Rebecca* as a metaphoric personification of the passionate and improper feminine, the heroine's unexpressed libido.[11] Whilst she is absorbed by Rebecca's anima, the girl's desire for her husband intensifies and her apprehension of her own sensual identity correspondingly becomes more complex. Significantly, in the climactic dream sequence discussed above, the girl flees from the evidence that she has appropriated Rebecca's tantalising and flaunting sexuality, together with its connotations of menace. The scene follows the disclosure of the secret of Rebecca's murder and the reburial of her corpse. It is as if the nightmare resurrects her presence only to presage her ultimate symbolic annihilation, for it immediately prefigures the sight of the burning of Manderley, with which the novel closes, as the house and its threatening occupant are destroyed in a single act of conflagration. As in *Jane Eyre*, by erasing the location of transgressive feminine desire, the heroine is released from the unpalatable past and evidence of her own subliminal proclivities in order to participate in a tranquil future with her husband.[12]

But how high is the price of tranquillity? It could be argued that the endings of both *Jane Eyre* and *Rebecca* involve a degree of compromise and that the heroines' final equanimity is only achieved at a cost of loss and consequent self-damage. There are few readers who find the mutilated and docile Rochester in the Ferndean chapters of *Jane Eyre* a totally satisfactory companion for the ardent young woman of the earlier episodes. Similarly the immediate condition of the de Winters' marriage, which forms the point where the story begins, is highly suspect. Their relationship is bland and passionless, dominated by the experience of exile as the couple wander rootlessly through the hotels of Europe, co-existing rather than interconnecting. Indeed, as Alison Light has recognised, the self-imposed banishment of the de Winters is both over-determined and unrealistic in its motivation. Rather, 'Maxim's loss of place, of Manderley itself, is a social, psychic and fictional necessity within the terms set up by the girl's assumption of Rebecca's position.'[13] It is this primary situation of displacement, both literal and symbolic, that shapes the narrative of *Rebecca* and creates the framework to implement the romantic quest. That quest incorporates a search for the unexplored dimensions of the self. The pluralistic landscape of female desire which Rebecca represents and with which the girl is obsessed, hints too at the potential eruption of lesbian impulses, rendered more explicit through Mrs Danvers' intervention, and adding a further level to the multi-layered notion of female deviance which the novel navigates.

For *Rebecca* is story upon story. The intertextuality of the work with its self-conscious recall of popular fictional forms, the romance, the detective story and the Gothic novel, reflects its ongoing internal dialogue about gender and genre. In her biography of the writer, Margaret Forster describes du Maurier's own resistance to attempts to label the book within existing conventions and notes especially her objection to its being read as the 'exquisite love story' her publishers claimed.[14] Its hybridity disturbs strict generic categorisation, and its textual liminality conflates the borderlines between popular and serious literature. The always tenuous frontier between 'high' literature and 'popular' genres virtually collapses when scrutinised in relation to the romance, as Harriet Hawkins' analysis of 'classics and trash' confirms.[15] For while *Rebecca* adheres firmly to the conventions of middle-brow romance fiction, it also registers its modernist legacy through its elaboration of the psychoanalytic and cultural subtexts that remain latent but unexplored in *Jane Eyre*. In addition it constructs a narrator who is herself a reader and whose experience of consuming fiction determines the direction and substance of the narrative. As Nicola Beauman observes, 'the nameless heroine of *Rebecca* ... *is* the young reader: she is professionally downtrodden, constitutionally crushed, and would not venture to do more than expect the worst of life and love'.[16] The received and hackneyed format of romantic fiction thus establishes a blueprint for her personal journey. It also creates a further dimension to that journey as being resolutely textual. Peter Kemp has remarked that the 'gothic imbroglio' of *Rebecca* gains its intensity from the fact that it houses the two personalities of its author. 'The second Mrs de Winter is the conventional du Maurier, conscious of acting a part, feeling almost an impostor on social occasions. Rebecca is the reason for this unease.'[17]

While it is dangerous to engage in over-strenuous biographical speculation, the point raises important critical questions. If to some extent the narrator is an authorial projection – and recent biographical research would indicate that such a supposition is not unreasonable – her role in constructing fictions, which are generated and effectively defined by her literary experience, postulates a searching enquiry at the heart of the novel into the intricate relationship between reader, writer and text.[18] Romance fiction, its production and reception and the immediacy with which it speaks to women readers, becomes itself a site of serious investigation.

If romance narrative continues to enthral women readers in part because of its continuous reconfiguration of womanhood and its liberation of multiple female selves, then *Rebecca* pursues that process of enthralment through its evocation of past scripts of the feminine. These scripts emerge through the heroine's fantasies as she builds on stories imperfectly related to her and only half understood, on overheard rumours and oblique conversations as well as on visible signs of the previous incumbent whose story she tries to piece together and re-enact. As has already been established in the introduction to this collection, romance is above all a discourse, a fabricated nexus of narrative codes which constitute interpretative paradigms, self-renewing and infinitely susceptible to modification. *Rebecca* is a novel which deals directly in textualities and in the prototypes of love, marriage and femininity which the discourse of romance inscribes. By locating the examination of romance within the framework of marriage rather than as a transaction which precedes wedlock, *Rebecca* rejects the normal narrative progress of the courtship plot, which is here collapsed into a few pages in the second chapter. The ensuing sustained enquiry into what it means to be an adult woman forces unavoidable confrontation with the confusing and competing scripts of femininity that face the heroine in a life where she is required to play roles dominated by the ghosts of pre-existing narratives.

From the very first pages of *Rebecca* the narrator is in the business of constructing conjectural scenarios and of proposing hypothetical explanations for fantasies which require only the most meagre stimulus to take off. For these purposes fantasy can be defined as 'not simply the mental image of a desired object; [but] it involves the total context and activity in and through which the object may be attained'.[19] It could be argued that fantasy motivates the entire central enterprise of *Rebecca*, through establishing as its fallible narrator one whose imagination is predicated on the restrictive and cliched features of contemporary popular fiction. Like *Jane Eyre*, the novel is a retrospective autobiographical account, written supposedly from the perspective of middle age. Unlike *Jane Eyre*, however, it begins with a dream, a nightmarish and distorted hallucination of place that produces images of isolation and which reconstructs in fantasy terms a visionary setting perfect for a Gothic romance. The nostalgic landscape evinced by the recurrent dream – 'Last night I dreamed I went to Manderley *again*' – poses a psychological complement for the heroine's own sense of social and psychic dislocation. The images of loss reflect the girl's quest for a home which will concurrently restore her to an identity, but the images envisioned are those subsequently associated with Rebecca. They are images of nature run riot, redolent of a disturbing and overblown sexuality and anticipating the references to the 'massed', 'slaughterhouse red, luscious and fantastic' rhododendrons and the heavily perfumed lilac with which she fills the house (p. 70). Just as Rebecca transfers the wild and sexually resonant into the cultivated, domestic environment, so her agency also releases the energies dormant in the unassuming English rose who is the novel's protagonist.

In a persuasive Freudian reading of the novel, Elisabeth Bronfen has referred to the initial representation of Manderley as a barred Other. It is both the forbidden place and the girl's fantasy space, which frighteningly incorporates the terrifying actuality of arrival at the place which in the fantasy remains constantly and tantalisingly out of reach.[20] The twinned motifs of desire and quest also invite a gendered inflection. They are a crucial factor in determining and sustaining the impetus of the romance. In a state of negation herself, never given a name but existing as a permanent blank canvas on which others (such as Maxim and Mrs Danvers) can make their imprint, the girl's desire for a convincing subjectivity is projected through her visualisation of a home, a sexuality and a dominant identity. Her psychic exile can only be ameliorated through the consolation of fantasy, but her fantasies form a perpetual reminder of what she lacks.

For the second Mrs de Winter, who is without significant identity and who is denoted only through the name of her predecessor, Rebecca functions conveniently as an Ur-text, and Manderley evolves into a palimpsestic labyrinth which the girl is continually striving to decipher. All around her are tangible signs of Rebecca's pre-existent personality but her attempts at decoding are entangled with her own imaginative limitations, which interpret the signs according to the romantic scripts she is familiar with. Importantly, throughout the novel the girl is represented as an avid consumer of popular fiction, of sentimentalised romances which programme her expectations and nourish her delusions. The disparity between those delusions and the reality of her experience is all too apparent: 'In books men knelt to women, and it would be moonlight. Not at breakfast, not like this' (p. 57). It is as if Maxim's proposal of marriage can only be authenticated by being filtered through the chimera of textuality, generating in turn a pre-packaged scenario with its own validating discourse.

> Romantic, that was the word I had tried to remember coming up in the lift. Yes of course. Romantic. That was what people would say. It was all very sudden and romantic. They suddenly decided to get married and there it was. Such an adventure. (p. 61)

The girl's preconception of married life forms an ironic presentiment of the unfolding of Rebecca's story, but preternaturally conditioned by a cliched and mass-marketed image:

> I would be his wife, we would walk in the garden together, we would stroll down that path in the valley to the shingle beach. I knew how I would stand on the steps after breakfast, looking at the day, throwing crumbs to the birds, and later wander out in a shady hat with long scissors in my hand, and cut flowers for the house. I knew now why I had bought that picture post-card as a child; it was a premonition, a blank step into the future ... He wanted to show me Manderley ...

My mind ran riot then, figures came before me and picture after picture ... (p. 58)

Living either in the future or in the past, the girl refuses to confront the present, and her experience is distilled through popular cultural artefacts, just as her relationship with Maxim remains a literary construct, 'like two people in a play' (p. 154). The text thus subverts at the same time as it affirms the power of the romance, concomitantly questioning whilst it dramatises the substance and impact of the cultural imagination in inscribing identity.

This dual process operates through a sophisticated critique of the contemporary aesthetic and its romantic heritage, a critique which reaches its climax when the narrator arrays herself for the costume ball, imitating simultaneously the portrait of a historic de Winter ancestor and the parodic travesty of that romantic image which Rebecca has previously and mockingly traduced. The episode strikingly recalls the *tableaux vivants* incident in Wharton's *The House of Mirth* (1904), where Lily Bart theatrically enacts a similar process of female adjustment to male fantasies of women as inviolable, untouchable and forbidden objects of aesthetic contemplation, deferred desire and erotic arousal, and by so doing renders explicitly the fetishised incarnation of the feminine to which her entire life has been devoted. In *Rebecca*, the stages on the route to the girl's choice of costume for the ball remain insistently textual. Her search for a prepared image which she can appropriate is conducted via the books of great paintings given to her as a wedding present by Maxim's sister, as if encouraging her to seek her identity in simulacra. Her exultant but transient moment of self-display exposes initially the inadequacy of her own status as a blank text, predisposed to adopt the deceptive resonances conveyed by a superficial reading of an aesthetic representation of femininity. It is the natural culmination of her prolonged self-positioning as object rather than subject, as she imagines herself being viewed, an object of envy, of beauty, or desire. Dressed so as to simulate a nostalgic echo of a romanticised past, she complies with the condition of what Laura Mulvey has described as 'to-be-looked-at-ness', her appearance 'coded for strong visual and erotic impact'.[21] Further, the complicated history of the portrait and its re-embodiment in Rebecca, the siren who is ultimately revealed as the antithesis of a romantic sensibility, serves to problematise the status of aesthetic objects in purveying cultural images and their equivocal relation to selfhood.

Feminist art historians have argued that cultural representations of female beauty are constructed within the assumption of a gendered gaze and an intricate nexus of responses to male sexuality which serve to negotiate and dispel fears of transgressive female difference or otherness. As Griselda Pollock suggests:

The terrors can be negotiated by the cult of beauty imposed upon the sign of woman and the cult of art as a compensatory, self-sufficient, formalised realm of aesthetic beauty in which the beauty of the woman-object and the beauty of the painting-object become conflated, fetishized.[22]

The classic love story is predicated on a conventional perception of female beauty as a pre-requisite for the arousal of male desire. In *Rebecca*, both the narrator and Rebecca engage in a convoluted process of self-displacement in order to reconstruct themselves through art as ciphers of femininity which will fulfil this purpose. In Rebecca's case the process is self-reflexive and deliberately ironising; she is *la belle dame sans merci*, who artfully adopts the posture of artlessness in order to seduce others. In contrast, the girl builds unintentionally on the successive layers of meanings already established, from the historicised referents of the original portrait through the collective memory of those who recall Rebecca's manipulation of its aesthetic reverberations to her own mimicry of a second-hand romantic femininity culled from an over-simplistic 'reading' of cultural icons. Her appearance, carefully orchestrated by Mrs Danvers, unsurprisingly has the opposite effect from that which she intends, horrifying her onlookers, who are in varying degrees attuned to the impact of sexual duplicity. The girl's adoption of Rebecca's pose and its accompanying cultural baggage merely compounds her failure to comprehend the full resonances of a female symbolism, as a product of its cultural antecedents, and its allegorised reception.

This failure is augmented by her corresponding misreading of masculine response. Maxim's status as romantic hero in *Rebecca* relies in part on his appetite for the fresh and unsullied as a counter to his disaffection with the artifice of schematic or performative femininity. The intensity with which the girl searches for textual clues, which will transform her into the worthy object of his ardour paradoxically blinds her to the source of her own appeal. Yet at the same time her search is an organic constituent in her search for a mature female self, vital if she is to escape the childlike mould in which her husband has cast her. In the absence of living role models, she can only resort to pre-existing inscriptions of 'woman' as an incarnation of what she can hope to attain, and in Mrs Danvers, a woman whose own interest in glamorous and calculated female sexuality is ominously enigmatic, she finds a sinister and potentially destructive guide.

The girl's naive reading of the signs and texts which surround her inevitably entails her complicity in their fabrication. Rebecca, whose equivocal but compelling presence in the novel comes to epitomise female allure, is for the narrator only an extrapolation of the semiotic evidence which is her bequest. Avril Horner and Sue Zlosnik, the title of whose study of du Maurier, *A Bold Slanting Hand*, makes explicit reference to the textual visibility which is the distinguishing mark of Rebecca, have drawn attention to the power of writing not merely as an informing principle in the text but in positively establishing the impact of Rebecca's presence. Her textual strength, they observe, 'is due not just to other characters' memories of her but to a sense of indelibility which continually surfaces in her signature and the "curious, sloping letters" of her handwriting'.[23] As they go on to argue, the act of writing is identified throughout the novel as a distinctively gendered activity, associated with women rather than with men. Its effeminacy is incompatible with an active masculinity but paradoxically it bestows strength on women who can use the pen to manipulate and assert control.

Rebecca's characteristically bold signature, which contrasts with the narrator's own 'cramped and unformed' handwriting 'without individuality, without style', recurs as a palpable challenge to the girl in her discovery of a series of texts: a scribbled dedication in a book, hand-written cards, initialled emblems, embroidered or engraved monograms. All these nourish her fantasies and reinstate Rebecca as authoritative mistress of Manderley, whose written imprint confers autonomy. Rebecca's writing table itself is a further indicator of the mastery which writing endows, recording for her successor the scope of her dominion and her definitive command over her life, for it is

> no pretty toy where a woman would scribble little notes, nibbling the end of a pen ... The pigeon-holes were docketed, 'letters unanswered', 'letters-to-keep', 'household', 'estate', 'menus', 'miscellaneous', 'addresses' each ticket written in that same scrawling pointed hand that I knew already. (p. 90)

Rebecca exerts a dual control: over the processes of writing which connote her individual space and over the aesthetic scripts of a romantic code of femininity, which she learns to manipulate to advantage but from which she deviates in reality. Her role in releasing the narrator's troubled unconscious is evidenced by the girl's admission that, 'I knew already', as she recognises what is uncomfortably familiar. This is endorsed by the final dream sequence when she finds herself reproducing Rebecca's 'long and slanting' handwriting with its 'curious, pointed strokes' (p. 396). Rebecca's personality and the transgressive potential she represents are tangibly imprinted on the narrator's unconscious, however strenuously she tries to deny the memory or erase the knowledge.

The twinned acts of writing and reading thus implicate their agents in gendered reflections of textual construction. The girl reads novels borrowed from the lending library, in contrast to Maxim whose reading is confined to newspapers or business documents. Her search of the house is analogous to the process of reading itself, likened to discovery of the forbidden, 'reminding me of a visit to a friend's house as a child, when the daughter of the house, older than me, took my arm and whispered in my ear, "I know where there is a book, locked in a cupboard, in my mother's bedroom. Shall we go and look at it?"' (p. 96). And Maxim's paternalistic and proprietorial attitude to his bride similarly encourages her in a state of textual/sexual immaturity, comparing their marital relationship to that of father and daughter:

> 'When you were a little girl, were you ever forbidden to read certain books, and did your father put those books under lock and key?'
> 'Yes', I said.
> 'Well, then. A husband is not so very different from a father after all. There is a certain type of knowledge I prefer you not to have. It's better kept under lock and key. So that's that.' (p. 211)

The locked texts of sexual discovery are reminiscent of the barred entrance to Manderley, the locus of the confrontation with the forbidden texts of the female psyche in the dream script with which the novel opens. Maxim compares his bride to Alice in Wonderland, another childish literary heroine, whose craving to enter through a locked door into a glimpsed forbidden place is also charged by imaginative curiosity. The nineteenth-century critics, who warned against the dangers of novel reading were similarly mindful of the sexual correlative of romantic fantasy on untutored female susceptibilities. So the narrator of *Rebecca* elides sexual and textual adventure in her pursuit of a mature self, which is, for her, embodied in the romantic quest and the attainment of desire.

The romantic quest thus incorporates a process of transformation, which requires the girl to construct a subjectivity in the presence of past models of mature womanhood. As an orphan, lacking parental or other familial precedent, she struggles to assert herself against a dead, powerful figure who keeps alive an alternative femininity against which she must prove herself. The model bears strong resemblances to the fairy-tale paradigm of the Cinderella and Snow White stories, those archetypal scripts of cultural and psychic discovery which incorporate the abiding spiritual presence of the buried maternal figure. In the Brothers Grimm version of *Cinderella*, for instance, the mother's ghost visibly materialises at key points in the narrative to guide her rudderless daughter, who is poised between the forces of good and evil, represented by two surrogate maternal figures, the fairy godmother and the wicked stepmother. The ambivalence with which *Rebecca*'s narrator reacts to the figure of Rebecca, who endures as her perpetual imaginative construct, fomented by the stories others tell about her, contains the characteristic ambivalence of the adolescent girl towards the mature woman who precedes her.

In *Rebecca* this ambivalence is ultimately crystallised as revulsion from the improper feminine. The girl rejects the transgressive femininity which

Rebecca deploys as a weapon in her campaign against social and gender conventions. The ideal of a companionate marriage, the nuclear family and the socially approved power relations which that encodes, provide the overt cultural norms of the text. But this does not in the slightest diminish Rebecca's power. She remains rightfully in the title role, the most compelling figure of the novel, the woman whose presence dominates the story and whose sexuality exerts an almost fatal attraction over the girl.

The search for an analogue of the self via the figure of the absent mother is paralleled by the love story's frequent conjunction of paternal and erotic scripts. In *Rebecca* this finds expression through the girl's combined sexual and social desire for a father figure, a desire which she projects on to her lover/husband. Indeed her first sighting of Maxim converts him into a mysterious, composite text of masculinity, 'a certain Gentleman Unknown', on to whom she imposes her romanticised longing for her lost father, 'my secret property', as she describes him, who forms the subject of their first conversation together. As with Jane Eyre's perpetually oscillating interaction with Rochester, male power, paternal authority and the accompanying inferences of repressed violence are critical ingredients of the sexual story to which the narrator subscribes. The relationship between the hero and heroine, which du Maurier depicts, conforms in a number of respects to the classic love story model of power and gender relations. The unnamed heroine, an unexceptional representative of the collective female readership, tries to assert herself against the massed forces of hereditary wealth and authority, personified by her husband. During her initiation into the public world of the institution of marriage, she is ground down by these symbols of his power and by his assumptions about her competence in the feminised world of household management. Her failure to cope with the protocol, with domestic details or with servants isolates her both from Maxim and from the environment which is designated as her womanly province. As Maxim withdraws into a masculine world, characterised by business affairs, by the official voice of newspapers and by trips to London for meetings with professional advisers, so he becomes further alienated from her as a lover. In this new world his place as arbiter is unchallenged and his removal from the private world of romance which blossomed in Monaco serves only to exacerbate her sense of displacement and isolation.

The girl's ultimate triumph over this divisive arrangement, as with Jane Eyre's conquest of the avatars of Thornfield Hall, signally fails to reward her with the satisfaction she seeks. The tension which sustains the romantic energy depends on the retention of the mystery, in part sustained through the submission to masculine power and the polarised gender roles which this subsumes. The return at the end of the story (the beginning of the novel) to the original European location, so conducive to the romantic ardour of their early encounters, does not resurrect the passion in a re-oriented relationship. Rather, in common with the readers who must put down their books and go back to the dusting, the romance which revivifies the narrator remains alive only in her dreams.

Notes

1 Gillian Beer, 'Representing women: re-presenting the past', in Catherine Belsey and Jane Moore (eds), *The Feminist Reader: Essays in Gender and the Politics of Literary Criticism* (London: Macmillan, 1989), pp. 63–7.

2 Janice A. Radway, *Reading the Romance: Women, Patriarchy and Popular Literature* (London: Verso, 1987), p. 214.

3 Kate O'Brien, 'Fiction', in the *Spectator* 12 August 1938, p. 277.

4 Basil Davenport, 'Sinister House', in the *Saturday Review* (24 September 1938), p. 5.

5 Avril Horner and Sue Zlosnik, 'Extremely valuable property: the marketing of *Rebecca*', in Judy Simons and Kate Fullbrook (eds), *Writing: A Woman's Business* (Manchester: Manchester University Press, 1998), p. 59.

6 Nicola Beauman, *A Very Great Profession: the Woman's Novel 1914–39* (London: Virago Press, 1983), pp. 3–4.

7 Rachel M. Brownstein, *Becoming a Heroine: Reading About Women in Novels* (Harmondsworth: Penguin, 1984), p. xxvii.

8 Alison Light, '"Returning to Manderley" – romance fiction, female sexuality and class', in *Feminist Review* No. 16 (April 1984) p. 13.

9 Daphne du Maurier, *Rebecca* ([1938] London: Arrow, 1992), p. 139. All subsequent page references to the text are to this edition.

10 Elisabeth Bronfen, *Over Her Dead Body: Death, Femininity and the Aesthetic* (London and Manchester: Manchester University Press, 1992), p. 294. See also pp. 291–323.

11 See particularly Harriet Hawkins, *Classics and Trash: Traditions and Taboos in High Literature and Popular Modern Genres* (Hemel Hempstead: Harvester Wheatsheaf, 1990); Alison Light, 'Returning to Manderley'; Tania Modleski, *The Women Who Knew Too Much: Hitchcock and Feminist Theory* (New York London: Methuen, 1988), pp. 44–55.

12 Sandra Gilbert and Susan Gubar's magisterial study, *The Madwoman in the Attic: the Woman Writer and the Nineteenth-Century Literary Imagination* (New Haven: Yale, 1989) has heavily influenced critical readings of the double and its presence in nineteenth-century representations of paired female characters. Gilbert and Gubar's analysis of that syndrome and its relation to writing, gender and autonomy underlies this discussion. See also Lyn Pykett, *The Improper Feminine: The Woman's Sensation Novel and the New Woman Writing* (London: Routledge, 1992) on the fictional pairing of 'proper' and 'improper' constructions of femininity.

13 Light, 'Manderley', p. 19.

14 Margaret Forster, *Daphne du Maurier* (London: Chatto and Windus, 1993), p. 137.

15 Hawkins, *Classics and Trash*.

16 Beauman, *The Woman's Novel*, p. 211.

17 Peter Kemp, 'Born to be a boy', in the *Times Literary Supplement* (9 April 1993), p. 23.

18 Note particularly Forster, *Daphne du Maurier*.

19 Victor Burgin, *Feminism and Psychoanalysis: A Critical Dictionary* ed. Elizabeth Wright (London: Blackwell, 1992), p. 85.

20 I am indebted to Elisabeth Bronfen's unpublished lecture on Alfred Hitchcock's film adaptation of *Rebecca* (1940), given at Sheffield Hallam University, 1995, and for subsequent discussions on the subject.

21 Laura Mulvey, 'Visual pleasure and narrative cinema', [1975], reprinted in Robyn R. Warhol and Diane Price Herndl (eds) *Feminisms* (New Jersey: Rutgers University Press, 1991), p. 436.
22 Griselda Pollock, *Vision and Difference* (London: Routledge, 1988), p. 153.
23 Avril Horner and Sue Zlosnik, '"Those curious sloping letters": reading the writing of du Maurier's *Rebecca*', in *Barcelona English Literature and Language Studies*, 1996, pp. 105–15.

9

Phyllis Creme

Love Transforms: Variations on a Theme in Film and Soap

There is an image on screen that we are all familiar with. The face of a woman in close up, in soft focus, with back lighting: 'radiant', 'rapt', 'transported' – transformed by love. It is a picture that is part of the history of cinema; and, as I write, some such composite image seems to loom up in front of me: a close up of a Mary Pickford-like face, with a blonde halo of hair, in soft focus, looking as much back into herself as at the camera-spectator or middle distance; Greta Garbo, softened at last; Marilyn Monroe with kissable full lips (encountering for, example, Napoleon in *Marie Walewska* (1937)). Today it will often be followed by a kiss that begins tenderly and lovingly, characteristically accompanied by the man touching the woman's face in a gentle, exploratory way, and then becomes passionate as sex as well as love is experienced. The image is usually part of a shot-reverse-shot sequence, the woman looked at by a man in a shot that is also given into the ownership of the viewer, held for a moment longer than is dramatically necessary, time briefly suspended, or repeated. The shot is always special: separated off in some way, it seems to capture the magic of cinema, in its ability to 'hold' the spectator immobile, transfixed, as Christian Metz puts it, in an instant of identification with herself ('pure act of perception'). The spectator also identifies with the character on screen and seeks her desires there. Film – the moving image on screen – is above all the medium that can give form to and concretise our fantasies: cinema as the dream factory.[1]

   This image seems to encapsulate a first magic moment of falling in love, a love that we all seek, that is absolute and unconditional and so complete that it seems to be only in film, in the power of the moving image to enthral us, that these moments of what we long for can be given to us. The romantic theme that this figures, I will argue, is that of the power of an unconditional love to transform: the woman is transformed, visibly, in front of our eyes. Often the transformation is so powerful that it enables her also to transform her world. The image marks a moment of magic. We might expect that this image of a woman who is looked at would have changed in films about 'strong' women, particularly in contemporary, 'post-feminist' films. Yet although the image itself may be modified, and the story may vary a little, broadly it seems to persist. I want to explore what there is in this by now composite image that insistently returns and resonates so strongly. I will look at three different instances in screen fiction, which all work rather differently but which also have striking similarities: *Now Voyager* (1942), a 1940s 'women's film' starring Bette Davis, scrutinised by film studies in the 1980s; *Frankie and Johnny*, a contemporary and popular romantic film from 1991; and a moment in 1992 from *EastEnders*, the BBC soap watched by millions, which weaves into its audience's lives twice, now three times, weekly. Why does an image of the woman transformed by love, *apparently by the look of a man*, continue as an emblem of romantic film, even in what purport to be 'women's', or 'new women's' films, or a soap that claims to be 'realistic' and non-glamorised drama? I will argue that it retains its appeal for us because, contrary to appearance, it is not only about adult, heterosexual love but it also summons up the trace of what we have lost and continue to long for: an experience of total, unconditional love that in real life is no longer attainable, but which has its origins in the mother–baby relationship.

This exploration will draw on concepts of D. W. Winnicott (1896–1971), an English psychoanalyst whose particular focus was the mother and infant couple. In his work, Winnicott de-emphasises the importance of the Freudian Oedipus stage and the emergence of the gendered subject. His focus shifts from the father to the mother, and it may be argued, from sex to love.[2] His major concern is with the developmental process as the baby gradually separates itself from its mother and becomes a person in its own right, able to recognise and relate to others, as a subject in a world of subjects and objects. He is best known for his work on 'playing', which he sees as both the precursor of cultural activity and as a general creative orientation to living, where the person experiences a connectedness between the inner and external world. As a result she can make a mark, have an impact, on her world. The ability to play comes from the earliest relationship of the baby to the mother.

In *Now Voyager*, Charlotte Vine, played by Bette Davis, is a young woman of a rich Boston family, who lives with her widowed mother, and is suffering from a nervous breakdown. Her mother (who is clearly a monster; the film, told from Charlotte's point of view offers her no sympathy whatsoever) has unwillingly agreed with Charlotte's sister to allow a 'psychiatrist' to visit her. Through his care she is gradually cured, and changes from her repressed, spinster-like identity into a woman in charge of herself and her destiny. She falls in love with Jerry, who is unhappily married, but at the end of the film, gives him up in order to care for his daughter (Tina, like her an unwanted child).

There are three different images in *Now Voyager* that represent Charlotte's progressive transformation through love, both the loving care of the psychiatrist and that of Jerry. The first is a famous shot of Charlotte making her way down the gangplank of a ship; Bette Davis, a film icon perhaps more for women than for men is visibly (even risibly), transformed, Cinderella-like, from her old maid disguise into an elegant image of 'herself', as star; in the story she has taken the place and clothes of a famous actress. As Charlotte emerges from the ship after a 'cure' voyage, we are given, teasingly, first an image of her high-heeled leg, and then of her face hidden by a wide hat. Charlotte the frump (although she appears intelligent and self-aware, able to articulate her hatred for her 'bad' mother) has been transformed by the doctor's care into the Bette Davis glamorous image that we know and expect.

The next image of transformation in the film occurs in the more traditional way within a series of exchanged looks between Charlotte and Jerry when she agrees to stay with him in Rio after she has missed her ship. This is the film's 'romantic' moment of acknowledgement of the woman's love and desire for the man, and it is marked by a shot of Charlotte in close up and soft focus, held longer than in the previous exchange of shots between the couple, when she was still uneasy about her looks and identity. The following sequence of the film shows Charlotte in another transformed appearance, in a shot that both develops and contrasts with the previous one of her leaving the ship. This time she is on her own, having said goodbye to Jerry, who is returning to his wife, and she is not only dressed up as before but is now also laughing and active. She has 'become' Charlotte Vale, and this time displays total confidence in her new role and appearance; she is outgoing, and surrounded by admirers who pronounce her the most popular woman on board. Her caring older sister and her previously unthinkingly teasing niece cannot believe the transformation – which does in fact lack the verisimilitude of a good deal of this film: it is a piece of cinematic magic, apparently the magic of love and romance.

There is a sense in which *Frankie and Johnny*, produced nearly fifty years after *Now Voyager*, is more traditionally romantic: the lovers find themselves not only through, but with each other. This film's narrative drive is the traditional one of the man's (Johnny/Al Pacino) pursuit of the woman (Frankie/Michele Pfeiffer) but the main characters are in some aspects deliberately deglamorised. They are 'ordinary'; they have had bad luck, they work in a cafe and have experienced difficult times. Frankie is thirty-six and can't have children, Johnny has been in prison. Frankie (although Michele Pfeiffer is famous for being unable to look unappealing) takes no care of her appearance. She is self-sufficient, and good at bowling but not at dancing. Both characters 'lack' something, which in the end turns out to be each other. Frankie's careless appearance is suggested to have its roots in her mother's alcoholism and the stifling family life from which she is trying to escape. More foregrounded is her recent relationship with a man who beat her up, causing an abortion and her inability to have children.

Bit by bit the film tells us that her apparent self-sufficiency is a defence. Through a series of parallel editing scenes the opening of the film shows the two travelling from quite different venues – she from her neurotic family, he from prison – and gradually ending up in the same cafe where Frankie works and Johnny finds a job. Glimpses of each character are caught by the other, but quickly this tentativeness is focused in shots of Frankie looked at, at first unawares, and then unwillingly, by Johnny. Johnny pursues Frankie single-mindedly and the film ends with the couple formed. This is a romantic film narrative which encourages acceptance with a contemporary, post-feminist overlay.

As in *Now Voyager*, the moment of transformation for the woman is crystallised in an exchange of looks that clinches the protagonists' love for each other. At a party Frankie watches Johnny dance; he displays himself for her in a temporarily contemporary reversal of the looking/looked at roles. But he also looks at her as he dances and in the intercutting between his energetic and flamboyant solo dancing, we are shown the familiar close-up face of a woman transformed by love, slightly dreamy, stilled, accepting his display as for herself. At last Michele Pfeiffer is looking beautiful, lit up, with only the vestige of her previous scruffiness. (She has previously 'dressed up', with amusing difficulty, for her date with Johnny, in a way to which the spectator has become unaccustomed in this film.)

In these film examples the urge towards the illusion of naturalism that is a hallmark of dominant narrative cinema may seem out of key with the magic of the moments of transformation that these separated-off images of women represent; on the other hand the verisimilitude may also encourage us to believe in the fantasy magic we long for. And even in *EastEnders*, I was surprised to find a similar image in the determinedly down-to-earth, even world-weary, Michelle, when she was moved unexpectedly by her feeling for Clyde, a young black man she had befriended.

A common film studies reaction to the image of a woman looked at by a man is that it encapsulates the whole of dominant cinema's representation of Woman. Since Laura Mulvey published her influential essay on 'Narrative cinema and visual pleasure' in *Screen* in 1975, the notion of Woman represented as an object of the gaze has become commonplace in film and popular culture studies.[3] Women as individuals are transformed into the icon/signifier 'Woman to be looked at', within a dualistic structure of looks where the male character or spectator 'owns' the look in a subject/object, male/female, active/passive, sado/masochist opposition. In the examples I am considering here, it is indeed the woman who is looked at: while both she and the man fall in love, and while this may be represented through an exchange of looks, the moment is crystallised into the image of the woman.

Although this fixed dualism has been contested, with a focus on 'differences' rather than 'difference' (and on men too as objects of the look), nevertheless film studies have largely ignored what happens when, instead of looking, we take the place of the looked-at figure on screen.[4] Feminists have been reluctant to explore the pleasures of narcissism, exhibitionism, even showing off, that being the object of the look implies, because they are too easily associated with (sado)masochism and objectification, or with conformity to men's desires and power.

However, it is the experience of any committed spectator that, as we engage with a film, we psychically move through the materially impassable screen barrier and step onto the screen to take a part in the action. In this way we become involved so that we take the place of the characters, even though, with another part of ourselves, we 'know' that what we are looking at (from a distance) is fictional. In our engagement with film, we never simply maintain the outside position of looking on (although this position also has its powerful pleasures, the theme, for instance, of Hitchcock's films); rather, in the unconscious fantasy structures that film mimics and elicits in us, we take on different subject positions, sequentially or simultaneously. In Melanie Klein's model of projective identification, meanwhile, a part of our unconscious fantasy is projected outwards and comes to rest in the figure that elicits that fantasy.[5] In the examples I am looking at here, are the women presented in close ups that traditionally invite the spectator to empathise and identify with them. At this point I move into the domain of the screenplay, away from my safe, distanced position outside it, controlling my objects. Instead I am there in the place of the one who is looked at.

In that place we all, whatever our gender, may take pleasure from being looked at as an object of desire, but the wish stemming from the experience from infancy of the exchange of looks between the baby and its mother can also be more far-reaching and fundamental. From this perspective, the image of the rapt woman on screen then becomes that of a fantasy for a regressive state of one who is loved unconditionally. What we may have once had (but it is mythical because the total experience has been lost if it ever existed), and may nostalgically long for and seek to replay, is that earliest experience of total love. In unconditional love we may do what we like, with no need to consider the real world, no need to be careful, no need to please; we please, anyway. This is the love that enables us to become ourselves, not for what we can give to the other, but for our simple existence. To gain this love we do not have to be special, do not have to take action, do not even have to give in return. Traditional narrative film, with its satisfying resolution together with the suspended and repeated images of being in love, suggests that the moment of transformation can last. However in the non-fictional world the couple is rarely the site of unconditional love; the mythical moment of falling in love may replicate it – the couple is so pleased with each other – but then the couple also has to face the compulsion of each other's needs. In 'real life', where our longings persist but are tempered, we know (but cannot quite accept) that in adult relationships we have to give and take, work at it, accept the rough with the smooth – all those cliches that sum up a kind of disillusionment that reality brings. Fiction film, however, still has the power to replay our deepest, unconscious fantasy wishes and so images on screen can retain their power even while in other frames of mind and, consciously, we might be inclined to reject them. The image of the woman who is looked at, the filmic magical moment of transformation may, then, reactivate the lost and longed-for experience of the person's relationship with the mother.

Such a process of transformation is suggested in Winnicott's 1967 essay, 'Mirror role of mother and family in child development', which explores the importance of the exchange of looks between the mother and baby as a part of the process of its becoming a person. The essay makes an interesting comparison with Lacan's 'Le stade du miroir' written in 1949 on the Mirror Stage, a major influence on film studies accounts of the look.[6] Winnicott himself acknowledges the influence of Lacan's essay on his thinking, but stresses that his understanding of the child's relation to the mirror is different: the influence has provoked divergences rather than imitation. For Lacan the baby's identification with its image of itself in the mirror is a *méconnaissance*; an identification with an ideal 'I' which forces a disjuncture between the perfect-whole-seeming image and the reality of the baby's experience of itself as uncoordinated and incomplete. The sense of a unified self offered by the image in the mirror is a fundamental, decisive and enduring delusion for the subject. There always remains this gap between two 'I's' in Lacan, as if the self is projected outwards, but only to a false identificatory image, leaving the experiencer empty.

Winnicott's view of the person is quite different from that of Lacan's view of the subject-in-language, the speaking subject for whom the splits multiply at the child's entry into language and sexual difference when the symbolic order is superimposed upon the illusory unified 'I' of the mirror stage: a view of the subject as decisively formed by a succession of splits and alienations. As Kaja Silverman puts it, for Lacan, if it were possible 'to probe to the deepest levels of the human psyche, we would find not an identity but a void'.[7] By contrast, for Winnicott there is the possibility of an innate, original 'self', or what he also terms the 'true self', which, at first merely a trace or potential, finds its expression and is actualised through the person's activities in the external world and through encounters with others. Whereas for Lacan the image as self in the mirror is essentially of an Other (a non-existent Other), for Winnicott there is the possibility of the seeing of one's own image as the discovery of one's true self in a transformational moment of self discovery.[8]

This experience which, I am arguing, is replicated for the desiring spectator in the character on screen has been given to the baby by the mother: *'The precursor of the mirror is the mother's face'*.[9] The baby's relationship to the mother's face aids the process of defining itself as separate and in the same process in forming its sense of self.[10]

What does the baby see when he or she looks at the mother's face? I am suggesting that ordinarily what the baby sees is himself or herself. In other words the mother is looking at the baby *and what she looks like is related to what she sees there*.[11] In a complex process of inter-identification, when the mother looks she reflects back the baby to itself, building up its sense of its self.

Winnicott explains further what he means by referring to cases when the baby sees not its reflection but instead sees the mother as herself; already and too soon an external object, outside and apart, before it has had the chance to experience itself-in-her. In these cases (when the mother is psychically distant from the baby) 'the mother is not then a mirror' and then if this experience is repeated the baby is unable to experience its true self, having to adapt too early to the emotional needs of the other. Some babies 'tantalised ... study the variable maternal visage in an attempt to predict the mother's mood, just exactly as we all study the weather, to determine whether it is "safe" to be spontaneous' (spontaneity was one of the criteria by which Winnicott judged psychic health); the baby withdraws into itself 'or will not look except to perceive (the object) for it cannot apperceive' – cannot, that is, make a relation between what it sees and itself.[12] For Winnicott the sense of a gap between inner and outer, between subject and object, is pathology, leading to an unnecessary sense of alienation, to the terror expressed by one of his patients: 'wouldn't it be awful if the child looked into the mirror and saw nothing?' Winnicott sums up his account of the essence of a good experience of looking in an aphorism:

When I look I am seen, so I exist.
I can now afford to look and see.
I now look creatively and what I apperceive I also perceive.[13]

Of Francis Bacon's paintings, he says; 'in looking at faces he seems to me to be painfully striving towards being seen, which is at the basis of creative looking'.

'Giving back to the baby the baby's own self': from this perspective, then, the joy at being looked at goes beyond the pleasure of being the object of the sexual gaze, to the experience of finding oneself, with a sense of creative connectedness to the external world.[14] Being seen for myself, having myself reflected back to me, similarly and reciprocally, enables

me to find myself in the external world, in what I too, in my turn, look at. In such creative looking the person continually makes and remakes her world. Being looked at in these terms is not passive; it transforms the person (into herself) which in turn enables her to transform the world around her.

This theme is explored further in Winnicott's case studies where the analyst functions as the 'mother' denied to the patient-as-child. The story of *Now Voyager* unfolds remarkably like a case study for Winnicott's proposal in that the therapist may fill the gap left by the distant mother. [15] Charlotte Vane is portrayed as a woman who has not been allowed the sense of her own existence by her mother and who is enabled to find and gradually remake herself and her world, initially through the unconditional love of her psychiatrist doctor (played by Claude Rains). Like Winnicott's baby who, refused its reflection by its psychically absent mother, defends its 'true self' by its 'false', defensive self, Charlotte has withdrawn, only allowing herself expression when alone. Otherwise she is in disguise. The doctor is a familiar cure-all, even God-like, figure in Hollywood women's films of the 1940s. In *Now Voyager*, the avuncular, reassuring figure of the doctor-psychiatrist quickly becomes exactly mother-like. He seems at first to love Charlotte unconditionally; later, like a mother with a growing child he becomes more demanding. When they first meet he comes to her room, colludes in her secret smoking, admires her handiwork and allows her to talk about her transgressive relationship with a young officer on the ship in which she and her mother were making a cruise. The doctor, then, becomes the real mother; the blood mother, a false one, who dominates and represses Charlotte, insisting simply on her own needs and standards of behaviour. The doctor validates Charlotte's illness as the terrible, self-destructive frustration of someone who has not been allowed to be herself, or allowed the expression of her desire, but who has been turned into a flat-shoed, bespectacled 'old maid' by her mother's tyrannical, repressive regime. He becomes the all-loving mother that Charlotte has been denied.

Being looked at is an issue for Charlotte: she cannot take it for granted. Her first appearance in her new glamorous guise (in the shot discussed above) is a deceit – she is literally wearing the borrowed clothes of a glamorous actress – which she acknowledges by talking about her 'real', 'spinster aunt' self to Jerry. When she first appears in this disguise she hides her face. At several points after their first meeting we are shown Jerry looking at Charlotte in reverse shots where the camera moves away from her more quickly, as she looks down, unsmiling, ill at ease. So far her transformation has been into a false image. She has been released from her mother's construction of herself but has not yet found her own identity. As if trying on new personalities, she has first taken on and then refuted the disguises of the actress whose place she had taken on the cruise. Her next step is to move out of this stage, to become truly independent of her mother/doctor by finding 'herself' as an adult.

Unlike the characters in *Frankie and Johnny*, Charlotte's trajectory through the narrative is to an identity that does not depend on another for her happiness. The doctor's cure enables her to get rid of her borrowed clothes and gradually to appear as herself. As Lea Jacobs notes in an analysis of a sequence early on in the relationship between Jerry and Charlotte, in a series of looks between the man and woman the usual shot-reverse-shot structure is interrupted as Charlotte sees herself in the mirror. Within this one shot she becomes both object and subject of her own look and for this one shot the man is excluded.[16] This pre-figures the final episode of the film when Charlotte again gives up Jerry, to take over his child and bring her up.

She has given up her lover, has more or less killed off her mother (she has a heart attack when her daughter finally stands up to her and refuses to marry the 'suitable' man she finds boring), fulfilling one of the film's fantasies – to kill the false mother and release the daughter. Now a woman of independent means, Charlotte changes further from her timid persona to a new self, an outspoken woman who can organise her own life and that of others. By the end of the film she has become a surrogate mother, ostensibly a second best substitute for the man, but it is possibly a more satisfactory resolution: for Elizabeth Cowie this exclusion of the man by the mother–child duo is the fulfilment of a different wish, the return to a pre-sexual relation with the mother.[17] Having 'found' herself, through the love of the doctor and Jerry, Charlotte does not need the other half of the couple. Her happiness no longer depends on either her doctor or her lover, since she has been released into finding herself as a woman and as a companion to her lover's child. In a camping scene the two are portrayed as asexual girl companions, but she has also become the 'good' mother that neither of them has had. In the final sequence of the film, the forbidding house in which Charlotte was brought up and with which the film opens is transformed at a Christmas party into a place of colour, laughter and happiness. Having found herself, like Winnicott's baby, she can now remake her world. In this scene, which has a sense of a circle completed, the child Tina (Charlotte's alter-ego) is shown on the same flight of stairs, where Charlotte was shown in her original 'ill' guise. Tina too has been transformed into a 'pretty' (rather over-pretty for today's audience) image, through Charlotte's love.[18]

In *Frankie and Johnny* both of the couple have insisted in different ways that they want to be loved and recognised 'for themselves'. This is maintained and elaborated in the final sequence where they sleep together and form as a couple: Frankie's acceptance of Johnny is signalled by her offering him a toothbrush; she stands brushing her teeth and wearing bed socks in another contemporary and tender, rather than traditionally romantic, love scene. Frankie in love is 'herself' without glamorous trappings; she has 'confessed' both her age and her inability to have children. Love has enabled her to 'be herself', a self however, who, more traditionally, perfectly 'fits' her lover. A recurring motif in *Frankie and*

Johnny is that the relationship between the Al Pacino and Michele Pfeiffer characters is uniquely right; Johnny insists that they 'fit' each other – are a perfect match. The mutual caring of the relationship, where tenderness, talking and acceptance become more important than the passion, is particularly marked in Johnny who (mother-like) will look after Frankie in her 'bad' moments. In a humorous and endearing fashion this film speaks to our longings and seems to tell us that even today, even for the disadvantaged and psychically wounded, love can cure, and unconditional love is attainable. In giving a traditional romantic story a contemporary gloss, the spectator may be led to believe more thoroughly in its magic and to wish that we too may find a substitute for the original state of pleasure in being looked at.

The final sequence of the film shows that Frankie's transformation brought about by her falling in love, like that of Charlotte, enables her also to transform her world. In a series of beautiful tracking shots the camera takes us out of Frankie's bedroom, beyond Frankie's view, to the bedrooms of some of the characters in the film; they all seem to have come under the same benign influence that she is experiencing. True to film's ability to give the same status of reality to characters' fantasies as to external 'reality' it is not clear whether these transformations have indeed happened, or whether we are simply witnessing her imaginative reconstruction; in film the distinction is not made. What the film does make clear is that we seem to be witnessing a moment of magic, both in our being able to witness these characters, as if from an aerial viewpoint, and in what has happened to them, their ordinary lives invested with a new contentment, their quarrels ended. The film ends with a shot of the moonlit sky, in a shot which visually recalls Bette Davis's final question: how can she want the moon when she has the stars? Both of these film characters have what they want. Charlotte's cure and 'sacrifice' of her lover for his child have given her herself, and her world. Frankie, too, finally loved for herself, casts a benign spell on those around her, in another instance of looking.

Michelle in BBC1's *EastEnders* was known to British viewers for many years before finally leaving for a new life in America (when the actor had had enough). The interest for the spectator in a long-standing soap is precisely that it doesn't come to an end and the characters have to grow older. Michelle visibly matured from the anxious, pregnant sixteen-year-old to a mother-student and, above all, reliable friend and daughter; following, like all good daughters, her mother's footsteps, she evolved into a 'tower of strength'. It was of course 'love' that determined the course of Michelle's life, from her premature launch into teenage motherhood as a result of her affair with her friend's father, Den Watts, the landlord of the local pub. This, we were given to understand was her 'real' love. (Never mind that 'dirty' Den of tabloid fame was a bad lot; even he had a moment of tenderness for Michelle and her baby.) Being a teenage mother, it is suggested in *EastEnders*, transformed her, turned her from a girl confused and depressed by her motherhood to the adult who was competent, bettering herself, and caring of her friends and family; and who has a series of relationships. She continued to fall in love, both before and after her relationship with Clyde, which was signalled in that familiar close up, softened and lit up. Over the years viewers came to expect that Michelle, usually harassed, with a dogged, anxious expression, would continue to replay for us the transforming experience of being seen, and of seeing. Soap operas make use of repetition, and each repetition of the sight of Michelle once again falling in love confirms the power of love to transform both her own life and that of others.

The naturalistic mode of *EastEnders* discourages the kind of glamorisation allowed even in the ostensibly realistic *Frankie and Johnny*; the touch of cinematic magic of this film could never make an appearance in *EastEnders*, whose only departure from its determined naturalism is to veer towards a thriller or gangster genre. Yet as a soap, even one committed to a naturalistic style, it is already related to melodrama, which, as Ien Ang points out, elevates all daily emotional life into exaggerated high drama, validating our subjective knowledge that our inner lives are important and that our fantasies are 'real' (even as we fear that they are not).[19] Moreover the blurring of fictional characters and real-life actors in television soaps that the press presents also persuades us that, with that part of ourselves that believes in what we see on screen, 'they' are like 'us'.[20] So Michelle's recurring, small and progressive transformations from relationships that end, but that we come to expect will be replaced, persuade us that we too can be transformed through love. Even in our real world we may after all continue to find ourselves in the look of another.

In discussing these three examples of filmic romantic narrative, I have taken an imaginative leap on to the screen, to get involved in the film story. I have argued that the pleasure of romantic fiction comes from our involvement in its scenarios which speak to our unconscious fantasies. I have explored one fantasy that may underlie the image of a woman falling in love: the fulfilment of our regressive, but always present, desire for unconditional love, where we find ourselves in the look of the other. These stories suggest that the couple is the basis of community and that, coming together, can repair all hurt. This idealised image is seductive because it overlays the treatment of an adult's relationship, beset by normal difficulties, by another that lies behind and is still longed for in the sexual encounter: the one relationship that was entirely without strings, when the mother's look bestowed on the baby its identity and sense of self. For a moment those images on screen of women transformed by love return us to that mythical state which we imagine existed once and could exist again. Founded in the early mother–baby relationship this is a desire that is gender-free: mothers look at sons as well as daughters, men as well as women seek love. But this seems to have been forgotten in our cultural images, and certainly awaits futher theorisation.

Notes

1   The history of this term is traced in the Introduction to James Donald (ed.), *Fantasy and the Cinema* (London: BFI, 1989).
2   Winnicott, D. W. [1967] 'Mirror role of mother and family in child development', in *Playing and Reality* (London: Tavistock Publications, 1971).
3   Laura Mulvey, 'Visual pleasure and narrative cinema', in Beverley Nichols (ed.), *Movies and Methods* ll (Berkeley: University of California Press, 1985).
4   Ann Kaplan offers a 'reading against the grain' from the mother's point of view, in 'Motherhood and representation: from post-war Freudian figurations to post-modernism', in Ann Kaplan (ed.), *Psychoanalysis and Cinema* (London: Routledge, 1990).
5   I am indebted to Elizabeth Cowie for this point and others in her analysis of *Now Voyager* in 'Fantasia', *m/f* (1984).
6   'Le stade du miroir' [1949], in Jacques Lacan, *'Écrits*, trans. A. Sheridan (London: Tavistock Publications, 1977).
7   Kaja Silverman, *Male Subjectivity at the Margins* (London: Routledge, 1992), p. 4.
8   The notion of the mother as a 'transformational object' is explored in C. Bollas, *The Shadow of the Object: Psychoanalysis of the Unknown Thought* (London: Free Association Books, 1987).
9   D. W. Winnicott, 'Mirror role of mother'.
10   Ibid., p. 116.
11   Ibid., p. 114.
12   Ibid., p. 113.
13   Ibid., p. 114.
14   Ibid., p. 118.
15   For example, 'Playing: the search for the self', in Winnicott, *Playing and Reality*.
16   Lea Jacobs, '*Now Voyager*, some problems of enunciation and sexual difference', *Camera Obscura*, (1981).
17   Elizabeth Cowie,'Fantasia'.
18   It is interesting, however, that the image carries much less charge and conviction than that of Charlotte/Bette Davis, indicating that it is the power of the spectator's identificatory stake in the image of the actress as much as the narrative content that arouses our fantasies.
19   Ien Ang, *Watching Dallas: Soap Opera and the Melodramatic Imagination*, trans. D. Couling (London: Methuen, 1982).
20   Or rather, as David Buckingham points out in his account of the *EastEnders'* audiences in *Public Secrets: EastEnders and its Audience* (London: BFI, 1987) we choose to pretend that we cannot tell the difference; in fact, he argues, audiences are merely playing with the relation between reality and fiction; audiences are not stupid, but they do enjoy fiction.

Filmography

Frankie and Johnny (dir. Gary Marshall, 1991).
Marie Walewska (dir. Clarence Brown, 1937).
Now Voyager (dir. Irving Rapper, 1942).

Further Reading

Hinshelwood, R. D., *A Dictionary of Kleinian Thought* (London: Free Association Books, 1991).

Laplanche, J. and Pontalis, J. B. [1968] 'Fantasy and the Origins of Sexuality', in Donald, J. Burgin and C. Kaplan, *Formations of Fantasy* (London: Methuen, 1986), pp. 5–34.

Rodowick, D. *The Difficulty of Difference* (London: Routledge, 1991).

10

Nickianne Moody

Mills and Boon's *Temptations*: Sex and the Single Couple in the 1990s

Lord, I love the nineties,' Duke chuckled. 'Women can finally be honest and say what's on their minds. Forget about being coy and childishly sweet about making love.

(Rita Clay Estrada, *Love Me, Love My Bed,* 1997)[1]

In February 1985, Mills and Boon launched their *Temptation* series of romances for British readers. Rather than the Mills and Boon 'Rose of Romance' the new series featured a rosy apple brand mark on the spines and in place of the 'o' in 'Temptation' on the front covers. The Virago Press had previously used the apple logo as a market identifier because of its connotation of knowledge and defiance. Mills and Boon however, preferred the sexual allusions of forbidden fruit, sinful carnality and the emblem of an ersatz battle of the sexes. The advent of explicit and extra-marital sex as a formulaic element in Mills and Boon fiction amazed both readers and writers.[2] These heroines were now uncharacteristically able to voice their desires and initiate sexual play. *Temptation* was marketed as offering sexual fantasy and although this may move closer to Tania Modleski's infamous charge of 'bad faith' or to accusations of publishing soft pornography for women, sex is not really the issue raised by these books.[3] The successful change in the company list during the 1980s and 1990s strengthened its market share and has had a definite effect on rival products as well as more recent subgenres published by Mills and Boon.[4] The significance of the new approach towards marriage and gender relations which has been taken by *Temptation* lies in the way it makes adjustments to the pre-1985 Mills and Boon romance formula. The new narrative structure is thus able to achieve narrative resolutions which are resonant with a hegemonic consensus of post-feminism.

Like science fiction, 'true romance' is a more complex formula to define than is sometimes imagined. Many different kinds of women's writing are grouped together under the term 'romance'. Traditionally, Mills and Boon romance has focused on the heterosexual couple to the exclusion of other roles and relationships experienced by women. Narratives culminated in the declaration of love and commitment; that is, they did not tend to explore the course of a relationship beyond the announcement of an engagement, a wedding day or honeymoon. The structural relation of romantic narrative will be examined in greater detail in a later discussion of Janice Radway's work on the 'narrative logic' of romance.[5]

Mills and Boon fiction is not itself homogenous and is particularly sensitive to changes in cultural climate. The company prides itself on its awareness of the 'changing face of romance'. A promotional history of the publishing house issued in 1988 declared: 'A Mills and Boon romance adapts to the society from which it takes its cues, but it still features a happy ending ... it is only by constantly updating its novels both outwardly and inwardly that Mills and Boon can continually woo its readers, for their tastes in, and requirements of romantic fiction are a publisher's vital barometer.' Yet I will argue that the distinction and continuity between Mills and Boon products in Britain before and after 1985 lies not in attitudes to sex, but those of marriage. Whereas some feminist critics have continued to debate the *Temptation* series with regard to the issues raised by the commercial production of 'pornography for women', this discussion does not. Instead it looks at the uneasy relationship between romance and marriage for the 'mature' Mills and Boon heroine in the 1990s.

Mills and Boon's commitment to 'change' is reflected in the marketing of the *Temptation* series which bore the legend 'Sensuous ... contemporary ... compelling ... a new romance for today's woman'. The typical cover design for the first series may have illustrated the moonlit desire of the heterosexual couple, but insets showed one of them at their respective and modern place of work. Frequently it is the expectations of work in the 1990s which threaten the institution of marriage. Deborah Philips has shown how in the post-war period, Mills and Boon 'bachelor girls' also devoted their pre-marital energy to their careers.[6] Here they learnt the virtue of service and the social skills necessary for the modern post-war world. In 1988 another Mills and Boon series, *Contemporary Romances*, specialised in 'Simple, modern love stories, focusing on hero and heroine. Rewarding happy endings for naive and sophisticated characters', which contrasted with *Temptation*'s: 'Passionate, sensual novels, where larger than life characters face temptation and make difficult choices. Compelling plots follow our heroines into unusual careers, as they tackle the dilemmas of life and love.' The distinction between these two is important. Mills and

Boon do not just have to update their *mise en scene*, but rather the narratives' actual cultural verisimilitude.

Unlike Mills and Boon's *Contemporary Romances*, *Bestseller* reprints and *Historical* romances of the 1980s and 1990s, or those specialist subgenres (e.g. *Starsign Romances*, *Faraway Places* and *Euromance*), which preserved a traditional investment in the discourses of virginity and its reward, *Temptation* focused on mature, sexually aware heroines whose social and personal identities were confirmed by their careers. The heroine's work is central to her life: it provides her with financial independence, friends, self-respect and both the opportunity to meet, and the means of sustaining, social intercourse with the hero. It is, however, usually the case that she has achieved the pinnacle of her success at work by her thirties, and we meet the heroine *in medias res,*when she is looking for, something else, in the continuation of her life story.

There are no changes in the overabundant, somewhat florid, Mills and Boon style: in the 1980s special writers' workshops were held to enable authors to incorporate thoughts and emotions with the description of sexual activity. Such terms as 'throbbing manhood', the ability to speak 'in a husk' and 'rough elegance' are still endemic. Femininity is marked by the changing out of work clothes into those of leisure, licensing the heroine to be mysterious, contrary, intuitive and emotional in contrast to her cool and competent career demeanour. Despite remaining tall, physically attractive and masterful, the construction of masculinity now includes a newly emphasised trait of choosing to abstain from sex until lust has been declared love. The interesting development here is that the focus and personal intensity of the heterosexual romance is broken up by clearly defined roles and relationships with other people, i.e. members of the family; these may conflict with the heroine's romantic destiny. Sex, desire, masculine and feminine identity are governed by these roles which have to be negotiated before the heterosexual affair becomes prominent. For example, the heroine of *Twice a Fool* has to be assured of her brother's happiness before she can concentrate on her own; in *The Perfect Mix* the heroine is entangled with the many people with whom she shares her apartment; in *A Private Passion* the heroine has to be certain about her younger sister's career before her own relationship.[7] In all three examples these relationships and responsibilities are resolved before, or precede, the dominant narrative consideration of marriage. Furthermore they emphasise the continuity and importance of the family in this fiction.

Other analyses of the *Temptation* series which have concentrated on the depiction of sexual acts in romance fiction, for example, Alisa Salamon, identify very specific change.[8] The heroine is most significantly no longer passive and denies the stereotypical image in these novels of one who is romantic and masochistic; Salamon argues that the heroine is now able to hold dominion over her male counterpart. She attempts to establish the *Temptation* novel as an aesthetic form of soft-core pornographic writing and does so by examining the way in which the series subverts phallocentrism. She is able to identify heroines who remain in a position of sexual power throughout their relationships which is particularly expressed in the accounts of their control during sexual intercourse and play. More particularly, in the work of Rita Clay Estrada, Salamon finds examples of heroines who reserve the right to refuse a romantic attachment to the hero while being sexually involved with him.[9] When she analyses the language used in these sections of the novels, Salamon concludes that the sexually authoritative *Temptation* heroine can take up the role of 'aggressor', confident that the hero will yield to her demands.

So although Mills and Boon has become more explicit, it has not really made a radical departure in style or content, particularly in comparison with other popular erotic texts marketed for women, for example Virgin's 'Black Lace' imprint. Earlier studies of Mills and Boon brought to light that the fantasies foregrounded in this fiction were those of class rather than sex, which is borne out by the five plot types in Mills and Boon fiction of the 1970s identified by Helen McNeil.[10] In the main her plot types are derived from literary romances e.g. 'Pamissa' which is a combination of Richardson's *Pamela, or Virtue Rewarded* (1740) and *Clarissa Harlowe* (1747). The plot acknowledges and resolves the different interests between genders which can be expressed economically or spiritually. The desirable, often working class, heroine has to resist the hero's advances until he has proposed marriage. McNeil's first plot type, the 'Cinderella', is purely a fantasy of class. McNeil sees the 'Cinderella' narrative as a derivation of the governess plot found in Brontë's *Jane Eyre* (1847). The heroine for this plot type is intelligent but poor, and McNeil suggests that before 1970, Mills and Boon featured many worthy shop girls who made good marriages. Moreover, the doctor/nurse romances so popular before that time also reinstate the governess plot. The 'Rebecca' plot, named after Daphne du Maurier's pre-war novel, is also a fantasy of class. The second wife or girlfriend is a quiet mousy type who has to live up to the sexual aggression of her predecessor. The narrative expresses both social and sexual unease. Such embarrassment and social anxiety is also found in the 'Masquerade' plot. The heroine finds herself in a situation where she pretends to be engaged/married to her social superior. The 'Bartered Bride' plot reverses marriage and courtship as the heroine is traded, usually by her father, to a man she hates but eventually comes to love and respect.

In *Reading the Romance*, Radway draws upon her interaction with readers to produce an ideal type for the Harlequin romance, which she refers to as 'the narrative logic of romance'.[11] Through the extensive questionnaire and ethnographic interviews which oriented her textual analysis, Radway produces a set of Proppian narrative functions for these romances. She demonstrates that these stories have a shared narrative structure; following the precedent set by Wright's structural analysis of the Western, she argues that the narratives comprise three essential stages: an initial situation, a final transition of that situation and an intermediary intervention that causes and explains that change (p. 134).[12] What Radway was especially interested in was the narrative actions in the romance formula which lent a sense of coherence to this transformation. In looking at these romance stories she established thirteen logically related functions which led to the gradual transformation of the heroine from 'an isolated, asexual, insecure adolescent who is unsure of her own identity, into a mature, sensual and very married woman who has realised her full potential and identity as the partner of a man and as the implied mother of a child' (p. 134).

In her discussion of the ideal romance, Radway states that what women are offered by Mills and Boon is a means to ideologically resolve the contradictions of patriarchy. The romance structure provides a means to read male behaviour and make sense of it rather than demanding change (p. 181). The heroine retroactively reinterprets the hero's offensive behaviour as acquainted to his basic feelings of love and affection towards her. Readers are thus encouraged to engage in the same rereading process in order to understand properly what is being offered in their own relationships. A major part of the heroine's continued acceptance of brutal, masterful and childish aspects of idealised romantic masculinity comes from the representation of the unique feminine power of understanding, tolerance and conciliation upon which the narrative structure rests. Romantic fiction renegotiates the difficulties posed by male autonomy while denying the worth of complete female autonomy. It does this to maintain a particular status quo which Radway describes as the construction of 'a particular kind of female self, the self-in-relation demanded by patriarchal parenting arrangements' (p. 147). This is an ideology that *Temptation* is still attempting to rationalise.

Radway's approach expands upon McNeil's textual survey and begins to provide us with the necessary evidence to show that Mills and Boon have not made a radical change with the introduction of sex to their formula, but rather that the changes occur in the structural portrayal of the gender relations found in the *Temptation* series. Where the *Temptation* novels deviate most significantly from Radway's ideal type (p. 134) is in their adherence to 'function 10': 'The heroine reinterprets the hero's ambiguous behaviour as the product of a previous hurt.' Interpretation, miscommunication and misunderstanding are still key features of the Mills and Boon plot, but it is predominantly the heroine who now has to negotiate the previous hurt, be it divorce, collapse of parent's marriage, disappointed first love, relationship with parents/grandparents or ultimately the decision, made prior to the narrative action, to live singly and opt out of heterosexual relationships altogether. The heroine has to be persuaded about marriage itself and not necessarily the suitability of the hero to be a husband, which is more typically the dilemma in earlier narratives. The novels still concentrate on the declaration of love and commitment, but the denouement of the story is cogently emphasised not as a mutual physical (and/or emotional) attraction, but as the realisation of a possible compromise between the two parties which would enable their marriage.

McNeil has a very interesting fifth plot type which she calls 'Masquerade'. Once again the narrative is class oriented. The heroine lays claim to a man above her station by pretending or being forced to act as the wife/girlfriend of the hero even though she is not.[13] The significance of the 'Masquerade' plot is that the heroine has to be humiliated in the process of this farce before the happy ending can take place. Feminist critics at the beginning of the 1980s were particularly aghast at the ritual humiliation and suffering of the heroine as she privately came to understand the hero's motivation and masculine behaviour.

Sex in the *Temptations* series is remarkably unproblematic. It is usually premeditated and therefore it is represented as normal, satisfying, without regret, without consequences and responsive to the heroine's fantasies. However, sex is *less* the issue in Mills and Boon romances; rather it is marriage and it is the concept of matrimony which is self-consciously being updated in this fiction. This takes place by using the style and *modus operandi* of a much earlier narrative discourse on marriage, women and work: one which presents a strong contrast between a perception of nineteenth-century ideals of marriage, i.e. passive womanhood and domesticity ('Find yourself a sweet young thing and train her right from the beginning') with a more favourably viewed 'modern' notion of the 'companionate marriage' of complementary opposites, fun and relative equality ('He wanted someone who had a life of her own; someone with a strong sense of herself and her place in the world').[14]

Relative equality and mutual interests are expressed as shared goals and values. In turn, as a basis for marriage they suggest, that the pleasures of courtship can be sustained. As did the 'screwball comedies' of 1930s Hollywood, the *Temptation* series of the 1980s and 1990s redefines the notions of masculinity, femininity and marriage for its own time. Both romantic narratives respond not to a perceived moral crisis about divorce, which is seen as a necessary evil, but to anxieties around the state and desirability of marriage.

Temptation narratives address six main areas of contention in asexual (especially work) or heterosexual gender relations. These are represented as the common experience of women in their late twenties and early thirtiess who have often been brought up by single mothers during the 'feminist' 1970s and early 1980s. The narratives take on issues of life after divorce, financial insecurity, chauvinism, the transition from work to marriage and the undervaluing of female personal achievement by patriarchal criteria, but they are more interested in rectifying selfish and 'unnatural' female independence. To realise these considerations the romance formula is required to explore a range of 'heroines' and compromises which is in itself extremely interesting. This is not to say that the fantasy, coincidence and 'consensual harmony' which belie capitalist economic and social relations are no longer predominant components or elements of the romantic narrative, but that they lead us to start assessing very specific hegemonic negotiations.[15]

The 'Masquerade' plot seems to stand out from the others identified by McNeil because it is a *comic* form of misunderstanding and the ensuing social situations it engenders also have comic dimensions. In this respect it does, indeed, have much in common with the plots of Hollywood screwball comedies of the 1920s, 1930s and 1940s, for example the Paramount social comedies and Fred Astaire musicals. In overcoming the obstacles she is faced with, the heroine wins the hand of the eligible bachelor who is marrying beneath him. The crucial difference between the 'Masquerade' plot and the screwball comedy is that the former is born out of a fear of social embarrassment and not the fun which is the *raison d'être* of relationships in the latter.

Effective comparison between *Temptation* and the screwball comedy arises through consistently shared characteristics between the two modes of romantic storytelling. *Temptation*'s emphasis on small-town America is not just to provide a suitable location, but to facilitate the reaffirmation and reinscription of its values in the face of urban and modern lifestyles.[16] Both narrative types advance the idea that one of the protagonists has become too involved in their work at the expense of the rest of their life: 'Loving moments cannot be born when both people are totally involved in a career.'[17]

This absorption is resolved through the character or couple gaining a new perspective and healthier world view. The choice of comic rather than melodramatic mode for this debate is extremely significant. Musser argues that in silent cinema 'Melodrama intensified feelings of guilt and anxiety, while comedy could address the deep structure of social crisis and make it vital to social well-being.'[18] The belief that a woman is free to choose a partner and, if necessary, to divorce him has become an important part of the ideology of bourgeois marriage.[19] The *Temptation* narrative is able to accommodate the experience of failed love and marriage within its romantic discourse.

Mills and Boon novels not only enjoy the comic small-town characters of screwball comedy: for example, the heroine's mother in Engels' *Hard to Resist*[20] who with the support of the ladies in the 'Crazy Quilters' (rather than that of her daughter) stands for election to the exclusively male and influential 'Rogues Club', but also overtly absurd and comic situations such as the delivery of the upstairs divorcee's bed to the heroine's apartment in the later *Love Me, Love My Bed* (1997). Further shared aspects include the common image of consumerism. Lent has proposed that screwball comedy redefines relationships through consumption, which in Mills and Boon is a motif of pleasure and identity.[21] Luxury and the appeal of middle-class privilege and upper-class social events are central elements of these fictions; for example parties, marriage, fashion, shopping and travel, and Cavell sees such luxury as 'essentially an expression of eroticism'.[22] For Mills and Boon it is a code of femininity denied by the austerity of the work world.

The heroines of screwball comedies – Claudette Colbert, Irene Dunne, Rosalind Russell, Katherine Hepburn – are a little more sure of themselves than those of Mills and Boon romances. Nonetheless *Temptation* heroines share the same vitality, physical freedom, spontaneity and ultimately the inability to challenge the conventions of matrimony and the economic dependence of parenthood. However, the difference between *Temptation* and screwball comedy is that in the former the woman's submission is not required for the marriage to take place. *Temptation* is not a comedy of conquest, but of compromise.

How this compromise is reached is through the way in which both narrative forms equate and resolve sexual tension as ideological tension. This is the most significant similarity between the two narrative forms, although *Temptation* romances do not need to be so madcap as they do not have the same limitations imposed by rigid adherence to the mores of pre-marital chastity. Lent describes the plot to a screwball comedy as one which 'involved a sexual confrontation between an initially antagonistic couple whose ideological differences heightened their animosity'.[23] The courtship then demands physical and verbal sparring until mutual love is declared and the decision to marry taken. Cavell's study of the Hollywood comedies of remarriage describe the characteristic sound of screwball comedy as bickering. The prominence of verbal wrangling as a mode of exchange reaches the point where 'high spirited, intelligent repartee was a new symbolic language of love' (p. 82).

It is important that the hero and heroine have equal billing in the screwball comedy. Similar to the Mills and Boon text, consensuality is achieved by looking at both points of view and the mediation of self-reflexivity. In the *Temptation* series we are party to the hero's deliberations concerning the heroine and his growing respect for her as a woman and partner. If we consider the way that marriage is reinstated as one of companionship in these texts we can begin to explain the immense popularity of BBC1's mid-1990s adaptation of *Pride and Prejudice*. Rather than the Brontë governess plot, the heroine has to be convinced that *marriage* is an attractive long-term proposition. In North America, and increasingly in Britain, romance in the Mills and Boon format is blended with suspense and detection, which again reproduces the commonality of purpose which drives the plot of the screwball comedy.

Ideological tension in screwball comedy is mainly found in disputes concerning the binary oppositions of city/country, home/work, reason/intuition and not necessarily or directly the clash of gendered interests, for example who is going to give up work to follow the other partner and whether the woman should give up a dangerous or demanding career. These oppositions are resolved through the new idea of love as companionship. The 'temptation' (from a feminist perspective) experienced by the 1990s heroine is not to surrender her precious virginity, but to commit the post-feminist sin of giving up her hard-won independence. The enticement to do so, and thus justify the social placement of women under patriarchy, is the fun and play present in the banter of screwball comedy; not status or security or desire, but an alliance with the enemy – an alliance against a hostile and bewildering modern world. In *Temptation* novels the heroine needs to be reassured that the companionship she enjoys and the potential she sees for her own personal development through this relationship will not terminate at the altar. More essentially she has to be convinced that the problems which beset her parents' generation or her peers' (for example, dependent economic position, relegation to the domestic sphere, lack of freedom and personal space, mental/physical abuse, lack of communication, boredom, insecurity and infidelity) will not be *her own fate* if she marries.

As Radway's discussion of the ideal romance develops she advances the thesis that despite the stories' apparent preoccupation with the heterosexual couple the ideal romance attempts to recover 'the lost mother' (p. 156).[24] The romance ideologically positions women in patriarchal relations which have a definite narrative logic:

> Although it is tempting to interpret this distaste for women as evidence for female masochism and of a desire to see feminist tendencies succumb to the power of love, it can be explained more fully by connecting it with the heroine's and the readers' impulse toward individuality and autonomy, a step that must be taken, at least within patriarchy, *against* the mother, that is *against* women. (Radway, p. 126)

This is essential to an understanding of *Temptation*'s articulation of a post-feminist sensibility and how the romance is reinscribed for the contemporary cultural climate. The hero must contrast with the ideological construction of a nineteenth-century patriarchal malefactor, but the heroine is required to overcome the influence of her mother's damaging 'old fashioned' *feminism* as witnessed in the following observation of a 1985 Mills and Boon protagonist:

> I get it from my mother, whose main goal in life has been to succeed. And success to her is career. I find myself at times mirroring her – shall we call it her middle class disdain for the careerless multitudes? And when I catch myself at it, I hate it.[25]

By considering this statement from a Mills and Boon heroine we can see how *Temptation* rewrites the formula of heterosexual negotiation. Radway identifies that social status is extremely important to the romantic plot: the heroes in the successful romances identified by her readers, in the early 1980s, are all aristocratic. In the *Temptation* series, however, this is not necessarily the case. The heroine's career gives her status which threatens to price her out of the marriage market; quite a lot of the *Temptation* stories dwell on crises of male insecurity when faced with a woman who is successful at work or who owns her own business. The compromise that leads to marriage needs to resolve the possibility of work within a marriage which legitimates not sexual relations, but parenthood.

To assure the heroine about marriage it is the *hero* who abstains from sex (even in the face of the heroine's desire) until it is declared love and it is the heroine who has to resolve her previous hurt. The hero frequently retains the moral highground and the heroine is positioned as being actively in the wrong and not the arrogant hero; the heroine wilfully labours under misapprehensions about the hero. Rather than having to prove her innocence, devotion or loyalty and thus provide evidence that she is worthy of marriage, she has to recognise that marriage is worth personal risk or sacrifice. It becomes her responsibility (with the hero's help) to redress her 'dysfunctional' personality traits. It is the heroine's past which prevents her from making a commitment to monogamy and the responsibilities of marriage. Just as in the screwball comedy, the traditional gender roles of the Mills and Boon romance are reconfigured and made more flexible in order to accommodate the enduring ideology of romance and gender equality through marital harmony.

The semblance of gender equality is very significant to the *Temptation* narrative. *Temptation* heroes are not necessarily 'new men', but they have undergone some processes of reconstruction through their dealings with an aggressive *modern* world. They compare favourably with other men who inhabit the 'real' world and who are presumably recognisable to the reader. They are divorced or have had significant previous relationships in which they have found that women have not been able to take the strain of what is demanded of them: that is, they die, become ill or have psychological breakdowns. The heroine of *Temptation* is different because she can be healed and he can help her.

The plot to *An Imperfect Hero* (1991), for example, is one of remarriage as the couple have to reorder their relationship which suddenly finds itself on the borders of divorce.[26] The heroine, married in her teens due to unplanned pregnancy, finds that now her children are growing up and she has the luxury of time and money, she can contemplate a very different equation of marriage. However, the readers' attention is drawn to the experience and point of view of her husband as he comes to terms with the fact that he has kept his wife through her financial dependence and 'physical need'. During their separation the narrative focuses on his suffering and not hers and the heroine is thrown off balance when she renegotiates her marriage with the new reasonable, rational version of her husband.

In *An Imperfect Hero* it is the heroine's work which has caused the rift in their marriage as he has no share in it. Work and the stress of a successful career at the expense of a private life is a key motif in these romantic narratives. *Spring Fancy* (1985) uses a traditional structure of a heroine choosing between two suitors. Her fiancé is very work oriented and she personifies his computer terminal as a rival for his affections. She turns to her second suitor when it is he who appreciates her need to talk about her own work-based problems. Her choice between potential marriage partners is complicated by her relationship with her mother. Her mother was abandoned by her boyfriend while they were dating, leaving her to bring up the heroine on her own. The mother put herself through business school and educated herself for a career with 'steel trap deadliness'. Thus the mother was able to support herself and her daughter at the expense of her emotional life. The sizeable social wedding of her daughter to a professional man is her mother's dream and threatens the heroine's personal happiness.

The heroine of *Hard to Resist* also finds that her mother's insistence on marriage as a solution to her problems is unrealistic in the modern world. She finds that she is without support in her attempts to confront the daily chauvinism she experiences in her work situation. The men she deals with are irrational and unreasonable but must be endured in order for her to support her son. Alongside the heroine of *Legal Tender* (1988), she feels that she has to constantly prove herself and balance standing up to the boss with knuckling down under the weight of sexism.[27] *Legal Tender* discusses secretaries' rights and the Association for Law Office Administrators; however, such organisations hold no place in the narrative action. The heroine is driven by the memory of her mother's financial insecurity. Rather than any collective or political action it is her feminine understanding of the hero and her eventual marriage to him which presents a way out of an intolerable situation. Women in these novels are often made aware that the criteria for their success is judged by other standards and their personal achievement is not valued by patriarchal criteria. The heroine of *A Private Passion* can exclaim 'you've reduced my life's work to an avocation, at least in your assumption', and the hero has to incorporate an appreciation of a woman's life prior to his proposal into the marriage offer.[28]

The real challenge to the romantic formula is actually the divorcee who is at peace with, and enjoying, her new single status. In Estrada's *Love Me, Love My Bed*, the toast at the girls' night out is: 'And may the best woman win in the battle of the sexes ... and may the battle end soon so we can all get on with living and loving with those wonderful, sensitive, housebroken partners.'[29] However, the heroine is not in earnest when she raises her glass. Like the much younger independent heroine of *The*

Perfect Mix the women have to be convinced about marriage in contrast to the insincerity of modern values. These two stories exhibit the particular zaniness of the screwball comedy. Women's independence is frequently construed as incompatible with commitment: 'I'm talking about realising what's hidden deep inside you, sharing it with another person, not retreating into that mad cap world where everyone just accepts you at face value and no-one tries to probe beneath the surface.'[30] Unfortunately, although independence is seen as highly desirable it is also normally forfeited (along with the pleasures of the work environment) when the heroine marries. Therefore the new formula has to reinscribe these pleasures as the properties of marriage or inferior to those of marriage.

The 'companionate marriage' will not therefore tolerate the expression of male chauvinism, although other traditional aspects of masculinity such as 'physicality' are in evidence. Therefore, despite physical attraction, the heroine of *Wildcat* (1990) cannot negotiate a relationship with the hero until he has overcome his tendency to classify her independent behaviour as prurient.[31] This novel very closely conforms to McNeils's 'Masquerade' plot type (see above). The heroine is believed to be engaged to the hero and is humiliated at various stages of the story. She does not, however, take the traditional route of living up to his expectations regarding the speech, dress and conduct of a lady, all of which she demonstrates she is capable of in her professional life. The *Temptation* hero has to demonstrate not just tenderness, but that he is prepared to personally invest in the relationship. Ultimately this might extend to a vow made in *Finders Keepers* (1990) that he will never demand changes or attempt to curb the heroine's 'restlessness'.[32] More commonly however, narrative conclusions imply that the heroine's involvement in her work is limited after marriage to a few more years before the birth of her first child.

Some Mills and Boon authors vehemently denied that the 'new man' appears in their work. However, he could be a key to how and why the Mills and Boon romance has been modified. The recently established academic discipline of men's studies has noted a sexualisation of the male body in the post-1985 period which makes use of it as a passive sex object in advertising. The male body as an object of spectacle is also a characteristic of the *Temptation* novel. The images of 'men and babies' that we can point to as an illustration of the 'new man' also find themselves on the covers of contemporary Mills and Boon products, including *Temptation*, although, in the main, *Temptation* novels are distinguishable from other series because they choose to emphasise the strength and virility of the male body – men are presented déshabillé as much as their heroines. Nixon argues that this imagery is directly connected to changes in consumer markets, that is, the targeting of men in the 1980s.[33] The visual signification of the 'new man' (e.g. particularly in male fashion photography) presents an increasingly familiar new version of masculinity and masculine culture which has consequences for the meaning of masculinity and gender relations. It is this popular middle-class renegotiation of masculinity and gender relations that has demanded a response from Mills and Boon. In order to illustrate his discussion of plural masculinities, Nixon posits the imagery of the 'new man' operating in opposition to accounts of masculinity defined by feminists in the early 1980s. When the first books of the *Temptation* series were launched, feminist critics characterised masculinity as the image and experience of 'aggression, competitiveness, emotional ineptitude and coldness, and dependent upon an overriding and exclusive emphasis on penetrative sex'.[34]

In order to explain this version of masculinity, Nixon relates it to the requirements of the nineteenth-century, middle-class work environment and the relations of power that operated between men and women in the middle-class home. These are best expressed as feminine duty and masculine privilege, a dichotomy which is the bugbear of *Temptation*. As the division of labour changed to accommodate new demands on the middle-class professional employee, so did gendered power relations, roles and expectations. In this sense, it could be argued that it is a change in cultural masculinity, and not necessarily cultural femininity, which is being accommodated by the new romantic formula. Meanwhile, when 'new man' imagery becomes recognisable as an articulation of masculine identity, feminist cultural critics have shown us that it begins to steal the moral highground from women. This is indeed what has happened in the Mills and Boon novels, where the heroine is criticised for embodying the characteristics of assertive masculinity. Now it is the man who wishes to marry, settle down and have children. The ideology of post-feminism is an effective means of pacifying feminism so that it can be integrated into the *modi operandi* of consumer capitalism. The career woman does not threaten the capitalist system, especially in the way that it is currently geared to make high, short-term demands on workers in their twenties and early thirties. Work can be part of the *transition* to romance: the two are *complementary* stages, but not simultaneously compatible. Women have a higher duty to perform. Marriage equates to parenting and not sex in these novels.

By removing the central feminist demand of professional equality *for life*, a romantic account of the dynamic and functional wife and mother for the 1990s can be realised. On consideration, the Mills and Boon heroine is currently one who has been successful but damaged (often psychologically), but can heal and 'rediscover' herself with the love of a good man. The need to accommodate feminist ideology within the Mills and Boon diegesis is thus now outmoded. Society has changed, and heroines who have 'made good' in the public sphere must subsequently lay claim to their 'pre-feminist' heritage: the contentment of home and domesticity (albeit one run on a high budget). The novels visualise an idealised community which is very often rural, in contrast with the urban setting of work, and there is a persistent fantasy of the woman professional joining such a community following her experience of the loneliness and purposelessness of single life. Narratively, this is displayed not only in the pleasure of becoming a wife (status), but in becoming a 'daughter' or 'sister-in-law'.

The enunciation of cultural change is one of the fascinations of genre fiction, and Mills and Boon in particular. Whereas historical and regional sagas in the late 1980s and 1990s have expressed their relationship to recent transformations in gendered identity and gender relations through an up-front articulation of such cultural anxieties (for example, in their focus on homelessness, unemployment, one-parent families, domestic violence, illegitimacy and desertion) *Temptation* has concentrated on converting the anxiety into a new cultural *desire*. In this respect, texts that at first appear to be about a new level of sexual permissiveness for women are actually more concerned with the 'seductions' of marriage and domesticity. Romantic fantasy is thus purposefully incorporated into *domestic fantasy* and readers are shown a new 'sequence' of sexual, professional and family negotiations. The 'happy family' has always been the unspoken coda to the classic Mills and Boon romance, of course: the difference now is that it is part of the story that *has* to be told.

Notes

1 Rita Clay Estrada, *Love Me, Love My Bed* (Richmond, Surrey: Mills and Boon 1997).
2 Discussion with researchers who have taken a more ethnographic approach to Mills and Boon reception, Val Williamson and Mairead Owen.
3 Tania Modleski, 'The disappearing act: a study of harlequin romances', *Signs* (5) (Spring, 1980), p. 4.
4 As is well known Mills and Boon carry out extensive market research on their products. For instance, in R. C. Estrada's *The Ivory Key* (Richmond, Surrey: Mills and Boon 1992), the editor's introduction draws the readers' attention to an eleven-question survey at the back of the book. The questionnaire introduces itself as follows 'the storyline of this book was slightly different from other books in our *Temptation* series because it featured a ghost as the hero, we would like to know what you think about it'. Offering a free book in exchange for the readers' views, among other questions Mills and Boon asked: 'Would you like to read more books with a supernatural element in the storyline?' and 'Would you like books in the *Temptation* series to include other elements as well as the romance? Please tick those that interest you: Action/Adventure, Spooky/Sinister, Murder Mystery, Glitz/Glamour or Other'. The design for the new covers for the *Temptation* series in 1992 was announced as being in accordance with readers' wishes.
5 Janice Radway, *Reading the Romance: Women, Patriarchy and Popular Literature* (Chapel Hill: University of North Carolina Press, 1984).
6 Deborah Philips, in a paper given to the Association for Research in Popular Fictions Conference 'Romance and Roses', November 1995.
7 C. Zach, *Twice a Fool* (Richmond, Surrey: Mills and Boon, 1986); C. McLean, *The Perfect Mix* (Richmond, Surrey: Mills and Boon, 1988); C. G. Thacker, *A Private Passion* (Richmond, Surrey: Mills and Boon, 1986).

8   Alisa Salamon, 'Can women resist *Temptation* novels? A study of the romance fiction genre as a form of soft core pornography'. Unpublished paper, 1995.
9   Estrada has also been included in the survey of Mills and Boon undertaken for this discussion.
10 Helen McNeil, 'She trembled at his touch', *Quarto* (May, 1981), pp. 17–18.
11 Radway, *Reading the Romance*, p. 150. Further page references to this volume are given after quotations in the text. N.B. Mills and Boon financed their move from hardback library stock to paperback publishing and distribution by selling their backlist to the American company Harlequin. In 1972 the companies merged.
12 W. Wright, *Six Guns and Society* (Berkeley: University of California Press, 1975).
13 Not to be confused with the *Masquerade* series title given by Mills and Boon to their historical romances in the 1980s.
14 Estrada, *Love Me*, p. 137.
15 See Roger Bromley, 'Natural boundaries: the social function of popular fiction', *Red Letters*, No. 7, 1978.
16 It was rumoured in the writing sorority that *Temptation* manuscripts would only be accepted if they were postmarked from the USA.
17 Estrada, *The Ivory Key*, p. 170.
18 C. Musser, 'Divorce, De Mille and the comedy of remarriage', in K. B. Karnick and H. Jenkins (eds), *Classical Hollywood Comedy* (London: Routledge, 1990), p. 289.
19 D. Shumway, 'Screwball comedies: constructing romance, mystifying marriage', *Cinema Journal*, Vol. 30, No. 4, (Summer, 1991).
20 M. Engels, *Hard to Resist* (Richmond, Surrey: Mills and Boon, 1991).
21 T. O. Lent, 'Romantic love and friendship: the redefinition of gender relations in screwball comedy', in K. B. Karnick and H. Jenkins (eds), *Classical Hollywood Comedy* (London: Routledge, 1990).
22 S. Cavell, *Pursuits of Happiness: The Hollywood Comedy of Remarriage* (Cambridge, Massachusetts: Harvard University Press, 1991), p. 313. Page references to this volume are given after quotations in the text.
23 Lent, 'Romantic love', p. 315.
24 Salamon ('Can women resist', 1995) also finds this consideration in the work of Melanie Klein where this same desire is described as a condition of benign sanctum '... that what we want we can get, and then we feel secure against the danger of the emptiness and destructiveness which arise if we cannot get.'
25 L. Spencer, *Spring Fancy* (Richmond, Surrey: Mills and Boon, 1985), p. 170.
26 J. Morrison, *An Imperfect Hero* (Richmond, Surrey: Mills and Boon, 1991).
27 A. Fox, *Legal Tender* (Richmond, Surrey: Mills and Boon, 1988).
28 Thacker, *A Private Passion*; p. 194.
29 Estrada, *Love Me*, p. 56.
30 McLean, *The Perfect Mix*, p. 140.
31 C. Schuler, *Wildcat* (Richmond, Surrey: Mills and Boon, 1990).
32 C. Neggers, *Finders Keepers* (Richmond, Surrey: Mills and Boon, 1990).
33 S. Nixon, 'Exhibiting masculinity', in S. Hall (ed.), *Representations: Cultural Representatives and Signifying Practices* (London: Sage, 1997).
34 Here Nixon (ibid.) is referring to books like A. Metcalf and M. Humphries (eds), *The Sexuality of Men* (London: Pluto Press, 1988), from which this quote is taken (p. 296).

Further Reading

Aspinall, S., 'Women, realism and reality in British film 1943–1953', in J. Curran and V. Porter (eds), *British Cinema History* (London: Routledge, 1983).

Chapman, R. and Rutherford, J. (eds) *Male Order: Unwrapping Masculinity* (London: Lawrence and Wishart, 1988).

Geraghty, C., 'Diana Dors', in C. Barr (ed.), *All Our Yesterdays* (London: BFI, 1986).

Harvey, J., *Romantic Comedy* (New York: Knopf, 1987).

Marks, E. and De Courtrivon, I. (eds) *New French Feminisms: An Anthology* (Hemel Hempstead: Harvester Wheatsheaf, 1981).

Meaney, G., *(Un)like Subjects: Women, Theory, Fiction* (London: Routledge, 1993).

11

David Oswell

True Love in Queer Times: Romance, Suburbia and Masculinity

'You know, Changez, love can be very much like stupidity.'
'Love is love, and it is eternal. You don't have romantic love in the
West any more. You just sing about it on the radio. No one really
loves, here.'
'What about Eva and Dad?' I countered jauntily. 'That's romantic
isn't it?'
'That's adultery. That's pure evil.'[1]

Hanif Kureishi's *The Buddha of Suburbia*, published as a novel in 1990 and
presented as a television serial in November 1993 on BBC2, is a
(post)modern romance, which traverses some of the most contentious fault-
lines of modernity: gay/straight, black/white; urban/suburban and
highbrow/lowbrow. It is set primarily in 1970s London. Karim, the
central character, narrates a 'coming of age' story, and yet his romantic
quest is far from settled on either side of the fault-lines.

It might seem strange to talk about *The Buddha of Suburbia* in relation
to 'romance'. Most of the reviews of the television serial referred to it as
a 'rite of passage' drama.[2] Only Peter Paterson, in an enthusiastic review
in the *Daily Mail*, used the term 'romance', and then only in passing, to
describe Karim's brief relationship with a woman called Helen. Paterson
describes Karim's encounter with Helen's racist father ('We're all with
Enoch here') outside her suburban dwelling and the subsequent sexual
assault on Karim's jacket by the family dog. ('The dog was in love with
me – quick movements against my arse told me so.') Paterson says: 'And
the romance had started so well, at one of Haroon's seances, where Helen
had gazed into Karim's eyes ...'[3]

Given this, why talk about *The Buddha of Suburbia* in relation to the traditions of romantic fiction? Why, when, as numerous critics have argued, this is a genre primarily written by, and addressed to, women and one which is contained within the limits of heterosexuality? Why, when only one critic obliquely refers to one scene in terms of romance (a failed romance at that)? Perversely, it seems to me that *The Buddha of Suburbia* works precisely because it celebrates a *failing* of what we might consider as the limits of traditional romance. The novel's and the television serial's presentation of masculinity and non-normative sexuality foreground, I want to argue, a different way of thinking about 'love'. Central to this is the way in which *The Buddha of Suburbia* picks up on, or is symptomatic of, a reformation of gender and sexual politics in the late 1980s and 1990s: namely the story's relationship to 'queer' politics, its relocation of queer within the 'suburban' and its figuring of forms of masculine self-government.

A Queer Romance[4]

The Buddha of Suburbia is two narratives running side by side: one which is marginal, and follows the trajectory of traditional romance, and the other which is central, and steers a perverse course of 'queer love'. The formulaic patterns of traditional romance can be found in the love between Haroon, the Buddha of the title, and the upwardly mobile Eva. He leaves his wife, takes up hybrid ('Eastern'/'English' suburban) mystical teachings, moves to the city, leaves his clerical job in the civil service and finally arranges to marry Eva. Haroon's and Eva's love for each other is paraded within settings which foreground traditional romantic interests in 'furniture, clothes and gourmet foods'.[5]

The *dramatis personae* of this story equally follow that familiar path.[6] The love of Haroon, *the hero*, for Eva, *the heroine*, is threatened by her possible desires for *the rival* Shadwell (or 'Shitwell' as Karim often refers to him). Likewise 'Mum' (Margaret), Haroon's separated wife, remains in the background as the constantly remembered potential *rival woman*. As with the conventions of the romantic genre, the main problematic and pleasure is heterosexual love.[7] The Buddha's romantic desire for the heroine, though, is never hidden and drives the narrative progression toward marriage and the path of success from suburb to city.

Nevertheless, although these characters are tied to the narrative conventions of romantic fiction, their display disturbs the progression towards a conservative resolution. Eva's interests in interior design, 'tasteful' clothes and dinner parties do not merely visualise the *mise-en-scene* of this love. These traditional romantic interests are heavily encoded as signs of Eva's desire to succeed in the city. They externalise her desire for status and, in doing so, upset their more formulaic connotations.

Likewise Haroon's mystery is not deep within his masculine or Indian identity. It is not an expression of his being nor is it an expression of a 'pathological experience of sexual difference'.[8] Instead the text (both novel and television serial) makes it clear that the character of 'the Buddha' is a foil. Haroon plays the mystic to his suburban sitting room gathering in order to escape the dull routinisation of the office in which he has no control. He plays upon their prejudices in a bid for freedom. Eva is not foiled by this, rather she is complicit in the construction of Haroon. She plays the otherness of an exotic and romantic masculinity in her bid for metropolitan status.

In this way, although the story has all the hallmarks of traditional romance (its narrative structures, characters and *mise-en-scene*), it does not play them straight. Moreover, it is Karim's story, the story of a second Buddha who takes the middle path between black/white and gay/straight, which is the main narrative of the text. His romance begins when he goes with his father to Eva's house and meets her son, Charlie. Charlie goes to the same school as Karim, but is a year older and a figure of awe and splendour. Charlie is an archetypal romantic hero, whose 'spectacular masculinity', to use Janice Radway's phrase, is an object of fascination and lust: 'every aspect of his being, whether his body, his face, or his general demeanor, is informed by the purity of his maleness'.[9]

He was a boy upon whom nature had breathed such beauty – his nose was so straight, his cheeks so hollow, his lips such rosebuds – that people were afraid to approach him, and he was often alone.[10]

However, unlike the hero of traditional romantic fiction, Charlie is first and foremost a queer icon: whereas women 'sighed in his presence', 'men and boys got erections just being in the same room as him'.[11] And although his perfection is clearly something to be desired, 'the terrorizing effect of his exemplary masculinity', as Radway suggests, 'is always tempered by the presence of a small feature that introduces an important element of softness into the overall picture'.[12] For Charlie, his vulnerability is displayed through the very ostentatiousness of his performance. At school his pranks get him publicly caned in front of all the other pupils and, when older, his masquerades as 'glam-rocker' and then 'punk singer' barely conceal his need for public attention and the affection of a crowd. But although this makes him approachable and although the recognition of his egotism makes it possible to criticise him, it is not, in the end, what makes him desirable. Karim's love for Charlie is driven by fascination and by the threat of his rejection. Charlie is always on the move both geographically and as a person. He is always moving on and leaving people behind. And it is this dialectic, in a similar fashion, that drives the narrative along. It is no coincidence that in the first few pages, after we are introduced to Charlie, Eva offers to Karim Voltaire's *Candide* as a better read than Kerouac's existentialist version, *On The Road*.

Similarly, Karim's story is both an escape and a quest, in which the question of *identity* is up-front. His journey is not so much a quest *for* identity as a search for a way *out* of identity.[13] In the opening paragraph of the novel, Karim declares:

> Why search the inner room when it's enough to say that I was looking for trouble, any kind of movement, action and sexual interest I could find, because things were so gloomy, so slow and heavy, in our family, I don't know why. Quite frankly, it was all getting me down and I was ready for anything.[14]

Creamy (Charlie's nickname for Karim, which carries the connotations of both sex and race) is not searching for psychological explanations. He is not searching for 'the inner room'. His ostensible anti-psychologism is deployed as a narrative technique for critiquing a 1970s and early 1980s form of identity politics. This form of identity politics, aided by an earlier existentialism, constructed 'political commitment' through the managing of one's self in terms of one's 'correct credentials' and one's place within the essentialised categories of class, race, gender and sexuality.[15] It drew upon the language and the techniques of a psychotherapeutic discourse. Talking about oneself, or even better expressing oneself to others through role-play, was a way of 'getting in touch' with one's *real* being. The *truth* of one's identity was discussed and acted upon in terms of one's ability to express and confess. In the field of sexual politics Foucault has rightly identified the technique of the confessional as a modern form of power/knowledge through which our conduct is governed.[16] Instead of seeing this as a reactionary form of privatisation or an unhelpful obsession with the self, to the extent that the 'political' is ignored, the language of psychotherapy, which gained credibility across the political spectrum, provided a way of governing the relationship between the personal and the political and setting in place new regimes of expertise.[17]

The critique of this earlier identity politics is brilliantly played out in *The Buddha of Suburbia* within the context of a radical theatre group, which uses the language of therapy as politics. In one scene in the television serial, an actor by the name of Richard talks about his coming out and confesses his desire for black men and his disgust for white men. Pyke, the theatre director, also referred to in the novel as 'the Judge', asks the actors to reflect upon the way in which their position in society had been fixed. He asks Karim what he thinks, to which Karim replies that he doesn't think he thinks deeply enough about these things. Karim throws the question back to Richard. Pyke intervenes and asks Karim, 'Who do you fuck Karim? Blacks or whites? Do you feel comfortable sleeping with white women?' Karim replies, 'I don't know. I'll fuck anybody!' The cast burst into sympathetic laughter. Creamy, through articulating his diverse sexual desire, implicitly sidesteps the technique of the confessional and disarticulates the question of sexual desire from the question of identity.

Unlike the heterosexual narrative progression of Haroon and Eva's story, Karim's story is episodic, marked by his multiple desires for, or encounters with, both men and women: Charlie, Helen, Jamila, Terry, Eleanor, Matthew and Marlene. The construction of Karim draws upon the figuring of bisexual masculinity in popular 'glam rock' discourses in the 1970s (e.g. Mick Jagger, David Bowie, Elton John and Rod Stewart). The use of Bowie's music within the television serial is a clear indication of this. In a review the *NME* described the serial as 'a warm celebration of radical, multicultural, polysexual, class-hopping London before and after punk rock' and stated that Bowie 'personified many of the above elements'.[18] Dick Hebdige, in *Subculture: The Meaning of Style*, refers to Bowie's 'camp incarnations': Ziggy Stardust, Aladdin Sane, Mr Newton, the Thin White Duke and 'more depressingly' the Blond Fuehrer.[19] The masculine performance of Bowie drew upon an earlier Edwardian foppishness. The disguise of the *dandy* was displayed, through dress and gesture, as a way of negotiating gender and sexual identity. This performance, especially in the figure of Bowie, was as Hebdige argues, 'devoid of any obvious political or counter-cultural significance'.[20] Although glam rock implicitly contested existing images of youth, the figure of the dandy ostensibly marked a retreat from politics into an aestheticism of the, predominatly, *white self*. However, *The Buddha of Suburbia* draws upon this reservoir of past images and reconstructs that masculinity and refigures it in relation to a notion of multi-ethnicity. The *NME* quotes Bowie: 'It is our innate sense of mix that could be our saving grace, if only some elements would stop refusing to recognise what a fantastic cultural invention we're becoming.'[21] Although the review downplays the question of sexual ambivalence and emphasises the problem of 'Englishness', it is clear that *The Buddha of Suburbia* does not simply repeat the figure of masculine bisexuality as 'withdrawn aesthete'.

Karim is neither 'straight' nor 'gay' nor simply 'bisexual'. His love for Charlie, Jamila, Terry and Eleanor is not prescribed within fixed categories of identity and community. His sexual identity is not explained in terms of his personality, but in terms of his playing with identity. Karim is neither simply 'English' nor 'Indian' neither 'black' nor 'white'. Karim is an actor, a mimic man, who adopts roles. In doing so he reveals how our *character* is no more than a mask to be worn, copied and repeated. This is most explicit in Karim's mimicking of the characters of Uncle Anwar and of Changez.

The notion that identity is not fixed but can be played with and contested has been a central element within the recent formation of 'queer politics'.

For example, a group called 'Queer Power Now' produced a leaflet in 1991 which stated:

> Queer means to fuck with gender. There are straight queers, bi-queers, tranny queers, lez queers, fag queers, SM queers, fisting queers in every single street in this apathetic country of ours.[22]

The Buddha of Suburbia explicitly draws upon this politics. In the title song Bowie sings: 'Screaming along in South London. Vicious but ready to learn. Sometimes I feel that the whole world is queer. Sometimes ... but always in fear.' Ellis Hanson defines queer as:

> ... that no-man's land beyond the heterosexual norm, that categorical domain virtually synonymous with homosexuality and yet wonderfully suggestive of a whole range of sexual possibilities (deemed perverse or deviant in classical psychoanalysis) that challenge familiar distinctions between normal and pathological, straight and gay, masculine men and feminine women.[23]

Queer has become visible in the late 1980s and early 1990s from the resistant celebrations of Act-Up and Outrage to the mainstream images of Madonna. Perversity has become paraded in the streets and other public places as a form of metropolitan vanguardism: for example, Bret Anderson, lead singer of Suede, declaring his bisexuality, or *Skin Two* magazines in W. H. Smith, or the countless articles in the press, women's and men's magazines and even morning television about S/M, cross-dressing, bisexuality, androgyny and so on. And yet these practices are far from unified and there is clear disagreement about the meaning of the term 'queer'. Anna Marie Smith, academic and queer activist, identifies queer politics as a resistance against the normalising discourses and practices of 'straight' sexuality and a struggle for a new politics of sexual diversity.

> 'Queer', and 'Outrage' slogans such as 'Queer As Fuck!', announce to both the straight bigots and the homosexual men and women who are content to work toward their inclusion in an otherwise unchanged sexist, racist, class oppressive society that queer activists are taking a militant anti-assimilationist stance.[24]

Isaac Julien uses the term to encompass the hybridity and ambivalence enunciated within postcolonial discourse:

> When I think of Queer cinema, I think of it as having a much wider sense than films made by lesbian and gays. I think also, in some instances for me, it replaces the notion of 'Third cinema'.[25]

And Richard Smith, in *Gay Times*, calls for a post-queer politics of multiple identification:

It's time to start looking post-queer, to begin to use all those wonderful words we have, both rediscovering our own and stealing theirs; homo, poof, dyke, cocksucker, faggot, queen, fairy, the list is endless. This is more than an appeal to some wanky liberal credo of each-to-his-or-her-own-ness. It's about the need not only to recognise how different we are from straights but how different we are from each other.[26]

Although the term 'queer' is used to articulate a range of political positions, it has clearly come to signify an assault both on 'straight' sexual discourses and practices and on an earlier moment in lesbian and gay sexual 'identity politics' which called upon individuals to express the truth of their self. Despite the ambivalence of Richard Smith's use of the term 'straight', the queer politics of the late 1980s and 1990s has been deployed against the binary divide between heterosexual and homosexual and in favour of an enunciation of the pluralisation of sexual identities.[27] In contesting the 'epistemology of the closet', queer politics disrupts both normative heterosexual identity formation and the notion of a fixed and essential lesbian and gay community. It has foregrounded the ambivalence of sexual identity and the heterogeneity of community. Likewise it has also come to define a wider articulation of 'perverse' sexual identities, communities and practices. Sex-workers, lesbian and gay identified men and women, practitioners of S&M, body piercers and so on are articulated within the category of 'queer'. In this sense the politics of queer is neither assimilationist nor separatist. Queer quite explicitly picks up from the 1970s Gay Liberation Front's anti-integrationist stance but does not ghettoise itself into a 'natural community'.

The problematisation of a fixed gendered and sexual identity, which is foregrounded in queer politics, brings with it *a playing with identity*. Joseph Bristow, although not commenting on *The Buddha of Suburbia* or explicitly on queer politics, provides a useful way of thinking about this issue. He has argued that 'the chance of imagining what it is like to be other identities' allows the possibility of 'creating alliances with them'.[28] It provides a way of thinking about and acting upon the relationship between pleasure and politics, such that identity is no longer fixed and essentialised. Bristow argues: 'The opportunity exists for *everyone* to be camp and to practise sado-masochism.'[29] This 'opportunity' exists not simply in *actual* encounters, but also in the *imaginary* space (or the imagined communities) of the text. For Bristow the meeting of others through the space of the text can be seen, in some sense, in terms of the process of self-invention. For example, in *The Buddha of Suburbia* we are able to identify with Karim, the narrator, and through this identification we are able to cruise other characters and form ourselves in the process. Bristow argues that the text is a 'cruising-zone'. It is:

A site where desire charts its spaces for others to share the pleasures of contact: contact between those who are able to identify each other but who have not – as with most cruisers – ever met before.[30]

In the process of this self-invention we identify with others and we become a little bit different: 'we re-present the desire to find out who we "are" in an unpredictable location where unforeseen *jouissance* may be created'.[31] We become constituted within other communities and constituencies. However, Bristow's analysis of the text as 'analogous to an urban map of sexual desire' is only partially useful in describing the romance of *The Buddha of Suburbia*. First, the characters cruised by Karim are not *of* a fixed community. None of the characters cruised are simply 'straight' or 'gay'. For example, Karim sleeps with Jamila who sleeps with Joanna. The focus is much more on sexual practices than on sexual identities. Second, Karim is uncomfortable in the constituencies within which he finds himself. He is clearly troubled by Terry's revolutionary politics, with Matthew and Marlene's sexual libertarian therapies and Charlie's S/M scene. He is made uneasy by Eleanor's aristocratic community of stories and interests: 'It was her stories that had primacy, her stories that connected to an entire established world.'[32] This sense of unease is located for Karim within power relations of class and race. Karim's 'past wasn't important enough'. It was not 'substantial'.[33] It was the story of the suburbs, his dad and his mum. Although Bristow's analysis of gay identity and textual pleasure shifts away from a notion of the formation of alliances as a conscious political project and towards a more sustained link between pleasure and politics, the metaphor of 'cruising' is deployed within the context of the urban and also leaves unquestioned the gendered nature of this metaphor. The practice of cruising, for example, is a particular form of metropolitan masculine gay sexual practice. As with queer politics the sexual geography of the suburban is left unexplored.

Living with Suburbia

For the perfect *flâneur*, for the passionate spectator, it is an immense joy to set up house in the heart of the multitude, amid the ebb and flow of movement, in the midst of the fugitive and the infinite.[34]

It is not simply the 'multitude' or the 'crowd', but the suburban which invokes contemporary pleasure, fear and concern: the suburban as a vast array of privatised lifestyles, serialised individuals, within a mass of architectural uniformity. In the last scene of the television serial, we see

Margaret Thatcher on a television screen in an Indian restaurant on the day of the 1979 general election. Karim foolishly predicts: 'Nobody is going to vote for that cow – she's suburban!' Eva retorts, 'Don't we live in a suburban country?'

The creation of 'queer' as a form of metropolitan identity is constructed, not so much in opposition to the popular (within the metropolitan, queer has become popular, even trendy), but against a notion of the ordinary and the suburban. The suburban has been historically zoned within the specific power relations of class, race, ethnicity and sexuality. Suburbia was developed in the nineteenth century as a consequence of the gendered division between 'work' and 'home' and as a result of the improvement in communications which made travel possible between these two sites. It was constructed as a means of escape from the 'lower orders' and the dirt, noise, disease and crime which was seen to accompany them.[35] A late nineteenth-century commentator, Mrs J. E. Panton in her book *From Kitchen to Garret* (1888), states that in the suburbs 'smuts and blacks are conspicuous by their absence'.[36] Understandably, black film-maker Isaac Julien argues that:

Suburbia, to put it crudely, has been the place where white people moved to get away from blacks ... It's something I can't really take seriously – especially in relation to 'gay culture' ... what would be my investment in appealing to suburbia or countryside places.[37]

It is precisely this suburban world, with its relatively uninterrogated ethnicities, which queer politics has been so distanced from in terms of its vanguardist approach to the political. It is the metropolitanism of queer politics which Alan Sinfield sees as particularly problematic:

And it depends on where you live. In rural Shropshire say ... just to keep going at all may require more courage than getting arrested on a demo in central London. And if you are struggling to be Gay, the last thing you want is someone living in more fortunate circumstances telling you that you don't measure up because you can't think of yourself as Queer.[38]

The Buddha of Suburbia, especially in its televisual version, addresses precisely this non-metropolitan constituency. In speaking to this imagined community the gender and sexual politics of queer undergoes transformation. For example, *The Buddha of Suburbia* does not represent masculine desire in the manner of Isaac Julien's *Looking for Langston* (1989) or *The Attendant* (1993). On reflection we might argue, as Judith Squires does, that 'transgression' is in danger of becoming 'mainstream'. She states that:

There is a growing celebration of sexual subcultures and acts of transgression, not only within the subcultures themselves, but also in the dominant culture. Mainstream culture has always plundered imagery and ideas from those in the margins of society – sexual minorities and 'bohemians'. But recently, there has been a quantitative change. Perversity is becoming a commodity, which sells films, fashions, CDs, books and magazines.[39]

She then goes on to ask whether, as a result of this commodification, 'perversity' 'is still subversive'. I want to argue, rather, that this transformation cannot simply be seen as the 'mainstreaming' of a resistant and alternative discourse. The politics of the televised version of *The Buddha of Suburbia* is not a watered-down politics. The serial deals with the everyday of the suburban. For example, Karim's romantic encounters are not, on the whole, played out within avant-garde, fetishised, S/M scenarios. And yet its ordinary appeal and attempt to work within a consensual politics does not *impurify* its radicalness. Rather, in locating this address within the suburban, the text begins to reconstitute the cultural geography of this previously uncontested domain and to problematise contemporary straight masculinity.

Television has historically addressed, and does still predominantly address, the suburban, the ordinary, and a normalised version of the family audience.[40] The presentation of *The Buddha of Suburbia* on the BBC, rather than commercial television, meant that the straight masculinity constructed within this address could be problematised within the heartland of conservative middlebrow culture. It was not simply, then, that *The Buddha of Suburbia* unsettles the traditional hallmarks of romantic fiction, but that its queer romance has a specific cultural and geographical location. There was one scene in particular which upset the more conservative critics of the tabloid press. In episode three, Karim's love for Eleanor is manipulated within an orgiastic world of sexual experimentation and power relations. Matthew, the theatre director, and Marlene, his wife, use sex to 'discover themselves'.[41] Matthew says at one point to Karim: 'I'm on the look-out for a scientist – an astronomer or nuclear physicist. I feel too arts-based intellectually.'[42] In this scene Matthew, the Judge, *gives* his wife to Karim, as if she were a gift, and *takes* Eleanor. Karim is clearly troubled by this situation. Then Eleanor, white, English and upper class, *offers* Karim to Matthew. The final scene of this episode shows Matthew smiling with pleasure as Karim sucks his cock.[43] The positioning of Karim within this scene vividly portrays the complex network of power relations which any queering of straight masculinity must negotiate.

The tabloid press reinterpreted the queering of straight masculinity in the television serial through the lens of a prurient, populist and moralist gaze. In this discourse, sexual invention and pluralisation are displayed as both an object of desire and derogation. The *Sun* displayed a nude shot from the serial on its front page and carried the headline, 'Shame of BBC's Porn Play' (17 November 1993). The *Daily Mail* splashed 'A Full Frontal Assault' on top of a story which included 'BBC bosses refused to make eleventh-hour cuts to last night's episode of the controversial sex drama *The Buddha of Suburbia* despite public concern over explicit scenes' (18 November 1993). This tabloid blast of disgust ricocheted within the wedding-caked walls of suburban England.

In the press, gendered sexual identities and modes of conduct were normalised within the terms of 'taste and decency'. The *Daily Mail* (18 November 1993) gave space to a number of its writers to respond to the serial. Graham Turner, 'married with three children', said: 'This is a seedy, sordid, violent and brutalising film.' Concerned about the 'degrading' sex scenes and the 'moral tone' of the programme, Turner stated that 'if it attracts large audiences, I fear for the mental health of those able to sit through it'. Likewise, Mary Kenny, 'married with two children', stated: 'It depressed me profoundly, when I began to think of what the BBC once stood for: culture, decency, dignity. And now here it is portraying the sex act explicitly.'

The Broadcasting Standards Council (BSC), one of whose tasks is to monitor 'taste and decency', received a number of complaints about this scene and others.[44] The Council did not seem to take into consideration the way in which the *Sun* and the *Daily Mail* had hyped up the concern. Nevertheless, it agreed that, in episode one, Karim's masturbation of 'a male friend' did not exceed 'limits reasonable for the portrayal of the incident within a work of this kind broadcast later in the evening and preceded by a warning' and it did not uphold complaints about 'nudity, homosexuality, nor the lovemaking between Karim and Eleanor'. However, it did uphold 'complaints directed at the act of group sex, believing it to have been treated at greater length than was necessary' (BSC, February 1994).[45]

It is precisely this suburban middlebrow culture that *The Buddha of Suburbia* addresses. James Saynor, in the *Observer* (31 October 1993), picked up on this point. He described Karim as 'a prisoner of a world located at the precise midpoint between heaven and hell – Bromley in South London, global capital of shoe shops and *Daily Telegraph* readers, where Kureishi himself grew up in the Seventies'. This sense of being a prisoner within the suburban, unable to escape from the middlebrow and the ideology of 'family values', provides the backdrop of a quintessentially 'English' suburban romance. *Brief Encounter* (1945), directed by David Lean and scripted by Noel Coward, immediately comes to mind: the furtive meetings between the married Celia Johnson and her 'lover' Trevor Howard, in the train station (the train being one of the conditions of existence of the suburban); the blossoming of love which carries the two characters into the countryside; the curtailment of this love as the two recognise their respective responsibilities; and the return to normality, the ordinary, the fireside, marriage and the suburban. Dreams of escape, of romance and of adventure are both created and cured within the suburban. Even the out-of-the-ordinary is, in the end, very ordinary. And yet the sense of restraint, of discreteness and of gentility exhibited within this romance cannot simply be typified as an 'English' repression of desire. On the contrary, desire is produced out of these refined morals and manners: a kind of sexual etiquette of teatime foreplay. The two characters in David Lean's adaptation of an earlier Noel Coward play are not imprisoned within the suburban, rather the suburban provides the necessary setting (its rules, modes of conduct and tensions) for such a romance. These suburban dreams for the non-suburban are not, to use Modleski's phrase, a means of innoculation. The failing of *Brief Encounter* is that it produces a narrow incarnation of sexual desire and romance. Similarly, Karim, in *The Buddha of Suburbia*, is only a prisoner of the suburban inasmuch as the suburban provides the setting for his desires (the tension between creativity and constraint).

Kureishi's fictions are resonant of the suburban domestic dramas of Alan Bennett or Mike Leigh (the 'English tradition of comic realism'): the idiosyncrasies of a Croydonesque world.[46] Kureishi states that:

> Looking back on the novel – though I might not like to admit it – I was more influenced by books like Lucky Jim and the early Evelyn Waugh than I was by *On the Road*. You know, funny books about boys growing up and getting into scrapes.[47]

The Buddha of Suburbia, then, draws upon those established narrative conventions of the suburban drama, more recently televised in the serialisation of Nigel Williams' novel *The Wimbledon Poisoner* (BBC1, 1994).[48] The 'boys growing up' in *The Buddha of Suburbia* are both escaping from the 'spiritual desert of suburban Kent' and its domestic 'banalities' (*Daily Telegraph*, 4 November 1993) and yet they are caught up in the mix of 'the mundane with the mindbending' (James Saynor, *Observer*, 31 October 1993).[49] We might argue that these dramas *expose* the hidden secrets of suburbia. But this returns us to a therapeutic and confessional discourse about sex. Or we might argue, instead, that they *produce* the suburban as being circumscribed by a rigid divide between the public and the private. Whereas its public space is conservative and heavily policed, beneath the closed net curtains a whole host of debauched and sinister activities are allowed to take place. The suburban becomes the representational site upon which the troubles of liberalism can be played out.

Chris Savage-King, writing in the *New Statesman* and *Society*, argues that '[t]he conviction of the suburbs that it houses no one special means that everyone works overtime at self-creation'.[50] In the television adaptation of Kureishi's novel this aspect of suburbia is clearly signalled through the use of David Bowie's music. As I argue above, the ambivalent star image of Bowie, himself a Bromley boy, constitutes the suburban as perverse and hybrid.[51] What is quite clear though, is that *The Buddha of Suburbia* makes visible these acts of self-creation and in doing so reconstitutes the suburban as *visibly* hybrid. It then begins to shift the terms and conditions of participation within this suburban public space: a space in which the dialogic relations within and between race, ethnicity, gender and sexuality are, not disavowed, but ready to be contested.

A Modern Masculinity: Queer, Dandy, Flâneur ...

Dandyism appears above all in periods of transition, when democracy is not yet all-powerful, and aristocracy is only just beginning to totter and fall.[52]

In reading *The Buddha of Suburbia* in relation to queer politics and in relation to the process of self-creation, it is difficult not to see Karim both as modern-day *dandy*, flamboyant and transforming himself in the process of acting, and as *flâneur*, traversing the suburban in the manner of Baudelaire's 'passionate spectator'. Both camp and queer, Karim seeks pleasure and reinvention. Foucault, in his later work on the aesthetics of existence, reads Baudelaire's description of the dandy as a way of understanding and rethinking the relationship between self and community in terms of self-creation:

To be modern is not to accept oneself as one is in the flux of the passing moments: it is to take oneself as an object of a complex and difficult elaboration: what Baudelaire, in the vocabulary of his day, calls *dandyisme.*[53]

Foucault talks about the practices of the self through which we can rethink ourselves and move beyond the historical limits of our existence. The critical practice of genealogy, he argues, makes possible a way of thinking outside of the normalising relations of power/knowledge. Critical thinking becomes a way, not of affirming identity, but of problematising our sense of who we are. Although Karim is in no way presented as being *conscious* of his past and *conscious* of his self-invention outside the limits of 'normal' sexual identity, the character of Karim, in being placed in the 1970s, begins to rework an earlier identity politics. Through Karim we reinvent the 1970s and the relationship between ethics, identity and politics. The dandyism of Karim allows us to reinvent a politics of selfhood.

However, even though Karim allows us to do this, I cannot help feeling ambivalent about a 'queer' reading of *The Buddha of Suburbia*. Karim, in seeing Charlie and Frankie in New York engaging in S/M sex, realises that he no longer loves Charlie. In this moment of realisation, any romantic narrative closure is foregone. There is no 'marriage' of Charlie and Karim. And yet the closing scenes of the text, perhaps, do offer some form of narrative resolution: a coming of age, a rejection of the playfulness of queer. Are we to read these scenes as Karim becoming 'mature' (where 'maturity' is read in terms of a reaffirming of heterosexual identity)? Karim's recognition that Charlie is not for him is set in relation to the closure of traditional romance (the proposed marriage between Haroon and Eva). Moreover, the final scene of the drama places Karim, Haroon, Eva, Shinko, Allie and Changez in an Indian restaurant. It is the day of the general election of 1979. As Haroon announces his marriage to Eva, the television screen in the corner of the room begins to herald the end of an era: the coming of the long winter of Conservative government and the coming of Aids.

Is *The Buddha of Suburbia*, then, merely another form of 'white flannel' romance? Is it in many ways no different from *Brideshead Revisited* (1981) or *Maurice* (1987)? Is the suburban queer of Karim contained as a set of youthful experiences, a pre-lapsarian fantasy? or does the reinvention of the 1970s provide a utopian site of resistance for the present, connecting the 1990s revival of 'flower culture' (rave, crusties, hallucinogens and so on) to a more imaginative sexual and gender politics which had been lost in the 1980s: an attempt to imagine a post-Conservative era? But perhaps this question is too much for one text to bear?

What is clear, though, is that *The Buddha of Suburbia* is a reworking of an earlier masculinity. In a similar fashion to Isaac Julien's *Young Soul Rebels* (1991), Kureishi's fiction critiques the narrative of male, working-class, subcultural rebellion. It rewrites the popular archives of music and subcultural imagery which are still resonant today (the hippy, the punk, the rasta). Julien's film provides a critique of the hard masculinities, of the rasta and the punk, which cultural studies had, in an earlier era, previously heralded as agents of resistance, and it makes central questions of gender and sexual identity. In *Young Soul Rebels* the infusion of soul and funk unsettles the hard masculinities of white and black subcultural forms and poses a more hybrid set of points of identification. As spectators we are offered both Caz (who is gay) and Chris (who is straight). Both characters are close friends and dress in punk/funk style. And yet their sexual identities are never questioned. It is a case of 'either/or', no 'and'. But in *The Buddha of Suburbia* there appears, as I argue above, both a critique of an essentialist politics of race, gender and sexuality and also a problematisation of fixed sexual identity.

Toward the end of the novel and in the final episode of the television serial, there is an increasing criticism of the proposition 'I'll fuck anybody'. There is an increasing criticism of Karim as simply queer, dandy and *flâneur*, seeking only pleasure and recreation. After his acting success with

Pyke's theatre company, Jamila confronts Karim for his non-attendance at an anti-fascist demonstration. At the time of the demonstration Karim had been pursuing his failed love for Eleanor. In the television serial, Jamila displays the wounds of her new lover, Simon, and calls out to Karim: 'Where are you going Karim ... as a person.' Karim's *becoming*, his masquerade, now begins to negotiate the difficult terrain of ethics and politics. Across the breakfast table in New York, Charlie declares: 'I love money'. To which Karim melancholicly replies: 'I used to think that pleasure was all there was ... When my father talked about the spirit I thought it was bullshit. ...' This is not a return to the identity politics of the 1970s and early 1980s, a search for essential being, but a recognition of the costs of being queer, an understanding of those left behind: Changez left by Jamila, Mum abandoned by Haroon and Karim ditched by Eleanor.

The dandy is, as Baudelaire reminds us, only transitory. This figure of masculinity merely signals the *possibility* of a better future, of different forms of loving and romance. The process of self-creation and of recognising the full weight of the *modern* does not mean that we should adopt the *attitude* or the *ethos* of the dandy. On the contrary the dandy is only a *pose* to be studied. It is a figure to be worked through in the face of modernity. It is a mask, which partially and fleetingly defines a masculinity which refuses to be named.[54] In the serial, we are left with Karim looking past the television screen, which displays Prime Minister Thatcher. He is melancholic and yet hopeful. Bowie sings: 'Sometimes I feel that the whole world is queer. Sometimes ... but always in fear.'

Acknowledgements

Thank you to Sean and Mona for their expertise and friendship.

Notes

1   Hanif Kureishi, *The Buddha of Suburbia* (London: Faber and Faber, 1990), p. 223.
2   For example, James Saynor in the *Observer* (31 October 1993) entitled his review of the serial as 'Rites of passage in my beautiful decade'.
3   Peter Paterson, *Daily Mail* (4 November 1993).
4   I should say here that the title for this section was invented for a conference paper in March 1994 and that this article was written before the publication of Paul Burston's and Colin Richardson's wonderful edited collection *A Queer Romance: Lesbians, Gay Men and Popular Culture* (London: Routledge, 1995).
5   See Ann Snitow, 'Mass market romance: pornography for women is different', in Ann Snitow *et al.* (eds), *Powers of Desire: The Politics of Sexuality* (New York: Monthly Review Press, 1983), p. 261 and Mandy Merck, *Perversions* (London: Virago Press, 1993) p. 56.
6   Merck, *Perversions*, p. 48.
7   See Tania Modleski, *Loving With a Vengeance* (London: Methuen, 1982).
8   Snitow, 'Mass Market Romance', p. 260.

9   Janice Radway, *Reading the Romance: Women, Patriarchy and Popular Literature* (London: Verso, 1987), p. 128.
10   Kureishi, *Buddha*, p. 9.
11   Ibid, p. 9.
12   Radway, *Reading the Romance*, p. 128.
13   In the opening lines of the novel this 'search' is discussed in relation to both postcolonial hybridity and suburbia. Karim states: 'My name is Karim Amir, and I am an Englishman born and bred, almost. I am often considered to be a funny kind of Englishman, a new breed as it were, having emerged from two old histories. But I don't care – Englishman I am (though not proud of it), from the South London suburbs and going somewhere. Perhaps it is the odd mixture of continents and blood, of here and there, of belonging and not, that makes me restless and easily bored. Or perhaps it was being brought up in the suburbs that did it.' (Kureishi, *Buddha*, p. 3)
14   Kureishi, *Buddha*, p. 3.
15   See Kobena Mercer, 'Welcome to the jungle: identity and diversity in postmodern politics' in Jonathan Rutherford (ed.), *Identity: Community, Culture, Difference* (London: Lawrence and Wishart, 1990).
16   Michel Foucault, *The History of Sexuality*, Vol. 1 (London: Allen Lane, 1979).
17   Nikolas Rose, *Governing the Soul* (London: Routledge, 1989).
18   *New Musical Express* (6 November 1993).
19   Dick Hebdige, *Subculture: The Meaning of Style* (London: Methuen 1979), p. 60.
20   Ibid, p. 61.
21   *New Musical Express* (6 November 1993). In this sense the use of Bowie's music also becomes a way of refiguring the star image of Bowie and of reinventing his less-than-radical past. For example, Hebdige quotes Bowie reported in *Temporary Hoarding*, a Rock Against Racism periodical: 'Hitler was the first superstar. He really did it right' (Hebdige, *Subculture*, p. 61).
22   Quoted in Cherry Smyth, *Queer Notions* (London: Scarlett Press, 1992), p. 17.
23   Ellis Hanson, 'Technology, paranoia and the queer voice', in *Screen*, Vol. 34, No. 2, (Summer 1993), p. 138.
24   Anna Marie Smith, 'Outlaws as legislators: feminist anti-censorship politics and queer activism', in Victoria Harwood *et al.* (eds), *Pleasure Principles: Politics, Sexuality and Ethics* (London: Lawrence and Wishart, 1993), pp. 23–4.
25   Isaac Julien, 'Performing sexualities: an interview', in Harwood, *Pleasure Principles*, p. 131.
26   Richard Smith, 'Papering over the cracks', *Gay Times*, (May 1992), p. 29.
27   It is not clear from Smith's comment whether we are to take 'straight' as a political position (i.e. as a point of contest which can be rearticulated) or as an essential and fixed class of sexual being.
28   Joe Bristow, 'Being Gay: Politics, Identity, Pleasure', New *Formations*, No. 9 (1989), p. 79.
29   Ibid., my italics, p. 79.
30   Ibid., pp. 78–9.
31   Ibid., p. 79.
32   Kureishi, *Buddha*, p. 178.
33   Ibid., p. 178.
34   Charles Baudelaire, 'The painter of modern life', in *The Painter of Modern Life and Other Essays* ([1863] London: Phaidon Press, 1964) p. 9.
35   John Burnett, *A Social History of Housing* (London: Methuen, 1986), p. 191.
36   Quoted in Burnett, *Housing*, p. 192.
37   Julien, 'Performing', p. 127.
38   Alan Sinfield, 'What's in a name?', *Gay Times* (May 1992), p. 26.
39   Judith Squires, Editorial, *New Formations*, No. 19, Spring, 1993.

40   See David Oswell, 'All in the family: television in the 1950s', *Media Education Journal*, No. 17, Winter, 1994; Richard Paterson, 'Family perspectives in broadcasting policy', paper presented at a BFI Summer School, 1988; Roger Silverstone, *Television and Everyday Life* (London: Routledge, 1994).

41   In the novel Karim describes Marlene and Matthew as 'more like intrepid journalists than swimmers in the sensual'. He perceives them as separated from the world and that 'their obsession with how the world worked just seemed another form of self-obsession' (Kureishi, *Buddha*, p. 191).

42   Kureishi, *Buddha*, p. 190.

43   The novel presents this scene slightly differently. Matthew inserts his cock in Karim's mouth without being invited. Karim gives his dick a 'South London swipe' and Matthew withdraws. It is only later that Eleanor puts Matthew's fingers, recently withdrawn from Eleanor's cunt, into Karim's mouth and suggests that the two men touch each other. Karim has little he can say with Matthew's fingers in his mouth (ibid., pp. 202–4).

44   Other complaints were made to the Council concerning Karim's masturbation of Charlie in episode one and the blasphemy of phrases such as 'Jesus fucking Christ'.

45   The BBC, in its statement to the BSC, argued that the programme was about 'the search of a young man ... for his sexual and cultural identity'. It continued by saying that: 'The theme was explored frankly within the context of a satirical treatment of attitudes prevalent at the time, seeking to convey the current moral confusions and uncertainties.' (BSC, February 1994).

46   See James Saynor, *Observer* (31 October 1993).

47   Ibid.

48   Nigel Williams, *The Wimbledon Poisoner* (London: Faber and Faber, 1990).

49   Chris Savage-King, writing in the *New Statesman* and *Society*, states that both Kureishi and the director, Roger Michell, juggled with 'the wish to be loyal to the suburbs in the face of a sneering metropolis, and a need to depict the frustration of a place you moved on from' (5 November 1993).

50   Savage-King argues that: 'Karim ... views Bromley as a phantasmagoria. The suburbs, as a cliche, are reinvented, and shown more as a seat of possibility, less a death sentence' (ibid.).

51   Both Kureishi and Bowie went to Ravenswood Secondary School in Bromley.

52   Baudelaire, *Painter*, p. 28.

53   Michel Foucault, 'What is enlightenment?', in Paul Rabinow (ed.), *The Foucault Reader* (New York: Pantheon, 1984), p. 41.

54   Foucault misreads Baudelaire when he focuses on the dandy as the heroic figure of self-creation (*Foucault Reader*, p. 41). For Baudelaire, C.G. (Constantin Guys, the artist who remains anonymous) is not a dandy because this mask is too blasé, insensitive and unaware of the 'world of morals and politics' (Baudelaire, *Painter*, pp. 7–9). Likewise, C.G. has 'an aim loftier than that of a mere flâneur' (ibid., p. 12).

Filmography

The Buddha of Surburbia (BBC TV, 1993).
Brideshead Revisited (Granada TV, 1981).
Brief Encounter (dir. David Lean, 1945).
Looking for Langston (dir. Isaac Julien, 1989).
The Wimbledon Poisoner (BBC TV, 1994).
Young Soul Rebels (dir. Isaac Julien, 1991).

12

Barbara Creed

Abject Desire and *Basic Instinct*: a Tale of Cynical Romance

Much has been written about the meaning of romantic love. Whether it is seen as a deep fulfilling passion, a kind of madness, an elusive fantasy, or a compulsive unfulfilled yearning, love has been depicted in the Western world as a central and necessary part of life. From the classics, opera and theatre to popular fiction, music and film, the quest to find true love is represented as a normal and natural pursuit. The lover's dream of unity and wholeness is the central theme of countless narratives from fairy-tales to film.

But love does not necessarily assume a normal face nor follow a socially acceptable trajectory. Tales of love and desire also embrace the darker side of human nature and include narratives of Gothic horror (*Gaslight*, 1944), masochism (*The Night Porter*, 1974), sadism (*Peeping Tom*, 1960), fetishism (*Vertigo*, 1958), and necrophilia (*Bad Timing*, 1980). Narratives such as these do not explore the lover's dream of unity and wholeness; instead, they argue that such a union is not possible, and that romantic love is a myth that masks the true nature of desire. The nexus between sex and death is central to cinematic tales of love and has been explored – throughout the history of the cinema – in films such as *Pandora's Box* (1928), *Double Indemnity* (1984), *The Night Porter* (1974), *Maitresse* (1976), *The Conformist* (1971), *Last Tango in Paris* (1973), *9½ Weeks* (1986) and *Bad Timing* (1980). All of these examine – and to some extent, celebrate – the erotic in relation to sex and death. In *The Night Porter* and *Maitresse* the couple (in both instances engaged in a sado-masochistic relationship) freely embrace death.

Luis Bunuel's famous 1929 avant-garde film, *Un Chien Andalou* was one of the first to draw the connection between desire and death. The film begins with the famous moon/eye/razor sequence in which a man (played by Bunuel) stands on a balcony by a window, sharpening a razor while looking at the moon. As a cloud crosses the moon, we see the razor slice through the eye of a woman. Eight years later a series of strange events take place – also by a window. A couple watch an androgynous woman, on the street below, poking a severed hand with a long stick. A crowd gathers. A policeman places the hand in a striped box and gives it to the girl who clasps it to her breast. Suddenly and unexpectedly, she is run over by a car.

The response of the man on the balcony is one of intense sexual excitement. He grabs the woman with him, and caresses her breasts which suddenly appear naked and then transform into buttocks. A close-up reveals his eyes rolled back into his head so that the pupils are no longer visible; a line of blood drools from the side of his mouth as if he were a vampire. As in the opening sequence with the moon/eye/razor, man's desire for woman is imbued with sadism and cruelty and stimulated by an odd event – a car accident.

Bunuel presents two scenarios: romantic and anti-romantic. He savagely undercuts the conventional view of romance (lovers, a moonlit night) by slitting the woman's eye – an action which suggests that desire is aligned with darkness, aphanisis and cruelty. These themes have recently been re-examined by David Cronenberg in *Crash* (1996, based on J. G. Ballard's novel) in which the male protagonist, and a band of vampiric followers, haunt the city's highways looking for accident victims as a necessary stimulus to sexual pleasure.

The vampire film also draws connections between sadism, death and the erotic. Dracula's victims, almost always female, become willing followers, energised by sexual desire only after they are first bitten and then bleed. Having joined the ranks of the undead, their sexual desires – mingled with a desire for blood – are represented as insatiable. The vampire genre represents sexual desire as the antithesis of so-called normal desire. This is also true of the lesbian vampire film (*The Vampire Lovers*, 1971; *Vampyres*, 1974; *The Hunger*, 1983) in which Dracula is a woman. Day is replaced by night, life by death, human by animal. The vampiric holes – usually two rounded black pits sunk into the neck – replace the wholeness of self, of the union promised by romantic love. Once bitten the subject can never return to life above ground.

The deadly *femme fatale* of film noir (*Double Indemnity*, 1984; *Out of the Past*, 1947; *Sunset Boulevard*, 1950; *Body Heat*, 1981) also offers the promise of taboo sexual passion. Dwelling in bars, motels, gambling joints, anywhere but the family home, she lures the man into her sticky web with the promise of forbidden pleasures and sexual excess. Like her sister, the black widow spider, the *femme fatale* invariably devours the male, encasing him in a trap that leads to his death. The *femme fatale* is seductive, deadly, abject: her victims, willing accomplices in their fate.

Georges Bataille explored the connection between desire, death and the erotic.[1] He drew an important parallel between the lovers' conflicting desire to *lose* themselves in each other while also desiring to *find* themselves, to establish themselves as a couple. Bataille was particularly interested in what he saw as a loss of intimacy in relationships, which he defined as a sacred, animal state of being. Rationalism and human self-consciousness (awareness of death) means that we see ourselves as objects rather than existing in a boundaryless or oceanic state of being. In his view, the only way to erase our boundaries, to engage in a primal confrontation with the self, is through violent, perverse excess and debauched behaviour – anything that challenges normality.

> The union of lovers is confronted by this unending question: Supposing the unified being they form counts more for them than love, they are condemned to the slow stabilisation of their relationship. The vacant horror of steady conjugality has already enclosed them. But if the need to love and be lost is stronger in them than the concern with being found, the only outlet is in tearing, in the perversities of turbulent passion, in drama, and if it is of a complete nature – in death. I would add that eroticism constitutes a sort of flight before the harshness of this dilemma.[2]

Bataille, then, sees desire or the 'perversities of turbulent passion' as the only way to obliterate one's boundaries – a central theme of film noir and the horror genre.

Even the woman's romance, whose intention is to bring about a romantic union of the lovers, seeks pleasure in perversity, that is, the desire to lose oneself by traversing boundaries. In *The Dark Abyss*, the hero is described as a 'primitive', animalistic being. There are references to his 'animal magnetism', predatory manner and to the 'latent cruelty' beneath his civilised veneer.

> Held by the sensual snare of his eyes, she felt like a rabbit entranced by a stoat, powerless, pushed by the sexual charisma of the man into a bondage more fearful than that of her empty mind.[3]

In response to his animalistic sexuality, she is forced to forsake all moral precepts – anything that would hold her back from plummeting into the 'dark abyss' of uncivilised desire. The animal-hero says:

> 'I'll show you what it's like to lose your mind completely. I'm going to make you forget that you're anything but a collection of sensations and needs and desires that will eat you up if you're not satisfied.' The hard passion in his voice forced an answering hunger deep inside of her.[4]

In *The Interloper*, the heroine is also freed from the constraints of conventional morality so that she can surrender to the hero's sensual onslaught.

> His attack, for that was what it had been, had opened to her a world of sensation she had never imagined. A world where the values and principles so carefully instilled by her mother had been swamped by a raw sensuality, as primitive as it was powerful.[5]

Not all romance novels explore primitive forms of desire, but there is certainly what might be described as a soft-porn subgenre of Mills and Boon tales which examine taboo forms of sexual pleasure, particularly those associated with the bondage fantasy and loss of identity.

The fantasy of being overpowered is central to both soft- and hard-core pornography for men and women alike. It creates a space in which the heroine (and reader), who has been brought up to obey strict moral dictates (such as the one which holds that women cannot enjoy sex outside of true love) can temporarily abandon such values and surrender, instead, to the dictates of the body – frequently described as a 'traitorous body'. Mills and Boon thus explores the notion of 'limits' and 'boundaries' in relation to normal and perverse desire.

In her study of the abject, Julia Kristeva writes about the link between the erotic abject and the notion of the boundary.

> The eroticisation of the abject, and perhaps any abjection to the extent that it is already eroticised, is an attempt at stopping the haemorrhage: a threshold before death, a halt or a respite?[6]

Kristeva defines the abject as that which does not 'respect borders, positions, rules' that which 'disturbs identity, system, order'.[7] The romantic hero of Mills and Boon deliberately sets out to challenge rules, cross borders and disturb identity. For the place of the abject is 'the place where meaning collapses', the place where 'I' am not.[8] In surrendering to the hero (the bondage fantasy leaves us no choice), the heroine is 'forced' to experience a loss of subjectivity; the self is the final obstacle to an encounter with the erotic in those situations where the erotic is transgressive or abject. The heroine willingly enters the 'abyss', the black hole at the centre of subjectivity, the wounded eye fetish of the surrealist film and painting.

In tales of romantic love in which the couple take up conventional, socially-sanctioned roles, the lure of the abyss, loss of self and perverse desire are held off or denied. Although the subject must exclude the abject, it must nevertheless be tolerated, for that which threatens to destroy life also helps to define life. Further, the activity of exclusion is necessary to guarantee that the subject take up his/her proper place in relation to the symbolic. If, however, the subject desires to encounter forms of abject eroticism then she must be prepared to engage in what Bataille describes as 'the perversities of turbulent passion, in drama, and if it is of a complete nature – in death'.

Tales of romantic love, such as *Romeo and Juliet*, in which the star-crossed couple are doomed by forces outside their control, explore death as a tragic and unwanted end; some narratives, such as *The Story of O* (1977) and *The Night Porter* (1974) depict characters who set out to encounter the abject erotic in its final manifestation. A recent Hollywood film, *Basic Instinct* (1992), examined the tension generated by treading a fine line between tolerating and excluding the abject erotic. The film was highly controversial, supposedly because of the scene in which the heroine displayed her genitalia (pornography's 'beaver shot'); in my view, the reason for its notoriety had more to do with the manner in which the text linked desire to death, and both of these to woman as the embodiment of the originating moment of loss and castration.

Basic Instinct is an erotic thriller; that is, a tale which sets its drama of human relationships, and its explicit depictions of on-screen sex, against a background of criminality or mystery. Set in San Francisco, it stars Michael Douglas as the edgy, hardboiled detective Nick Curran, who falls in love with a murder suspect, Catherine Tramell, a beautiful, blonde bisexual writer of mystery novels, played by Sharon Stone. The characters are generally too cynical or worldly-wise to embrace the possibility of love openly; instead they engage in sexual relationships in which the word 'love' is rarely used – in this instance, only Nick confesses his love, but in a throw-away line that is not allowed to mean anything too significant. He describes the possibility of a long-term relationship in an odd metaphor that masks his serious intent with frivolity. 'We might settle down, screw like minks and raise rug-rats.' Related to film noir, the contemporary erotic thriller (*Fatal Attraction* 1987; *Body of Evidence* 1993; *Body Heat* 1981) represents sex as deadly. The female and male protagonists are drawn to each other like sexual magnets; both cynics, neither is in the market for love – not at the beginning anyway.

In his fascinating analysis of contemporary culture, Peter Sloterdijk argues that the disintegration of romantic ideals in the twentieth century resulted in a pervasive cynicism which affected all areas of life – particularly the sexual. Referring to the anarchic philosophy of Dada he writes: 'Without a theory of bluff, of show, seduction , and deception, modern structures of consciousness cannot be explained at all properly.'[9] Cynicism became one of the central distinguishing features of the modernist impulse. In her discussion of Sloterdijk's theory in relation to *Pandora's Box* (1928), Mary Ann Doane makes the important observation that: 'Such a cynicism does not attempt to unmask or unveil the true sexuality but rather to demonstrate that sexuality resides in the mask, the game, the deceptiveness of vision associated with the crossing of the boundaries of sexual identity.'[10]

Basic Instinct is a classically postmodern text in that it plays with, and parodies, the modernist aesthetic of deceptiveness and the traversing of sexual boundaries. To achieve this, *Basic Instinct* constructs a world in which it is impossible to tell whether desire is real or a game of bluff and deception. On the one hand, eroticism is rendered abject – romantic love is an impossibility; on the other, it might be argued that a new form of romance has emerged, one which might be more aptly described not as romantic love, but as *cynical romance*. The couple – both loners – do not believe in love (although Nick is susceptible); instead, they believe in 'making love' and in pushing their erotic experiences to the limit.

The opening sequence of *Basic Instinct* emphasises themes of cynicism and deception, desire and death. Seductive music plays as the credits roll. A mirrored ceiling reflects images of a couple engaged in the throes of turbulent passion. Their writhing bodies slide across silken sheets. The camera moves to the head of the bed to reveal a woman – her face averted – astride the man, tying his arms to the bedposts. Long blonde hair falls across her face, signalling to the audience that her identity will remain anonymous while arousing the audience's desire to see her face. The anonymity, and subsequent interchangeability, of various female figures becomes a key theme of the film which deliberately fuels the cynic's response to Woman – 'Women, they're all the same. Dangerous. Untrustworthy.'

The camera focuses on her breasts and buttocks. As the music rises, the man moans ecstatically. The woman moves her body back and forth. His groans of pleasure intensify; in a reversal of conventional practices, sexual pleasure is registered on the male body and through the male voice. The woman suddenly leans back – not in response to the man's physical movements – but in order to search for an object beneath the sheets. Unexpectedly, she rises up; her body hovers momentarily over the man's before she descends, stabbing him with full force in the neck, the eye and across his upper body. It appears that she has – with careful deliberation – held off the moment of his death until he is at the point of orgasm. With her blade, she opens up his body, transforming it into a bloody, abject sight.

The fact that the man has begun to climax is later made clear; when the police arrive and begin to piece together the murder scene one remarks that there are 'cum stains all over the sheets'. 'He got off before he got off', another jokes cynically. A moment of pleasure and transcendence, orgasm marks both a sexual death ('*le petit mort*') and a literal death.

The cynic is always streetwise; he knows what it is like in the real world, particularly for the male silly enough to surrender power to woman. In its transgression of sexual boundaries, and its attitude of bluff and cynicism towards romance, *Basic Instinct* gives woman the agency. It is the male protagonist whose fate is left hanging in the balance. This play, or game of bluff, raises interesting questions for female, and male, responses in the audience – particularly as we soon learn that she is bisexual and that she controls every situation including, it seems, the fate of the male protagonist.

The opening murder scene is linked to another key sequence – the interrogation scene – in an important but oblique manner. The victim's girlfriend, a striking blonde, Catherine Tramell, has been taken in for questioning. The police and detectives are captivated by her blonde beauty and insolent, sexual posturing. She is like a female version of the 'cynical', 'arrogant' Mills and Boon hero. Detective Nick Curran, the senior investigator, is clearly aroused by the suspect, particularly by her audacious, flirtatious manner. The interrogating officers gather in a group around her. They fire questions: she fires right back. When she asks Nick if he has ever fucked on cocaine, the music (the same as that played in the opening murder scene) rises – along with the sexual temperature. There is a clear sense that anything is possible, that this woman – to whom sex and death appear to be a game – holds the key to the mystery. Having graduated from Berkeley with a double major in literature and psychology, she taunts the men with the fact she can read their desires like a book.

Parallels between the murder and the interrogation scenes are drawn: both are overtly sexual, both portray a mysterious blonde woman, both employ the same music, and both represent man as under the control of woman. The strongest parallel is, however, drawn by way of contrast. Whereas the murder scene represented the woman as having much to hide, the interrogation scene depicts woman as having nothing to hide. In the former she is masked, in the latter open. A sense of expectancy and excitement grows as Catherine Tramell, having verbally taunted Nick, slowly uncrosses her legs, opening them just wide enough so that her genital area is put on display. She is not wearing any underclothing. Positioned at a low tilt-up angle, the camera holds the shot then lets her long smooth legs fill the frame. As she crosses her legs, and talks of cocaine, she purrs: 'It's nice.' The rather overweight Detective Corelli begins to resemble a bowl of jelly, sweat glistening on his brow.

Lacan described the erotogenic zones as those areas marked by openings or cuts on the skin: 'lips, the enclosure of the teeth, the rim of the anus, the tip of the penis, the vagina, the slit formed by the eyelids, even the horn-shaped aperture of the ear.'[11] These openings on the body constitute a zone or boundary between inside and outside. They suggest areas of acute sensitivity which have the power to transform into abject sites. In mainstream public cinemas, the zones on display are primarily the facial ones – lips, eyes, nostrils, ears – sometimes nipples. The taboo zones of the genital and anal areas are usually only put on display in cinemas reserved for hard-core pornography. *Basic Instinct* was the first mainstream film to break this rule.

Nick is obviously in a state of full arousal; his response to Catherine Tramell's exhibitionistic display is controlled but obvious. Her act of exposure is too brief to reveal anything but a fleeting glimpse, a moment of shock. The thought that woman's genital – the forbidden erotogenic zone – had been screened in a mainstream film caused a public outcry and did wonders for the box office. But it was not the female genital which was opened up; in a perverse erotic display, the male body, cut and bleeding, offered itself as the film's prime erotogenic zone. Everything about woman remains a secret in the film: man is exposed, made vulnerable.

Catherine calls Nick 'the shooter', an ambiguous reference, first, to the fact he has killed innocent people in the line of duty; second, to his sexual intentions. She even implies that he has enjoyed the act of killing. Nick is captivated by Catherine Tramell but his cynicism prevents an open expression of romantic desire. Suspicion that she may be the deadly killer both curbs yet augments his passion. After all, a beautiful, dangerous woman offers a greater challenge. Nick's problem is that – unlike the male bondage victim of the opening scene – he is aroused by sadistic as well as masochistic urges. His anal/vaginal rape of Beth, the police psychoanalyst, testifies to his sadistic desires. Throughout the twists and turns of its complicated narrative, *Basic Instinct* plays on this dual perversion, suggesting that sex leads ultimately to death.

The film's argument that woman is the fatal sex is reinforced visually by the presence of four women all of whom are either bisexual and/or lesbian and all of whom are believed to be killers: Catherine herself; Beth, who slept with Catherine at College, and who may have murdered her husband; Roxy, Catherine's lesbian lover, who slashed the throats of her two young brothers when a girl; and Hazel Dobkins, an older woman and confidant of Catherine's, who was found guilty of knifing to death her entire family.[12] This doubling of the female figures – who seem to form a secret society from which men are excluded – creates a clear impression that the women are interchangeable; all signify the possibility of castration and death for man.

The look of desire constructed in *Basic Instinct* is a look of sexual ambiguity and abject eroticism, relayed between the main characters (Nick, Beth, Catherine, Roxy and Hazel) via an exchange of glances in which the dominant mode is one of cynicism. In the context of fantasy, the view of woman constructed in *Basic Instinct* is clearly a 'male' one. Tales of women as fantasy figures such as sex sirens, lesbians and whores is a favourite staple of pornography, film noir and the suspense thriller. But it is an unusual perspective in that the female figures are all-powerful, particularly Catherine, who is not even punished in the end for her 'deviant' sexuality and wicked way with the ice-pick. Images such as these, which draw attention to man's perverse desires, offer female spectators a rare opportunity to derive pleasure from an anti-romantic discourse.

In *Basic Instinct* woman – viewed from a male perspective – is even more dangerous than the man. After their first sexual encounter, Catherine tells him that an orgasm means nothing to her. Nick is clearly a cynic, a classic noir figure whose experiences with the underworld have led him to adopt a totally jaundiced view of human nature and women – or 'dames', as the 1940s hero liked to call the *femme fatale*. Catherine is the more interesting of the two. Like the classic cynic of modernity, Catherine is an urban being, a 'loose' woman, who is at home in the anonymity of the city: its nightclubs, fast cars, drugs and queer sex. She is a lone figure who is openly immoral and who has 'seen everything'. Sloterdijk describes the modern cynic as a 'borderline melancholic', borderline because such a figure is not immobilised by their cynicism; on the contrary, they continue to work, to function.[13] They also convey just the slightest suggestion of an inner despair which is veiled by an outer mask of toughness and an edgy manner. Catherine's fragility is revealed only once – when she breaks down over Roxy's death and says she always loses those close to her. Despite her wealth, power and cynicism, Catherine continues to write novels and to research human behaviour as a basis for her fiction. It is her borderline sexuality which constitutes her as both dangerous and fascinating.

In recent years, the temptress-as-lesbian has assumed a key place in popular culture. In her discussion of *Pandora's Box* as a modernist text, Mary Anne Doane argues that 'Sexual desire for the modern consciousness is never an entity in itself but the by-product of the moral ideals which will never fully and finally collapse and whose taboos engender its excitement and terror.'[14] Central to the modernist impulse which links sex and excitement, eroticism and death is the figure of new woman. As Patrice Petro points out in her reading of Walter Benjamin's *Central Park*, Benjamin's ambivalence and anxiety are inspired by the image of the new woman – 'an erotic, aggressive, and therefore profoundly "masculinised female figure"' who is linked to the prostitute and lesbian.[15] This image of woman was personified by Louise Brooks in *Pandora's Box* and by Marlene Dietrich in her cycle of 1930s films directed by Joseph von Sternberg. In these films, the erotic scenarios are imbued with images of lesbianism, prostitution, bisexuality and woman as a masculinised threat – motifs which are central to *Basic Instinct* made some sixty years later. The sexually enigmatic and dangerous woman is central to the representation of desire in narratives of abject eroticism.

Basic Instinct cynically plays with a series of images and events designed to 'shock' the spectator. These include the opening brutal ice-pick murder, the representation of all the female characters as lesbians and killers, and the notorious beaver shot. But *Basic Instinct* presents each of these, not in the form of a taboo (modern cinema audiences are themselves too cynical these days to be shocked), but as a 'staged' taboo, that is, the film offers the viewer pleasure in watching scenes that acknowledge (cynically) that sexuality is a game. Catherine Tramell makes this abundantly clear in her references to her latest book – a detective story – in which the hero's fate, that is Nick's fate, has already been written down. Nick's mistake is that he appears to fall in love with Catherine. In the final sequence he quips cynically that perhaps they will settle down and 'raise rug-rats'. It is Nick's reference to the possibility of love and family life (Bataille's 'vacant horror of steady conjugality') that seals his fate. Catherine scorns the very idea of procreation. The final shot – a close up of an ice-pick under the bed – recalls the film's opening murder and the alternative to 'steady conjugality' proposed by Bataille – 'the only outlet is in tearing, in the perversities of turbulent passion'. Like Bunuel's surrealist hero of *Un Chien Andalou*, the cynical, embattled hero of *Basic Instinct* has already demonstrated that he is aroused by sexual danger, but can he survive a game in which woman is the master cynic? In which woman has already written the script, and in which woman wears the mask? That is to say, a woman who moves freely – back and forth – across the boundaries of sexual identity. The female killer of *Basic Instinct* not only takes the male to the brink of extinction (the moment of orgasm) she also pushes him across the border into death. It is the abject form of erotic love which has been ignored in many discussions of romantic and Gothic love, despite various motifs which link the central character – even in Mills and Boon – to death and the abyss.

If the majority of Hollywood romances argue that the lack at the centre of human subjectivity can be made good, that a fulfilling union with the other is possible, what are we to make of that smaller group of films – of which *Basic Instinct* is exemplary – which emphasise the opposite, that the desire for union leads only to violence, disintegration and death?

In his late works, Freud examined how the human subject deals with the threat of dissolution and death. He came to believe that death was intimately bound up with the subject's desire for pleasure. The male seeks union with another who reminds him of his first love, his mother; the beloved stands in for the mother, their relationship a substitute for the infant–mother dyad. The lovers' desire for an imaginary wholeness, however, recalls the pre-birth state in which the unborn child was not only 'one' with the mother but that this unity existed because the child was in a state of inanimation or stasis. Pre-natal unity is preferable because it excludes the essential characteristics of life; that is, tension, striving, change and fragmentation.

Freud's theory of the death drive suggests that love stories which link desire to death represent an imaginary exploration of man's perverse desire to return to a state of non-differentiation, not through a happy, nurturing relationship but through a violent, erotic encounter with woman. Sexual pleasure is heightened through fear and knowledge that union with the woman will lead back to a state of originary wholeness and undifferentiated being. Man surrenders himself to the *femme fatale* as does a masochist to his mistress. In these narratives desire becomes abject yet erotic – the abject is eroticised.

Lacan also wrote about the infant's relationship with the mother but, unlike Freud, he did not define the pre-Symbolic mother as a figure who signified unity and wholeness, nor did he see the early relationship with the mother as one which represented these things. On the contrary it is the infant's encounter with the primordial mother, the original abyss, which Lacan named *la chose*, that leads to the infant's first awareness of loss and fragmentation and gives rise to the desire for unity. According to Lapsley and Westlake '*la chose* is thus the void around which the subject is structured'.[16] Thus, the infant desires an original unity which is an imaginary one. It desires to be the phallus for the mother where the 'phallus' signifies what the mother desires for her own fulfilment and completion and what the infant desires for its fulfilment.

In later life, the man demands of the woman that she represent the imaginary mother of unity and wholeness, but in the actual encounter with her, he experiences only lack. According to Lacan, 'desire is the desire of the Other': the couple-in-love can only offer each other what they desire; that is, that which can never be fulfilled. Elizabeth Grosz explains it this way: the sexual relation represents a futile attempt to 'satisfy this impossible demand, the demand to be/to have the phallus for and through the other'.[17] Love becomes a game in which each sex offers the other what they do not have. 'Any semblance of sexual rapport thus hinges on the phallus ... the man must pretend to have it, the woman must engage in the masquerade that she is it.'[18] Lapsley and Westlake also make the interesting point that in many films woman is represented as excessively beautiful, an idealised figure, whose function is to mask the lack and offer the promise that sexual unity is possible.

As feminist analyses of film have demonstrated, women are represented in terms of male fantasies about female sexuality: the exceedingly beautiful woman thus functions to cover over man's fundamental anxiety about lack, disintegration and death. 'It is because of this that Lacan could say that a beautiful woman is a perfect incarnation of man's castration and that beauty is "a barrier so extreme as to forbid access to fundamental horror".'[19] *Basic Instinct* plays on this opposition; Catherine Tramell's beauty wards off castration, yet the sight of her genitals, the originary abyss – offered as a brief, tantalising glimpse – threatens the subject with castration. Castration occurs at the moment of union, the moment of orgasm; this is why, in the opening scene, much is made of the fact that the man dies at the point of orgasm.

One of the most common ways of dealing with the lack in the other is through violence. In many films violence is directed at women who are seen to signify the original lack. *Peeping Tom* (1960), *Psycho* (1960), *Klute* (1971) and *Dressed to Kill* (1980) not only represent such violence, they also contain scenes in which the man's violence is analysed and pathologised along the lines of an originary experience of lack. It is this notion of lack and masquerade which helps us understand the sexual dynamics at work in films such as *Basic Instinct* which represent the end of desire as death. The majority of popular narratives do not push desire to the limit, do not cross the boundary between life and death in order to expose the abyss, the originary lack and the death of the subject. Those tales of love which do venture into abject territory – particularly noir and horror film – offer a different perspective on the nature of love and passion but one which is perhaps more compelling than the conventional love narrative with its impossible happy ending.

But why seek this state of lost unity through violence? In the conventional love story (*Camille*, 1937; *Dark Victory*, 1939; *Letter From An Unknown Woman*, 1948; *Beaches*, 1988), with death as its end, the beloved usually dies enfolded securely in the arms of the other, or fades away in a moment of aphanasis: in the tale of violent love, the lover meets death in a moment of extreme violence. The answer lies in the nature of desire and subjectivity as defined by Lacan; the end of desire is *la chose*, the abyss, separation, castration, death. The intensity with which the subject experiences desire shapes the intensity with which he/she rushes to confront their end. Just as lack and castration is a condition of the formation of subjectivity, so, too, is abjection.

Catherine Tramell's vocation as a writer is central to the film's narrative of death and desire and relates directly to the theme of abjection. A female *flâneur*, an observer of the human scene, Catherine claims to have written Mark into her narrative and, as such, is in control of his fate. Her latest novel involves a cop who falls in love with a woman he is investigating and is then killed. 'I'm using you for the detective in my book', she tells Nick. 'You're going to make a terrific character.' When Nick later asks how her novel is going, she replies, 'It's practically writing itself.' Catherine Tramell, the Woman, controls language and the play of signifiers; she pretends she is the Other for Mark, that she controls signification. 'You won't learn anything, I don't want you to know', she says. Living in anticipation of death at her hand, Mark is both castrated by his relation to language and by his relation to Woman. 'My book's nearly finished. My detective's almost dead', she tells him when he refuses to leave. The narrative of death and desire is being written from inside the text by woman herself. 'For cynics are not dumb, and every now and then they certainly see the nothingness to which everything leads.'[20]

For the subject/lover – constructed in/through language and through a desire for meaning – is also spoken by the abject, the place of meaninglessness; thus, the subject is constantly beset by abjection which fascinates desire but which must be repelled for fear of self-annihilation. The crucial point is that abjection is always ambiguous. Kristeva, like Bataille, emphasises the attraction, as well as the horror, of the undifferentiated:

We may call it a border; abjection is above all ambiguity. Because, while releasing a hold, it does not radically cut off the subject from what threatens it – on the contrary, abjection acknowledges it to be in perpetual danger.[21]

Abjection relates to eroticism through death; it represents 'a threshold before death, a halt or a respite'[22] If subjectivity is structured within and by the processes of abjection, and if the abject is 'already eroticised', this would suggest that a form of abject eroticism is also instrumental in the constitution of subjectivity and desire – that the subject takes up their proper place in the Symbolic order through/by the exclusion of a specific erotic practices which she/he finds both attractive and repulsive, alluring and deadly. Abject eroticism would then occur when the subject fails to expel the erotic, where eroticism is transgressive. For the abject erotic is the place where meaning collapses, where the definition of what it means to be 'human' is challenged, where the law is transgressed.

The abject erotic can assume many forms and would include the so-called perversions such as sadism, masochism, incest, necrophilia, coprophilia, anal eroticism, bestiality and in some societies where repression is strong, bisexuality, homosexuality and lesbianism. Its final, unanswerable form, however, is death: specifically death which occurs in a sexual context as does the ice-pick murder of *Basic Instinct*. The Gothic hero, deadly *femme fatale*, and dominatrix of pornography all represent – for their lovers – the possibility of death through desire which is why they are such compelling, yet ambiguous figures for the lover and the spectator alike.

Notes

1   Georges Bataille, *Death and Sensuality: A Study of Eroticism and the Taboo* (New York: Walker, 1962).
2   Georges Bataille in Denise Hollier (ed.), *The College of Sociology 1937–39*, trans. Betsy Wing (Minneapolis: University of Minnesota Press, 1988), p. 339.
3   Robyn Donald, *The Dark Abyss* (Richmond, Surrey: Mills and Boon, 1981), p. 53.
4   Ibid., p. 104.
5   Robyn Donald, *The Interloper* (Richmond, Surrey: Mills and Boon, 1981), p. 70.
6   Julia Kristeva, *Powers of Horror: An Essay on Abjection*, trans. Leon S. Roudiez (New York: Columbia University Press, 1982), p. 55.
7   Ibid., p. 4.
8   Ibid., p. 2.
9   Peter Sloterdijk, *Critique of Cynical Reason*, trans. Michael Eldred (Minneapolis and London: University of Minnesota Press, 1987), p. 402.
10   Mary Ann Doane, *Femmes Fatales: Feminism, Film Theory, Psychoanalysis* (New York and London: Routledge, 1991), p. 143.
11   Jacques Lacan, *Écrits*, trans. Alan Sheridan (New York: W. W. Norton, 1977), pp. 314–15.
12   For a discussion of the lesbian and gay male boycott of the film see Chris Holmlund's '"Cruisin" for a bruisin': Hollywood's deadly (lesbian) dolls', *Cinema Journal* 34, No. 1, Fall 1994, pp. 31–51. Holmlund also analyses the film in terms of its lesbian stereotypes and the pleasures it may hold for female spectators.

13   Sloterdijk, *Critique*, p. 5.
14   Doane, *Femmes Fatales*, p. 159.
15   Patrice Petro, *Joyless Streets: Women and Melodramatic Representation in Weimar Germany* (Princeton, New Jersey: Princeton University Press, 1989), p. 63.
16   Robert Lapsley and Michael Westlake, 'From *Casablanca* to *Pretty Woman*: the politics of romance' Screen 33, 1 (Spring 1992), p. 33. I am indebted to this excellent article for my discussion of Lacan.
17   Elizabeth Grosz, *Jacques Lacan: A Feminist Introduction* (London: Routledge, 1990), p. 133.
18   Lapsley and Westlake, 'From *Casablanca*', p. 32.
19   Ibid., p. 36.
20   Sloterdijk, *Critique*, p. 5.
21   Kristeva, *Powers of Horror*, p. 9.
22   Ibid., p. 55.

Filmography

Bad Timing (dir. Nicholas Roeg, 1980).
Basic Instinct (dir. Paul Verhoeven, 1982).
Beaches (dir. Bette Midler, 1988).
Body Heat (dir. Lawrence Kasdan, 1981).
Body of Evidence (dir. Uli Edel, 1993).
Camille (dir. George Cukor, 1937).
The Conformist (dir. Bernardo Bertolucci, 1971).
Crash (dir. David Cronenberg, 1996).
Dark Victory (dir. Edmund Goulding, 1939).
Double Indemnity (dir. Billy Wilder, 1984).
Dressed to Kill (dir. Brian de Palma, 1980).
Fatal Attraction (dir. Adrian Lyne, 1987).
Gaslight (dir. George Cukor, 1944).
The Hunger (dir. Tony Scott, 1983).
Klute (dir. Alan Pakula, 1971).
Last Tango in Paris (dir. Bernardo Bertolucci, 1973).
Letter from an Unknown Woman (dir. Max Ophuls, 1948).
Maitresse (dir. Barbet Schoeder, 1976).
The Night Porter (dir. Liliana Carani, 1974).
Nine and a Half Weeks (dir. Adrian Lyne, 1986).
Out of the Past (dir. Jacques Tourneur, 1947).
Pandora's Box (dir. G. W. Pabst, 1928).
Peeping Tom (dir. Michael Powell, 1960).
Psycho (dir. Alfred Hitchcock, 1960).
The Story of O (dir. Just Jaekin, 1977).
Sunset Boulevard (dir. Billy Wilder, 1950).
Un Chien Andalou (dir. Louis Bunuel, 1929.
The Vampire Lovers (dir. Roy Ward Baker, 1971).
Vampyres (dir. Joseph Larraz, 1974).
Vertigo (dir. Alfred Hitchcock, 1958).

Further Reading

Ackerman, Diane, *A Natural History of Love* (New York: Random House, 1994).
Barthes, Roland, *A Lover's Discourse: Fragments*, trans. Richard Howard (New York: Hill and Wang, 1982).

Belsey, Catherine, *Desire: Love Stories in Western Culture* (Oxford and Cambridge, Mass: Blackwell, 1994).

Creed, Barbara, 'The woman's romance as sexual fantasy: Mills and Boon, in Women and Labour Publications Collective *All Her Labours 2: Embroidering the Framework* (Sydney: Hale and Iremonger, 1984), pp. 47–68.

Foss, Paul, 'Eyes, fetishism, and the gaze', *Art and Text* 20, Feb–April 1986.

Fuery, Patrick, *Theories of Desire* (Carlton: Melbourne University Press, 1995).

Kristeva, Julia, *Tales of Love* (New York: Columbia University Press, 1987).

Masse, Michelle A., *In the Name of Love: Women, Masochism and the Gothic* (Ithaca and London: Cornell University Press, 1992).

Modleski, Tania, *Loving with a Vengeance: Mass-Produced Fantasies for Women* (New York London: Methuen, 1982).

Pearce, Lynne and Jackie Stacey, *Romance Revisited* (New York and London: New York University Press, 1995).

Silverman, Kaja, *The Thresholds of the Visible World* (New York and London: Routledge, 1996).

Singer, Irving, *The Nature of Love, 3: The Modern World* (Chicago and London: Chicago University Press, 1987).

13

Paulina Palmer for Cambridge Lesbian Line

Girl Meets Girl: Changing Approaches to the Lesbian Romance

> We can be an army of two. We can be Plato's perfect army: lovers, who
> will never behave dishonorably in each other's sight, and invincible.
> Let the world either kill us or grow accustomed to us; here we stand.
> (Isabel Miller, *Patience and Sarah*, 1969.)[1]

> Gael sat on the sofa beside Katherine and lit a cigarette. Katherine
> snuggled closely up to her and laid her head on her shoulder. 'I love
> you, Baby.' She batted her eyes until they created a breeze.
> (Deborah Powell, *Bayou City Secrets*, 1992.)[2]

The romance and certain genres related to it, such as novels with a
historical context and 'coming out' narratives focusing on the theme of
'girl meets girl', have achieved a notable degree of popularity with writers
of lesbian fiction.[3] Fashions in lesbian writing have changed considerably
in the course of the century but romance conventions and motifs continue
to play a part in the composition of novels and stories. The readiness of
writers to appropriate and rework them is illustrated by the fact that
texts as different in period and style as Radclyffe Hall's *The Well of Loneliness*
(1928), Ann Bannon's *I Am a Woman* (1959) and Isabel Miller's *Patience
and Sarah* (1969) have, in fact, one important feature in common: they
all represent lesbian variations on romance motifs and structures.[4] That
the romance should play a key role in lesbian fiction may come as a
surprise to the reader, since the heterosexist ideology informing the genre
and the emphasis it places on sexual difference make it appear, on first
impression, unsuited to lesbian appropriation. However, other features
it displays help to account for the appeal it exerts. The romance is a genre
which traditionally treats the theme of love and appeals to female

readership. It represents, in this respect, an obvious vehicle for the treatment and popularisation of lesbian themes. In addition, the idealised portrayal of a strong-willed heroine and her emotional development, which characterises twentieth century versions of the genre, allows for a celebratory portrayal of the female protagonist and her relationships. It also encourages a strong degree of reader identification. The varied use that writers make of these features is illustrated in the three works of lesbian popular fiction by Isabel Miller, Michelle Martin and Deborah Powell, on which I have chosen to centre my discussion in this chapter. The conventions of the romance furnish, as we shall see, both a frame and foil for the lesbian content of these novels. While exploiting the character stereotypes and structures of romantic fiction, the writers simultaneously seek to subvert the heterosexist ideology associated with the genre, transforming it into a vehicle for love between women.

Lesbian Romantic Fiction in the 1960s: Isabel Miller's *Patience and Sarah*

Miller's *Patience and Sarah* (1969), a fictional reconstruction of the relationship between the nineteenth-century American painter Mary Ann Willson and the daughter of a local farmer, employs the conventions of the romance with particular skill and originality.[5] Though writing in the hippie era of the 1960s, Miller avoids treating lesbianism 'as only an experiment and nothing more', the image which, as Lillian Faderman comments, typified the dismissive attitude to love between women current in the era.[6] On the contrary, she anticipates the political approach to the topic, with its emphasis on a feminist analysis of lesbianism, which was emerging towards the end of the decade. *Patience and Sarah* follows, on the whole, a typical romance trajectory, with the two young lovers positioned as the dynamic centre of the narrative. Their characterisation reflects, superficially at least, typical romance attributes and ideas of 'difference'.[7] Patience, in combining qualities of independence and sensuality with nurturing skills, resembles the heroine of mainstream romantic fiction. Like the heroine of the romance, moreover, she is portrayed at the start of the novel as emotionally isolated and suffering from a personal loss (her father's recent death). Sarah, in contrast, reproduces the attributes conventionally associated with the romantic hero. When first we encounter her, she is dressed as a boy and engaged in the typically male task of chopping logs. These roles have been assigned to her by her father who, since he lacks a son to help him on the farm, decides that her strong build and independent personality qualify her for the post. Though becoming increasingly critical of the psychological limitations and rigidities of the masculine role, she continues throughout the text to combine the contraries of strength and tenderness which, as

Janice Radway illustrates, the hero of romantic fiction generally displays.[8] It can be argued, in fact, that she unites them with a greater degree of success than the average male hero. As Radway points out, a feature of the heterosexual romance which frequently strikes the reader as unconvincing is the writer's attempt to graft on to the hero's entrenched masculinity qualities of tenderness and sensitivity.[9] Sarah's masculinity is, of course, by no means deeply entrenched. It is a role which she has assumed recently in the context of her 'man's' work – and, with Patience's encouragement, she has little difficulty in softening its contours. While the characterisation of Patience and Sarah reworks romance stereotypes, the various stages of their love affair, and the incidents of role reversal which it involves, also reproduce a typical romance trajectory. The sexual relationship between the two, one which Sarah, exploiting the privilege of her masculine role, initiates, is temporarily disrupted in the early stages by a period of misunderstanding and enforced separation. Conflicts of a personal kind, combined with the hostile reaction of relatives, upset the plans which the couple have made to elope. As a result, Sarah leaves home alone, leaving Patience to mourn her absence. However, after a few months of travelling, Sarah wearies of life on the road and, on returning home, seeks Patience out. An emotional reconciliation takes place – and the two pick up the threads of their relationship. This time, however, it is Patience who takes the lead. As well as reinitiating the sexual dimension of their involvement, she makes the move which eventually serves to liberate them from family control and enables them to fulfil their dream of setting up home together. By manipulating her brother and sister-in-law into discovering them kissing and, as a consequence, starting to regard them as a tainting influence on the family, she surreptitiously brings about their banishment. As a result, she and Sarah embark on the journey west, this time not separately but as a couple. After a series of further adventures introduced to illustrate their devotion and fidelity, they succeed in purchasing a farmstead in Greene County, New York State, and establish, in the words of the title under which the novel was initially published, 'A Place for Us'.

As readers familiar with the heterosexual romance will have recognised, the episodes summarised above reflect, relatively faithfully, its conventional stages and components. Even the incident of role-reversal which occurs around the middle of the novel when Patience, who up to now has played a somewhat passive role in the storyline, intervenes in the action and initiates the step which will eventually liberate herself and her partner from the restrictive influence of their families, is in keeping with romance conventions. Incidents of role-reversal are, in fact, a standard feature of the romance. When the hero shows signs of weakness and fails to act decisively, the heroine frequently steps in to perform some significant deed such as saving his life or nursing him through an illness. Patience's intervention serves a similar purpose. As well as convincing the reader of her loyalty and illustrating her initiative, it ensures that the love affair concludes on a positive note.

However, while modelling the lovers' trajectory on a conventional romance narrative, Miller simultaneously subverts the heterosexist ideology associated with the genre. In order to achieve this, she rewrites the patriarchal marriage plot which has dominated fiction for centuries and is the cornerstone of romantic fiction, by portraying her two central characters rejecting the role of 'wife'.[10] In refusing to marry, Patience and Sarah act in a manner quite at odds with the ethos of the romance. Romantic heroines, though women of spirit, do not generally take their independence so far as to criticise the family unit, reject relationships with men, and form partnerships with other women – as Patience, in fact, does. A critique of marriage appears on the novel's opening page in her ironically voiced comment, 'I'd never noticed that marriage made anybody else feel better!', expressed as she contemplates the oppressed marital situation of her sister-in-law Martha (p. 9). It is developed in the episode of the lovers' initial meeting where Patience, who associates marriage with suffering, is pleased to discover that, like herself, Sarah has no intention of becoming a wife; as she expressively puts it, she does not want to see 'that long light step made heavy with child and that strong neck bent' (p. 18). The critique of marriage and the heterosexual family in these episodes looks forward to the lesbian feminist analysis of the oppressive effect of patriarchal institutions which was to emerge in the early 1970s in essays by Sheila Cronan and Betsy Warrior.[11] Though anachronistic from the viewpoint of the nineteenth-century context of the novel, it encourages the reader to identify with the central characters and see their struggle to achieve independence as relevant to the feminist struggles of the present day. 'Wife' is not the only role assigned to women in life and literature which Patience repudiates. As well as spurning woman's conventional role of object of exchange or, as she grimly puts it, 'wards of males – neatly transferred from father to brother to husband to son to grave' (p. 137), she rejects the roles of 'spinster, sister and aunt' (p. 50) which Martha tries to foist upon her, relegating her to the position of unpaid skivvy. She also resists the role of 'madwoman in the attic', the common fate of the woman who transgresses patriarchal codes of conduct, to which her brother Edward threatens to drive her by proposing to incarcerate her in a cage in the loft. It is not only Patience's relatives who try to slot her into oppressive and restrictive roles. Sarah inadvertently does so too. Having returned from her travels and achieved a reconciliation, she appears perfectly content to allow Patience to continue playing the role of kindly friend and school marm, visiting her family and teaching them to read, while postponing making plans to live with her. And when eventually the two women do succeed in liberating themselves from family entanglements and travel west together, the people they meet on the journey again try to impose upon them conventional heterosexual identities. The female visitors to New York City whom they encounter at their lodgings, unaccustomed to seeing women travelling unescorted by men, weave around them a romantic fantasy portraying them as 'two heartsore maidens' forsaken in love 'seeking solace from mutual misfortune through mutual sympathy' (p. 177). By interspersing the text with references to conventional female roles and narratives, ones which the two lovers reject, Miller highlights the limited options open to women in nineteenth-century America. The references she makes to 'madwomen in lofts' and 'heartsore maidens' also hint at other storylines and scenarios, ones concluding with reference to suffering or death which, had she been constructing an orthodox narrative in which female transgression meets with punishment, she might have developed. This highlights the difficulty which she, and the characters whom she portrays, experience in resisting convention and creating innovatory narrative-lines/lifestyles. It also emphasises the radical nature of those they do create.

An obvious way in which *Patience and Sarah* differs from the mainstream romance is the limited roles which Miller assigns to men. Defining the distinctive features of lesbian narrative, Terry Castle describes the writer as substituting for the homosocial triangle of desire comprising two men and a woman, which characterises fiction reproducing hetero-patriarchal values, a triangle composed of two women and a man.[12] The narrative structure of *Patience and Sarah* agrees with Castle's blueprint since it is male characters, not female ones, who mediate in relationships and, having performed this role, are written out of the story. Edward, for example, eager to rid himself of the presence of the pair of lesbian lovers and the tainting influence they represent, assists them in organising their departure and, having escorted them on the initial stages of the journey, disappears from the narrative. The marginal position which men occupy in the novel is symbolically represented by the picture which Patience, on establishing herself in the farmstead in Greene County, paints to adorn her new home. It gives an unconventional portrayal of the biblical motif of Boaz, Ruth and Naomi. Ruth and Naomi occupy the foreground, while Boaz is portrayed 'distant, very small, his back turned leaving' (p. 186).

As is often the case with works of romantic fiction, lesbian as well as heterosexual, *Patience and Sarah* makes significant use of motifs appropriated from fairy-tale. The motif of the quest, reflected in the couple's search for 'A Place for Us', exemplifies this aspect of this novel. The story which Miller recounts displays interesting affinities with 'the tale of the two brothers' (or, more rarely, a brother and sister or two sisters), a quest narrative discussed by Bruno Bettelheim.[13] Bettelheim describes how the adventurous brother travels forth alone to seek his fortune, leaving his more cautious sibling at home. The two keep in contact by magic – and the tale concludes happily with their reunion.

Whereas in one version of the story, the stay-at-home brother risks his life to rescue his adventurous sibling when he runs into danger, in another, it is the stay-at-home brother who has to be rescued from the dull, monotonous life in which he has become entrapped. *Patience and Sarah* creates an innovative variation on this motif. The adventurous Sarah initially travels forth from home alone, leaving the over-cautious Patience behind. When, disillusioned with her travels, Sarah returns, it is the turn of Patience to step in and rescue her from the mood of despondency which has engulfed her. As a result of Patience's intervention, the two women eventually succeed in liberating themselves from family entanglements, embarking on a new life together.

Transformation is another motif with fairy-tale connotations which plays a key part in the novel. Sarah first appears to Patience in the guise of woodcutter, delivering logs to her home. This 'disguise' conceals the identity not of a prince, as is generally the case in fairy-tales, but a figure whom Patience and the lesbian reader find considerably more attractive – *a woman!* The treatment of gender and sexuality in the novel typifies, on the whole, a lesbian-feminist approach. Patience, who acts as the representative of this, is more amused than impressed by Sarah's somewhat ponderous performance of masculinity and succeeds in persuading her that 'It's better to be a real woman than an imitation man' and that 'when someone chooses a woman to go away with it's because a woman is what's preferred' (p. 23). In keeping with this remark, she insists that Sarah, when in her presence, remove her male attire and dress as a woman. Sarah comes to accept, partially at least, Patience's positive approach to womanhood. She starts to value her own body and see attraction between women in terms of identification, rather than difference. However Miller, while chiefly emphasising lesbian-feminist values of woman identification, signals on occasion a more pluralistic approach to gender. The association of the lesbian with role-play and cross-dressing, though ostensibly rejected, continues to recur throughout the text.[14] Sarah adopts the male pseudonym 'Sam' for purposes of finding work and, though complying with Patience's demand that she dress as a woman in her company, eagerly offers to cut her hair and reassume boy's attire to facilitate the purchasing of a farmstead. This focus on sexual difference is, in fact, essential to the novel's success. It maintains the romance conventions on which the narrative is structured and sustains the note of erotic tension in the couple's relationship. It also generates a lively storyline, since dressing as a boy confers on Sarah the privilege of initiating sexual encounters and entering the masculine sphere of paid work and independent travel.

Patience and Sarah is a pioneering work, remarkable for the time in which it was produced. It celebrates lesbianism in terms of ideas of women's liberation and political struggle in an era when the writer engaging in such a project had little social or cultural support and lacked literary models to emulate. Miller's most significant achievement is to transform the popular romance into a vehicle for an affirmative representation of lesbianism. In depicting her characters and their trajectory, she follows the conventions of the romance relatively faithfully. The narrative she creates offers the reader the pleasures traditionally associated with romantic fiction. These include imaginative involvement in a storyline which is easily accessible and emotional identification with a range of vividly drawn characters.

However, while utilising the romance format as a vehicle for lesbian themes, Miller does not entirely succeed in subverting the heterosexual codes and values which it conventionally inscribes. Her treatment of marriage is pertinent, in this respect. It might be criticised as confused and contradictory, since, while condemning the institution itself as oppressive, Miller concludes the novel by portraying Patience and Sarah engaging in a relationship which, in its emphasis on monogamy and its stereotypical division of roles, appears, in many ways, to replicate it. However, the issue is by no means clear-cut, and certain points can be raised in Miller's defence. In fact, she goes out of her way to distinguish between the oppressive nature of the actual institution of marriage, and the fulfilling relationship which Patience and Sarah enjoy. As Patience learns from observing the marital relations of her brother and his wife, the nineteenth-century American rural construct of marriage tended to relegate woman to the roles of breeder, maid of all work and sexual slave. The relationship which she forms with Sarah offers her, on the contrary, freedom from the obligation of childbearing, a division of labour which, though conventional, is at any rate equal, and a sexual partnership which is reciprocal and fulfilling. It also allows her time and opportunity to pursue her metier of painting.

Another criticism which the present-day reader is likely to direct at the novel is that Miller appears to equate childbearing and childcare with drudgery and, though portraying Patience as 'mothering' Sarah emotionally, treats lesbianism and biological motherhood as incompatible. However, to criticise the novel on this score is to ignore the historical context in which it was written. In identifying childbearing and childcare with women's oppression, Miller agrees with the feminist perspectives of the late 1960s/early 1970s. At this period no complex theorisation of sexual reproduction and motherhood existed, and the distinction between the fulfilling nature of 'the experience' and the oppressive aspect of the 'institution', articulated by Adrienne Rich in 1976, was as yet unformulated. The three major contributions to the analysis of the topic, Nancy Chodorow's *The Reproduction of Mothering* (1978), Dorothy Dinnerstein's *The Mermaid and the Minotaur* (1976) and Adrienne Rich's *Of Woman Born* (1976) were not to appear in print until later.

Judging from the comments of friends with whom I have discussed the novel, *Patience and Sarah*, as well as being of interest from a historical point of view, continues to furnish enjoyment for present-day readers. It is also significant in the sense that its publication prepared the way for a form of lesbian romantic fiction which, as we shall see from Martin's and Powell's novels, offers us pleasures of a very different kind.

New Versions of the Romance: Michelle Martin's *Pembroke Park* and Deborah Powell's *Bayou City Secrets*

In the 1980s and 1990s, with postmodern interests on the literary agenda and lesbian fiction achieving a new degree of sophistication, one might assume that the romance would be regarded as an outmoded form and would no longer exert an influence on lesbian writing. This, however, is not the case. The re-evaluation of genre fiction achieved by feminist/lesbian critics has resulted in the lesbian experimentation with popular forms such as the romance and the thriller gaining momentum while, at the same time, undergoing a degree of transformation.[15] With the commercial backing and promotional support supplied by feminist publishing houses and bookshops, lesbian fiction has achieved a wider readership and, as a consequence, has diversified into a number of different strands. Novels which appropriate and revise popular genres, such as the romance and the thriller, are regarded, on the whole, as the frivolous section of the market and are viewed in terms of entertainment. The ability of a work of lesbian genre fiction to hold the reader's attention and amuse her is, however, more complex than critics such as Bonnie Zimmerman, who write dismissively about novels of this kind, imply.[16] It requires not only the creation of a lively storyline but also – and this is more difficult to achieve – the inventive manipulation of cultural stereotypes and literary codes, and the skilful mobilisation of parody and pastiche. The writer has to display an awareness of the ideological significance of the genre which she is utilising since failure to do so results, as Anne Cranny-Francis observes, in her text 'being reappropriated by the discourses against which it is written'.[17] Like the tightrope dancer, she has to perform a precarious balancing act, maintaining an equilibrium between, on the one hand, respecting the conventions of the chosen genre and, on the other, subverting the attitudes informing it. These comments are relevant to the two texts discussed here: Martin's *Pembroke Park* (1986), a lesbian version of the regency romance, and Powell's *Bayou City Secrets* (1992) which is modelled on the format of the American crime novel.[18]

Both novels form a marked contrast to Miller's *Patience and Sarah*, in that they are written primarily for entertainment. Though influenced by women's/lesbian history and the debates it has generated (Martin is clearly aware of the increasing sexual restrictions imposed on women throughout the nineteenth century while Powell is familiar with present-day controversies about butch/femme role-play), they treat the issues, which they involve less explicitly, in a more playful manner. The sources to which they are indebted are, in fact, not so much the discourse of women's historical studies, and publications and workshops relating to it, as the realm of popular fiction and the media. The images of history they revise tend to be fictionalised, mythical ones, appropriated from popular novels and film. The regency scenario which Martin employs is familiar to the reader not only from the fictional works of Georgette Heyer and Jane Austen but also from the numerous film and television productions which either adapt them or reflect their influence. The gangsterland of Houston, with its associations of bootlegging and gunrunning, which Powell chooses as the location for her novel, is probably better known to the reader from American gangster movies than from the novels of Raymond Chandler and Dashiell Hammett which constitute its immediate source. Both the regency romance and the American crime novel are notorious, on the surface at any rate, for their heterosexism, and, in selecting them as material for revision, Martin and Powell commit themselves to taking on the ideological challenge they pose. The pleasure which the reader derives from their fiction, as well as reflecting the enjoyment of 'a good read' furnishing a quickly moving storyline, stems from the amusement and surprise she experiences in seeing the images of the past on which she has been reared transformed from a heterosexual to a lesbian context. Pleasure also stems from her admiration at the skilful use of parody by which the writer achieves this inversion of perspective. The fact that the two novels are intended primarily for entertainment does not mean, of course, that they lack political punch. If the reader, as is generally the case with women who identify as lesbian or bisexual, has ever felt excluded from mainstream culture and starved of an alternative, she finds it liberating and empowering, as well as fun, to see the images of history with which she is familiar transformed to incorporate a lesbian viewpoint.

Pleasures of this kind feature prominently in the reading of *Pembroke Park*, humorously advertised by Martin on the title page as 'A bit of a departure: the first lesbian regency novel'. While the novel's tone and style resemble the regency fiction of Georgette Heyer, the storyline and portrayal of character reveal affinities with Jane Austen's *Pride and Prejudice* (1813). Although the idea of reworking Austen's classic to focus on a lesbian love interest will no doubt strike some of her admirers as presumptuous, to judge from the remarks of certain commentators, it is, in fact, by no means as bizarre as it might at first appear. In an essay which, though unexceptional in scholarly terms, has been unjustly represented by journalists as scandalous, Castle draws attention to the preoccupation which Austen displays with the female body in both her letters and novels. She argues that 'sororal or pseudo-sororal attachments are arguably the most immediately gratifying human connections in Austen's imaginative universe', and points to the fact that many of the marriages with which her novels conclude 'seem designed not so much to bring about a union between hero and heroine as between the heroine and the hero's sister'.[19] Other women have also associated Austen's novels with lesbian interests. Although Martin is unique in publishing a lesbian version of *Pride and Prejudice*, her imagination is not the first to be fired by the idea. Alison Hennegan, in an essay aptly entitled 'On becoming a lesbian reader', describes how, in the 1960s when lesbian fiction was in short supply in bookshops and libraries, she compensated for its lack by creating in her imagination a lesbian version of Austen's famous novel. This, she recollects, gave rise to some unexpected partnerships: 'Charlotte Lucas had to be saved from Mr. Collins somehow and Elizabeth Bennett seemed to me the woman to do it. Sometimes I let Darcy have Bingley instead. If I was feeling really kind I invented an entirely new character for him, someone with Bingley's integrity and Wickham's profile.'[20]

Unlike Hennegan's transformation of *Pride and Prejudice* which remains in the realm of fantasy (as far as I know, she has never tried her hand at actually writing a lesbian version of the novel!), Martin's has achieved substance and form. She signals her debt to Austen by entitling her work *Pembroke Park*, which recalls the name of Darcy's country seat Pemberley, and by choosing as the setting for her storyline the village of Heddington, a community as conservative and close-knit as Austen's Meryton. The opening episode of her novel also displays affinities with *Pride and Prejudice* in that it centres on the arrival of an affluent visitor with aristocratic connections, and describes the gossip and conjecture the event generates. However, whereas in Austen's novel the appearance of the rich and handsome Mr Bingley inspires pleasurable excitement among mothers with marriageable daughters, in Martin's the arrival of the rich and beautiful Lady Diana March, who has recently purchased the local property of Waverly Manor, generates feelings of despondency and alarm. They are scared that her money and good looks will attract the local gentry and result in her stealing their daughters' suitors. Their fears on this score prove, in fact, groundless. Diana is portrayed not searching for a husband but recovering from feelings of grief occasioned by the death of her lesbian partner – and she clearly prefers women's company to men's. She acts as the chief signifier of lesbianism in the text and, as the narrative progresses, is portrayed as the centre of an upper-class homosexual coterie. Austen's influence on Martin is also apparent in the importance which feelings of prejudice assume in motivating the narrative, in the opening chapters of the novel in particular. Diana has lived in the Middle East and, when at leisure, likes to wear Turkish costume. On first encountering her, Joanna Garfield, the young widow who lives on a neighbouring estate and is assigned the role of romantic heroine, is shocked by what she sees as her outlandish attire and direct manner of speech. However, Joanna's initial feelings of prejudice are quickly (and predictably!) transformed into erotic attraction. This shift of response resembles not only Elizabeth Bennett's change of attitude towards Mr Darcy but also that of romantic heroines in general. It serves as a touchstone of Joanna's innocence, illustrating her lack of interest in fortune-hunting and her worthiness to win Diana's love. In romantic fiction, as Tania Modleski points out, 'The woman's determination to hate the hero' in the early stages of the narrative has a paradoxical effect, since it 'at once absolves her of mercenary motives and becomes the very means by which she obtains the hero's love, and, consequently, his fortune'.[21] In the case of Joanna and Diana marriage, of course, is out of the question, but the two women do embark on a love affair. The hostile reaction of Joanna's relatives and neighbours prevents the relationship from running smoothly, and an element of tension is introduced into the storyline by the intervention of her meddling brother Hugo, who makes an effort to disrupt the amour. Diana succeeds in outwitting his machinations, and the novel concludes in typically romantic vein with the two lovers turning their backs on the prejudiced society of Herefordshire and eloping to the continent – presumably to live happily ever after!

A species of genre fiction which has recently been appropriated by writers of lesbian fiction to treat issues relating to romance and sexuality is the thriller. The lesbian thriller, like its mainstream counterpart, includes within its parameters both the detective novel, which is characterised by an emphasis on the 'puzzle' aspect of the crime and a firm narrative closure resulting in an unequivocal reinstatement of social order, and the crime novel, which focuses on interests of a psychological nature and exposes acts of social injustice.[22] Powell's *Bayou City Secrets* is modelled on the latter. Appropriating the format of the 'hardboiled' crime novel, exemplified by the fiction of Raymond Chandler and Dashiell Hammett, Powell recounts the adventures of Hollis Carpenter, a lesbian news reporter in 1930s Houston. Powell's treatment of the period is postmodern in style, displaying an intelligent handling of pastiche and parody. Her representation of Houston, a city notorious in this era for its 'gangsters, guns, murderers and cheap gin', takes the form of a series of shifting vignettes which, as the references to 'Errol Flynn rolling dice' (p. 51) at the Lamar Hotel and '*Ceiling Zero* showing at the Metropolitan' (p. 93) indicate, is strongly indebted to film history. Her treatment of the the 1930s, while appealing on the surface to the reader's sense of nostalgia, is, in actual fact, highly critical. It establishes an ironic dialogue with the past, one which exposes the sexism, violence and corruption of American urban life at that time.

One of the hurdles which Powell, like other writers of crime fiction such as Barbara Wilson and Mary Wings, has to negotiate in attempting to transform the genre along lesbian lines is the portrayal of the figure of the sleuth and the attributes of ruthlessness and misogyny it reflects.[23] In depicting Hollis, Powell retains the hardboiled, wise-cracking persona associated with the male sleuth in American crime fiction but radically modifies the subjectivity and personal attributes which it masks. As Wings' protagonist Emma Victor and Rebecca O'Rourke's heroine Rats illustrate, one of the attractions which the figure of the lesbian investigator holds for the reader is her paradoxical combination of toughness and vulnerability – and Hollis is constructed on this model.[24] Her strength and independence are unrivalled, and in the gunrunning investigation on which the narrative centres she interrogates the suspects as ruthlessly as any man. However, as she herself admits, she is by no means a tough-guy movie hero. When unexpectedly confronted by the corpse of a friend, she vomits and, although she summons up the nerve to buy a pistol, notably refrains from using it. The tough persona which she assumes when making the purchase is humorously undercut by the patronising manner which the shop assistant adopts towards her during the transaction and by the fact that he addresses her as 'little lady' (p. 59). As this episode illustrates, Hollis, as well as occupying the role of hero, also plays on occasion the less dignified part of clown – the target of the reader's sympathetic laughter. In incorporating an element of humour into Hollis's characterisation, Powell follows the example of Sarah Dreher who centres her crime fiction on the naive but well-meaning Stoner McTavish.[25] The comic dimension of Hollis's portrayal is accentuated by the fact that, when pursuing criminals, she is generally accompanied by her dog Anice. Anice is no savage rottweiler, likely to inspire fear in the heart of gangsters and crooks, but a mongrel with a matted beard and floppy ears. She perches on Hollis's lap during car chases, sharing the thrills of the ride, and, like her mistress, who is too busy sleuthing to have time to make herself a proper meal, survives chiefly on a diet of brownies and ginger snaps.

Love affairs reveal Hollis at her most vulnerable, and in the romantic attachment which she forms with the glamorous Lily Delacroix, who unluckily turns out to be the criminal's wife, she unwisely allows her heart to rule her head. In portraying Hollis's infatuation with Lily, Powell amusingly parodies 1930s jargon. Hollis expresses her passion for Lily in suitably period terms, confessing that 'as I watched her talk I felt my heart do a Charleston' (p. 24), and, on anticipating a rendezvous with her, 'My mouth was as dry as a temperance hall' (p. 76). As these sentimental outbursts indicate, Hollis, though highly critical of male naivete and frequently disparaging her male acquaintances as 'stupid' and 'dumb', herself displays a pronounced element of naivete, an attribute which serves to endear her to the reader. While ostensibly contemptuous of wealth, and the greed which, she perceives, often accompanies it, she is overcome with wonder when confronted by the material possessions and affluent lifestyle it can buy. The mansion where the villain Delacroix resides is, in her eyes, 'only slightly smaller than Chicago' (p. 20), while the drawing room it contains resembles in decor and size 'a set for Jean Harlow' (p. 21).

Although Powell's aim in writing the novel is clearly entertainment, like her predecessors Chandler and Hammett she employs the format of the thriller to highlight injustices and social abuses. The illicit gunrunning in which Delacroix is discovered to be involved, rather than being represented as an occasional criminal aberration, is depicted as the tip of a pyramid of violence and greed to which society as a whole, the male members in particular, contribute. Relationships in both the criminal underworld and mainstream society reflect a hierarchy of power based on money and gender. This hierarchy forms the context of Hollis's romance with Lily, making the former uncomfortably aware of the immense gulf which separates her from her beloved. Lily, as Hollis discovers at their initial encounter, includes among her social perks the fact that she is distantly related to Mrs Simpson. As Hollis wryly puts it, commenting on the different social worlds they inhabit, whereas Lily's aristocratic ancestors 'had barely gotten out of France one step ahead of the guillotine ... my own family had waded out of the Irish bogs to get here' (p. 79).

In employing the thriller as a vehicle for lesbian romance, Powell creates a vivid delineation of 1930s constructs of lesbian sexuality. Her treatment of the butch/femme role-play which characterised American lesbian life in this period accords with the novel's postmodern style, creating an analysis of earlier modes of behaviour from the viewpoint of the present day.[26] Instead of portraying her characters expressing unease about cross-dressing and role-play, as is the case with Miller, she treats these practices unapologetically, accepting them as a feature of the 1930s social scene. Her perspective reflects, in this respect, the re-evaluation of lesbian role-play which has taken place in the 1980s and 1990s. Reacting against the lesbian-feminist critique of butch/femme roles as imitating heterosexual positions and promoting inequality among women, Joan Nestle defends them on the grounds that, in a homophobic era, they served a useful purpose by making lesbians visible to one another. Defining sexual attraction between women in terms of 'difference', she highlights their erotic dimension.[27] The discussion on the performative aspect of gender pioneered by Judith Butler has also contributed to the re-evaluation of lesbian role-play. Clare Whatling, drawing on Butlerian theory, observes: 'the butch/femme stance of the 1950s, instead of figuring as a rigid imitation of heterosexual roles, in fact plays with the visual assumptions about gender and sexuality, taking the limited erotic categories available to lesbians at the time and transforming them into something very different and highly subversive'.[28]

Powell's approach to butch/femme roles, though resembling Nestle's and Whatling's, is less idealised. Unlike the two theorists, she seeks not to defend the practice but to explore the complex sexual and social negotiations between women which it involves and to tease out the contradictions it displays. Hollis appears perfectly at ease in the role of butch, and the garb of slacks and saddle oxfords which act as its signifiers.

When her attire meets with disapproval, as it sometimes does from 'the old coots' whom she encounters in the course of her investigative activities, she nonchalantly shrugs off their criticisms with the common sense remark, 'I didn't dress to make them happy ... I dressed for myself' (p. 42). The butch Gael and her femme partner Katherine, the couple who befriend and support Hollis in her turbulent adventures, are similarly relaxed, and are portrayed on the whole, as 'equal but different'. Katherine is quite capable of holding her own in the playful arguments in which she and Gael engage, and is certainly no dumb blonde. It is she, in fact, who first perceives the connection between the theft of Hollis's address book and the murder of the police officer Joe Mahan, a vital clue in solving the crime investigation. The sparring matches in which the couple engage are represented more as a playful manipulation of gender stereotypes than as a straightforward imitation of heterosexual positions. The element of parody they reflect, though at times slipping into an essentialist stance, agrees in general with Butler's account of the performative aspect of gender. The episodes treating Hollis's involvement with Lily Delacroix, who is portrayed as an ultra feminine glamour girl, illustrate the way that, throughout the text, attraction between women is represented in terms of 'difference', rather than 'identification' as tended to be the case in the lesbian-feminist era of the 1970s. Powell emphasises that other forms of difference, such as personality and role, operate in sexual relationships than those pertaining to gender *per se*. Powell's focus, in this respect, agrees with the perspectives of Joan Nestle who explores the dynamics of butch/femme relationships, and with the queer theorist Sue Ellen Case who defines the sign 'lesbian' in terms of the butch/femme couple.[29]

The novels of Martin and Powell, published in the 1990s, form a marked contrast to Miller's, which first appeared in print in the late 1960s, the era anticipating the advent of the lesbian-feminist movement. Whereas all three writers rework conventions and narrative structures appropriated from mainstream romantic fiction, Martin and Powell treat them with a greater degree of radicalism. Miller's *Patience and Sarah* reproduces the format of the popular romance and the trajectory it inscribes relatively faithfully. By substituting lesbian characters for heterosexual ones, Miller transforms the romance into a vehicle for the treatment of lesbian-feminist themes, such as 'coming out', the search for a partner, and women's quest for liberation. As is the case with mainstream romantic fiction, *Patience and Sarah* plunges the reader into an emotionally powerful 'slice of life' narrative which enables her to enjoy the pleasures of character identification. This strategy, since it allows no distance between reader and character, permits little room for irony. It leaves the conventions of the romance unquestioned, appearing to endorse them uncritically.

Martin and Powell, on the contrary, influenced by the lesbian revision of popular genres which emerged in the 1980s, foreground the artifice of the romance format and subject its conventions to humorous parody. By placing characters who identify as lesbian in a heterosexist frame and highlighting the tensions this generates, they alert the reader to the ideological limitations of the romance genre and the social codes which it inscribes. The writers' parodic reworking of stereotypes from romantic fiction and the thriller, instead of representing character and subjectivity in terms of depth, signal that they are constructs which operate in terms of performativity. This agrees with queer and postmodernist perceptions. The two writers present the reader with a selection of transgressive sexualities, including lesbian, gay, butch and femme, while simultaneously parading before her a number of fictional stereotypes such as hero, heroine, villain, sleuth and gangster's moll. In this way, they encourage her to compare sexual constructs with literary ones.

The highly self-conscious approach to style and generic convention which characterises the novels of Martin and Powell not only transforms the romance into a vehicle for the treatment of lesbianism but also furnishes a critique of traditional concepts of romantic love and 'character', along with the works of fiction which popularise them.

Notes

1 Isabel Miller, *Patience and Sarah* ([1969] London: The Women's Press, 1979) p.101.
2 Deborah Powell, *Bayou City Secrets* (London: The Women's Press, 1992), p. 129.
3 For discussion of these genres see Paulina Palmer, *Contemporary Lesbian Writing: Dreams. Desire. Difference* (Buckingham: Open University Press, 1993), pp. 31–61; and Bonnie Zimmerman, *The Safe Sea of Women: Lesbian Fiction 1909-1989* (London: Onlywomen Press, 1990), pp. 33–118.
4 For reference to these writers see Jean Radford, 'An inverted romance: The Well of Loneliness and sexual ideology', in Radford ed., *The Progress of Romance: The Politics of Popular Fiction* (London: Routledge and Kegan Paul, 1986), pp. 97–111; Diane Hamer, '"I am a Woman": Ann Bannon and the writing of lesbian identity in the 1950s', in Mark Lilly ed., *Lesbian and Gay Writing: An Anthology of Critical Essays* (London: Macmillan, 1990), pp. 47–75; and Zimmerman, ibid., pp. 41–2, 47–9.
5 Miller, *Patience*. Further page references are to this edition and are in the text.
6 Lillian Faderman, *Odd Girls and Twilight Lovers: A History of Lesbian Life in Twentieth Century America* (Harmondsworth: Penguin, 1992), p. 203.
7 See Janice A. Radway, *Reading the Romance: Women, Patriarchy, and Popular Literature* (Chapel Hill: University of North Carolina Press, 1984), pp. 119–56.
8 Ibid., pp. 127–51.
9 Ibid., pp. 129–30, 147–9.
10 For reference to women writers transforming the patriarchal marriage plot see Rachel Blau Duplessis, *Writing Beyond the Ending: Narrative Strategies of Twentieth-Century Women Writers* (Bloomington: Indiana University Press, 1985); and Gayle Greene, *Changing the Story: Feminist Fiction and the Tradition* (Bloomington: Indiana University Press, 1991).
11 See Sheila Cronan, 'Marriage' (1970) in Anne Koedt, Ellen Levine and Anita Rapone (eds), *Radical Feminism* (New York: Quadrangle, 1973), pp. 213–21; and Betsy Warrior,

'Housework: slavery or labor of love?' (1971), in Koedt *et al.*, *Radical Feminism*, pp. 208–12.

12 Terry Castle, 'Sylvia Townsend Warner and the counterplot of lesbian fiction', in Joseph Bristow (ed.), *Sexual Sameness: Textual Differences in Lesbian and Gay Writing* (London: Routledge, 1992), pp. 128–47.

13 Bruno Bettelheim, *The Uses of Enchantment: The Meaning and Importance of Fairy Tales* (Harmondsworth: Penguin, 1991), pp. 90–6.

14 For a discussion of role-play in the novel, see Anne Herrmann, 'Imitations of marriage: Crossdressed couples in contemporary lesbian fiction', *Feminist Studies*, 18,3 (1992), pp. 609–24.

15 For reference to the feminist re-evaluation of popular genres see Helen Carr (ed.), *From My Guy to Sci Fi: Genre and Women's Writing in the Postmodern World* (London: Pandora, 1989).

16 Zimmerman, *The Safe Sea*, pp. 210–13.

17 Anne Cranny-Francis, *Feminist Fiction: Feminist Uses of Generic Fiction* (Cambridge: Polity Press, 1990), p. 9.

18 Michelle Martin, *Pembroke Park* (Tallahassee, Florida: Naiad, 1986). Further page references are to this edition are in the text; Deborah Powell, *Bayou City Secrets* p. 58. Further page references are to this edition and are in the text.

19 Terry Castle, 'Sister-Sister', *London Review of Books* (3 August 1995), p. 3.

20 Alison Hennegan, 'On becoming a lesbian reader', in Susannah Radstone (ed.), *Sexuality. Gender and Popular Fiction* (London: Lawrence and Wishart, 1988), p. 175.

21 Tania Modleski, *Loving with a Vengeance: Mass-produced Fantasies for Women* (London: Methuen, 1984), p. 49.

22 For discussion of the lesbian thriller, see Sally Munt, *Murder by the Book? Feminism and the Crime Novel* (London: Routledge, 1994), pp. 120–46; and Palmer, *Contemporary Lesbian Fiction*, pp. 63–77.

23 See, for example, Barbara Wilson's *Murder in the Collective* (London: Women's Press, 1984); and Mary Wings's *She Came Too Late* (London: Women's Press, 1986).

24 Rebecca O'Rourke, *Jumping the Cracks* (London: Virago, 1987).

25 Sarah Dreher, *Stoner McTavish* (London: Pandora, 1987).

26 Linda Hutcheon describes the writer of historiographic metafiction as engaging in 'a re-evaluation of and a dialogue with the past in the light of the present', in *A Poetics of Postmodernism* (London: Routledge, 1988), p. 19.

27 Joan Nestle, *A Restricted Country* (Ithaca, NY: Firebrand Books, 1987), pp. 78–109.

28 Clare Whatling, 'Reading awry: Joan Nestle and the recontextualization of heterosexuality', in Joseph Bristow, *Sexual Sameness*, p. 218.

29 Sue-Ellen Case, 'Toward a butch-femme aesthetic', in Lynda Hart (ed.), *Making a Spectacle: Feminist Essays on Contemporary Women's Theatre* (Ann Arbor, MI: University of Michigan Press, 1989), pp. 282–7.

14

Derek Longhurst

'They gotta do what they gotta do': Interrogating the Contradictions and Lasting Pleasures of Masculine Romance

The fact that most adventure formulas have male protagonists while most romances have female central characters does suggest *a basic affinity* between the different *sexes* and these two story types.[1]

Have I told you lately that I love you. (Van Morrison, 1989)

I believe in love. (Elton John, 1995)

Whatever I said
Whatever I did
I didn't mean it
I just want you back for good. (Take That, 1995)

Clearly it is somewhat unfair to John Cawelti to isolate a single quotation from his ground-breaking study of popular fiction published in 1976 and to place it in the context of a random selection of contemporary popular music. Strategically, however, it draws attention to a number of issues or problems in the critical assessment of popular forms.

First, and most obviously, there is the clear disjunction between the critic's voice and at least some of the (male) voices of popular culture. It may be objected that Cawelti is writing about different forms, specifically popular narrative rather than music, but taking the sentence as a whole reveals the dangers of reaching neat equations in the analysis and judgement of popular forms. Indeed, Cawelti almost suggests a kind of *biological* 'affinity' between what he terms 'the different sexes' and genres such as romance and adventure. It may be objected, again, that Cawelti is writing in the context of the 1970s and that twenty years of cultural analysis and feminist work have ensued, rendering critique of the kind I am conducting both redundant and even typical of male(?) academic practice. I would contend, however, that this hardly excuses the failure to discriminate between terms such as sex and gender. Moreover, and most important, Cawelti's assessment of adventure and romance reveals the problems endemic in a formulaic approach which does not adequately register both the fluidity and complexity of genre nor does it pay due attention to the social and historical contexts in which popular narratives are created/produced or read/consumed or to subtle analysis of gendered protagonists and processes of gendered identification.

Rather than assuming, then, a self-evident disjuncture between the genres of adventure, thriller and romance I wish to challenge simple dichotomies and pursue a line of argument that adventure narratives are deeply imbued with romance, and even are a mode of romance. Thus I will argue that they address the pleasures and dangers, predominantly but not exclusively, of male fantasy, wish-fulfilment and desire. Bridget Fowler has usefully outlined two major forms of contemporary popular romance:

> ... either the quest of the lovers to overcome obstacles to marriage, or the restoration of marital and family harmony after the threat of disintegration. In both forms, social unity, ethically correct action and individual happiness are simultaneously guaranteed.[2]

She goes on to argue that romance explores the conflicts surrounding patriarchy, sexuality and the family, ultimately celebrating heterosexual, monogamous relations. At first sight this may seem worlds apart from those genres associated with masculine narrative pleasures, but the question I wish to pursue is: are they? Clearly there are some important points of differentiation in that conventionally popular forms of romantic fiction focus upon the family and the domestic whereas masculine genres tend to be identified with the 'public' world of politics, with adventures in 'alien' locations, with war, 'action' and aggression rather than love and nurturing. It is frequently argued, also, that romantic fiction directed towards women readers addresses their desire for *relationship* (conventionally a kind of equal dependency heterosexuality) whereas narratives which fashion imagined masculinities tease at male fantasies of power and aggression.

This seems to me to be too simplistic in relation to much contemporary popular narrative as can most obviously be seen in what is, perhaps, a hybrid-gendered genre such as crime detection. Consider, for a moment, the case of Inspector Morse, in which the satisfaction of the desire for the resolution of the enigma of crime is paralleled by an unfulfilled and unresolved desire for relationship in the middle-aged eponymous 'hero'. One of the reasons for the success of the television series, I would argue, is that Morse's 'quest' for – and failure to find – relationship is frequently foregrounded, exploring a fractured vulnerability which conceals a depth of romantic feeling beneath a public brusqueness. Finally, Morse is left with opera as the only medium through which he can 'express' an inner passion and the visual and musical codes register a sense of sadness, loss and 'aloneness'.

This theme of the isolated hero has, I would argue, become particularly recurrent in the contemporary British thriller. It is absolutely central to Gerald Seymour's work, for instance, from *Harry's Game* (1986) through to *The Fighting Man* (1994) in which an ex-SAS man, feeling humiliated by his court martial for (justified) insubordination to an American officer during the Gulf War, leads a revolutionary group of Guatemalan Indians against the military dictatorship.[3] On the face of it this is a rather bizarre narrative which romanticises the man of action who is, of course, seen also by other characters as a mercenary. Seymour structures his narrative around a conflict between the duplicity and betrayals of international agencies (in this case American) and those who serve them, and the purity of motive of the 'fighting man', a common trope in the contemporary thriller. Seymour's protagonists, however, are always 'divided' in some way, in this case between the public persona of the hard, professional soldier and an internal 'world' of desire and feeling ('He had yearned to be wanted').[4] And, unlike James Bond, they never live to tell the tale; they perish in pursuit of some belief or imagined ideal which transcends the 'poverty' of their lives and the world which surrounds them. Consider, for instance, this passage from Seymour's *The Heart of Danger* (1995):

> It would be for her, Dorrie ... not for Mary Braddock in the Manor House, not for Basil and the creeps at Alpha Security, not for Arnold bloody Browne who had not lifted a finger when he'd needed help, nor for his Jane and his Tom and the paying of the mortgage for the roof over their heads, but for the love of Dorrie ... He thought that what he wanted, wanted most in the world, was to share in the love of Dorrie ... It was as if she called. It was as if he should follow. He knew that he wanted her love, certainty, more than anything he had wanted in his life. He craved the freedom that had been hers.[5]

In this case the protagonist, Penn, is no professional fighting man but a kind of anti-hero driven equally by his sense of the rejection of his potential through the operation of the English class system and by his pursuit of the 'truth' of Dorrie, whom he has never met, and uncovering the circumstances in which she has been murdered by a Serbian war criminal in the current conflict. The feature of the narrative I want to draw out here is the way in which Seymour explores the romance of sheer *irrationality* in his male protagonists and their frustrated desire for 'belonging' and relationship in some way which they struggle to define.

A somewhat different inflection can be traced in John Le Carré's *Our Game* (1995) which, in effect, focuses entirely around a quest by and within the protagonist/narrator for an understanding of relationships, past and present.[6] The dust cover is revealing in how the novel is represented to its prospective buyer in supermarket or bookstore: 'as Tim advances across the battered landscape of post-Thatcher England, into the lawless wilds of Moscow and then Southern Russia, we share with him also the dilemma of a dispossessed loyalist of our time, deprived of past and future alike, and grappling with his left-over humanity'.

Our Game is a novel of suspense in the great British tradition: now romantic, now tragic, now comic ... yet, even more than that, it is a novel suffused with magic. Clearly, in Le Carré's case there is the projection of his work as having achieved the status of 'crossover', bridging popular genre and the literary 'tradition'. The simple point to make, however, is that the narrative (of 'suspense') is focused upon a quest, an adventure circling around the search for the self, for moral value, love, national identity within societies which are depicted as Hobbesian in their loss of moral order. This seems a long way from Cawelti's encapsulation of the genre.

Masculine Identities

The heroes of the adventure or war genre, then, are often represented as idealised, strong, impervious to pain or danger: able to outwit the 'enemy' who generates the sense of risk and, therefore, excitement within the genre. The thriller narrative, it seems, plays upon the pleasures of conflict and danger while simultaneously reassuring the reader or audience that, no matter how hopeless the situation may seem, identification with the protagonist will not be disappointed in failure. In this sense the adventure thriller always engages at some level with the miraculous or magical and generates the pleasures of utopian wish-fulfilment. Frequently, of course, such representations are mobilised in the interests of national identity, as we shall see later, and need to be located in the context of specific political and historical contexts. It is also important to emphasise here that contemporary narratives explore a plurality of 'exemplary masculinities' rather than reproducing a single figuration which can be encapsulated in abstract, general terms.[7]

The tendency towards defining some kind of essential characteristic of masculinity is a widespread political and cultural phenomenon. For instance, Enoch Powell's contribution to the parliamentary debate of the

British Nationality Bill in the early 1980s gave a voice to a particular version of gender relations pervasive for his generation:

> Nationality, in the last resort, is tested by fighting. A man's nation is the nation for which he will fight. His nationality is the expression of his ultimate allegiance. It is his identification with those with whom he will stand, if necessary, against the rest of the world, and to whose survival he regards the survival of his own personal identity as subordinate.[8]

Women, on the other hand, serve their country by the expression of their 'specialised' function in 'the preservation and care of life'. It is, of course, possible to dismiss such views, like those of Norman Tebbit on cricket and nationhood or John Major on warm beer and cricket (again!), as the ramblings of a dotty Tory MP infamous for his role in the politics of British racism, but I would argue that it would be dangerous to underestimate the continued power of such representations especially in, say, the specific historical circumstances of the Vietnam War for America or the Falklands/Malvinas conflict for Britain.

It is also worth considering a representation of masculinity from the opposite end of the political spectrum:

> In Britain this direct sort of violence is limited mainly to police brutality, rape, incest, beating and individual murder by individual men. And from their fantasies, from the unavoidable beat-em-up cops and robbers series on television, the war comics produced just for boys and the phenomenal amounts of sadistic pornography produced for men, it seems that men don't feel at all guilty about their violence. Rather they seem to revel in it.[9]

I do not wish to quarrel with the anger which generates this passage but I do think that it is necessary, for political and cultural rather than merely 'academic' reasons, to question at least some of the assumptions of this argument. For a start, not to do so results, potentially, in sharing a platform on masculinity with nationalist jingoism while also failing to distinguish adequately between textual representations and 'real world' lived practices. The temptation to reify masculinity, in other words, undermines any analysis informed by *history* and specific social relations in the interests of assenting an ontology of innate characteristics of violence and brutality. Rather, I would argue, masculinities are constructed, created and recreated through processes of identification and social and cultural activity which are profoundly contradictory and far from uniform. Moreover, generation, class, ethnicity and regional cultures are only some of the more obvious factors which impinge upon gendered identities in addition to the mobilisation of discourses of nation. Thus, engagement with cultural forms is always a *negotiated relationship* not merely with the pleasures or idealising wish-fulfilling desires of a narrative but with how that narrative interacts with a selfhood which is never 'fixed' but enters into social life on an everyday basis. Clearly an important aspect of cultural analysis must be to tease out the complex ways in which the most public forms of representation – film, television, the press, popular fiction – seek to define the terrain of imagined identities. Thus we are all, in Anthony Giddens' terms, 'disembedded' – caught between local identities and globalised cultural industries which seek to market, among other things, forms of masculinity.[10]

One of the critical orthodoxies in such analysis is that 'male genres', with their attendant pleasures or fantasies, have little or nothing to do with the domain of the private, with emotional commitment, personal relationships or the domestic. An 'action-packed' narrative from *Boy's Own* to *Indiana Jones*, it is assumed, represses any such concerns. The closest male protagonists get to such experience is through male rivalry and bonding. While there is much evidence to support the appearance of such a disjuncture between romance and the adventure, quest or war thriller genres I think it is worth questioning whether there is not more relation than is commonly supposed.

What, then, are the most common characteristics of male genres of popular narrative which are inflected in specific ways within particular historical contexts? The obvious terms which come to mind are: action, danger, risk, loyalty and betrayal, suspense and resolution, the pursuit of 'fortune and glory' generally in foreign, 'alien' landscapes far removed – and, hence, safe from – domestic and familial relations which could undermine the virility of the narrative pleasures and representations of bravery, power and triumphant aggression. But is it all so very straightforward? After all, one of the most troubled frontiers traversed by masculinity is not that patrolled by armed border guards but the terrain between the public and the private, between 'society' and domesticity, between doing and being, between action and repression. I want to explore, then, a range of popular narratives produced over the last decade which seem to me to explore such issues and blur the disjunction between romance and fictions which, in different ways, are structured around a sense of a 'quest', through which masculinities are represented in contradictory ways.

Action Men

The Hollywood film industry in the last two decades has clearly sought to exploit 'sure-fire' successes at the box office in order to recover the massive investment involved in production. Nowhere is this more obvious than in the various sequences of films projecting male action heroes:

Harrison Ford, Sylvester Stallone, Arnold Schwarzenegger, Bruce Willis, Mel Gibson, Tom Cruise, Kevin Costner and so on.[11] Amongst the films which might be felt to be at the most extreme end of the spectrum from romance is the *Rocky* sequence.

Let me return for a moment, however, to the terms of Bridget Fowler's description of contemporary romance: the 'restoration of marital and family harmony after the threat of disintegration', 'social unity', 'ethically correct action', 'individual happiness'. There are ways in which this perfectly describes the structure of the narrative in *Rocky IV* (1985), for instance. Let me say at the outset that I have no wish to 'recover' the film for any kind of political or aesthetic value but I do think that it is worth examining the lines and tensions of its narrative. At one level this is a straightforward piece of jingoistic nonsense in which American masculinity ultimately defeats, against all the odds, its opposite Soviet number – so where, one might reasonably ask, does this involve elements of romance? The starting point is male bonding and national identity. The retired former champion, Apollo Creed (aptly named) challenges the Soviet champion Ivan Drago to a contest for no other reason than to defeat Soviet values and to assert his identity: 'we are warriors'. The contest is preceded by a bizarre song and dance routine involving James Brown and Creed, the two main functions of which are to demonstrate that blacks are clearly now sold on the American way of life and to assert American 'life' in general terms against the power symbolically represented by the massive Drago. Of course the contest ends with the death of Creed at the hands of the unscrupulous, ruthless Drago: 'If he dies, he dies' he sneers down at Rocky cradling Apollo Creed in *piétà* fashion.

There now begins Rocky's quest at the heart of the narrative. His search is for the masculine self buried within him through which Drago can be defeated ('I'm gonna take everything he's got', 'I'm a fighter – we gotta go with what we are', 'I just gotta do what I gotta do' and so on in predictably inarticulate fashion). In order to defeat Drago, Rocky embarks on a journey to the Siberian wastes and a central sequence of the film intercuts his self-training in a natural landscape and the honing by others of Drago as 'a perfectly trained athlete', a 'look at the future', using the full range of contemporary gymnasium machines pepped up by injections. Informing the conflict of values across 'super-power' identities, however, is the differentiation of hero and villain in the representation of their wives, their engagement with marriage and romantic love (and, in Rocky's case, significantly with fatherhood). Drago is equipped with a blonde supermodel whose main functions in the narrative are to act as his PR woman at press conferences and to 'look' arrogantly contemptuous of Rocky's wife. Where Drago's wife *accompanies* him and even participates in his training, Rocky carries his wife *within* him, represented in flashbacks of their relationship while he saws wood, lifts rocks and runs fully clothed up snow-covered mountains. Where Drago boasts 'I will not be defeated',

Rocky discusses being scared with his son ('goin' one more round when you don't think you can – that's what makes all the difference in the world'). Where Drago is promoted by sour-faced Soviet politicians (Gromyko and Gorbachev lookalikes) whom he rejects when being defeated by Rocky ('I fight to win for me'), the latter is supported by semi-comic friends whose main contribution is to tell him that he feels 'no pain' (the Don Kings of the contemporary 'fight game' and its notorious corruption have to remain an absence of this narrative in the interests of a manichean conflict between Reaganite America and the evil Soviet empire seeking world domination!). The final climactic brutality of the boxing match sees Rocky 'converting' the hostile crowd – initially, like Drago and his wife, represented through familiar fascistic imagery – to his side, presumably because his indomitable spirit in resisting the power of the automaton-like Drago provides them with a model which dredges up their repressed spirit in resisting the power of the state. Ironically, Drago shouts frustratedly 'He's not human. He's a piece of iron' but Rocky is constituted precisely as symbolic of an American humanity – the 'little man' with the will to succeed, combining aggression in the ring with a capacity for tenderness, love and friendship in 'life' – and it is this combination which generates the final (albeit absurd) scene of social unity in which the victorious Rocky tells the Soviet crowd that 'Two guys fightin' each other is better than twenty million' and that he has 'seen a lotta changin' during the fight so that 'If I can change, you can change. Everybody can change.'

The issue of the relation between nationhood and masculinity being tested is central, I would argue, to many other Hollywood films of the 1980s and 1990s. *Born on the Fourth of July* (1989) opens with the adult voice-over of Ron Kovic, the film's hero/victim, making a link between boyhood and a pre-lapsarian/Vietnam past: 'We turned the woods into a battlefield and dreamed that someday we would become men.' The narrative's trajectory takes us through Kovic's childhood of nationalistic parades, including glimpses of wheelchair veterans of the Second World War and Korea, through his adolescence during the Kennedy years in which context 'Ask not what your country can do for you, ask what you can do for your country' begins to take on a new meaning as Kovic feels himself pressured (but failing) to be 'the best' especially by his mother ('He wants to be the best ... That's what matters to God'). Indeed, the representation of the mother figure throughout the film is consistently hostile. Where she enunciates conventional political and moral platitudes ('It's God's will. Communism has to be stopped'), Kovic's assertion to his father 'I wanna go to Vietnam. I'll die there if I have to', causes his father to look out through his glasses helplessly at the rain and comment 'Not a nice night for the prom.' The film represents Kovic as repressing his inner confusion and publicly buying into the Marine recruiting version of history ('we have always come when our country's called us') and constructing the romance of masculine duty to sacrifice ('our dads got to go to World War 2. This is our chance to be part of history') and defending it against one of his friends' dismissal of volunteering for Vietnam in favour of completing his business degree ('Stevie, Stevie, it's okay. Someone's gotta stay here and look after the women and children while the men do the fightin').

The 'reality' of Vietnam, however, is depicted as a chaotic universe of 'accidental' My Lai-type massacres of women and children and Kovic, in the confusion of the battlefield, shoots one of his own platoon (Wilson) before being wounded himself. Returning home in a wheelchair, while his mother eats cake in front of the television, switching from a news programme about the anti-Vietnam war demonstration in Washington to 'Rowan and Martin's Laugh-in', Kovic is transformed from his position of 'respect for country, flag and religion' to a realisation that he had behaved 'like I was John fuckin' Wayne ... runnin' around in the woods again'. He identifies his paralysed state as castration and repeatedly identifies his feelings of loss around his 'dead penis' ('I look at my dick and my balls. I'd give everything – all my values – to have my body back again'). In despair he cries 'I want to be a man again ... Who's gonna love me?' Certainly not his mother in this film as she can only scream 'Don't say penis in this house' while his father pathetically tries to nurture him and take some care of his needs.

The sense of an inherited 'fathers' history' is reinforced when Kovic visits Wilson's family to tell them the 'real story' of how their son was killed. Here he finds a Georgia family sadly proud of their 'tradition' of having 'fought in every war this country's ever had'. Kovic finally becomes an anti-war veteran demonstrator against Nixon, gains fame for writing a book about his experiences and the film closes with an ironic fulfilment of his mother's dream that he will one day address a great crowd of people, 'saying great things'; he is wheeled on stage to address the Democratic Convention. Kovic no longer feels at odds with himself or with the society which surrounds him. As he puts it he has finally come 'home'.

The interesting feature of *Born on the Fourth of July*, then, is the way in which it explores the shaping and interaction of masculinities around 'everyday' cultural processes (parades, family traditions and histories, High School rituals, peer group pressure) allied to cultural forms of representation in the public sphere. Through Kovic the film deconstructs the 'romance of war' and locates his desire to live out ideals of masculinity in relation to his father, younger brother (for whom rejection of the war is as unproblematic as the Dylan music to which he listens) or to Stevie, whose single-minded pursuit of the American Dream of success in business can appropriate the symbolic forms (e.g. a parade float) of the nation for reasons of profit rather than ideals of 'death or glory'.

In these two films of the 1980s, then, the central configuration is of male subjectivity being tested and examined. In *Rocky IV* there is a focus on a fixed identity which is not, in fact, changed by its examination, merely reaffirmed. All that I would argue is that a kind of 'family romance' is intrinsic to the narrative of male aggression, bonding and the crassness of Reaganite cold war politics. In *Born on the Fourth of July* the male protagonist is represented as changing, the family becomes a negative 'romance' in relation to the politics of the film and the narrative focuses on constructed masculinity which is based upon repression. Thus, the central male protagonist is always *capable* of spontaneous emotion and while he enunciates learnt 'certainties' they are gradually eroded by his experiences (his letters to Donna from Vietnam carry 'feeling in the words') and in a sense the film's narrative pursues the trajectory of the eruption of this inner self into the public domain. And, finally, the film imposes, it seems to me, a 'magical' resolution to Kovic's sense of loss of male identity and the pain of his 'castration' can be reconciled by public accolades at the Democratic Convention. Is the 'quest' he pursues so bounded as to be registered by a transition from conservative Republican politics to liberal Democratic politics?

Family Pleasures

The last decade of Hollywood film production has witnessed not only the action-hero movies of Stallone, Willis *et al.*, but also a realisation that, commercially, the cinema must address family entertainment not only on the big screen but for the profits to be made from home video purchase/rental. The result has been a plethora of 'smart kid' movies, typified most notably by Macaulay Culkin, men swapping places with kids, men faced with bringing up babies and so on. In most of these films the comedy arises out of playing variations upon a theme: masculine identity is more fragile, more easily undermined, than the bravado with which it is asserted would suggest. In the process men discover their 'real' selves and arrive at some kind of 'new' identity.

Such reflections do not play a large part, however, in the adventure narrative which has enjoyed a revival, particularly through Spielberg's Indiana Jones sequence. In a way, Harrison Ford's portrayal of Jones takes up where Roger Moore left James Bond – a knowingly ironic all-action hero magically protected against the most extreme forms of hazard or danger. The relation between the Indiana Jones and Bond sequences of films is most obvious in *Indiana Jones and the Last Crusade* (1989) in which Sean Connery appears as Indiana's father. Throughout the film he plays the bumbling 'academic, a bookworm' who repeatedly 'screws things up' and has to be repeatedly rescued by his son. Here there is a 'knowing' interplay between the Connery persona, his Bond identity and the figure of Professor Jones who burns his fingers with a lighter rather than succeeding in burning through the ropes which bind him and his son. In the sequence women are feisty (*Lost Ark*), feminine and, therefore, repeatedly humiliated (*Temple of Doom*), or beautiful but treacherous (*The Last Crusade*). The 'romance' of the narratives lies in the 'quest' and the way in which Indiana Jones can pass through and 'own' a range of 'exotic' cultures. It could be argued, perhaps, that the films recover a tradition of narratives in which the white man rescues a vulnerable, weak society (such as the Hindu village in *Temple of Doom*) from a threatening force beyond its power to resist. Any number of colonial narratives come to mind here.

A different kind of 'quest' is pursued in *Field of Dreams* (1989) in which Kevin Costner plays an Iowa farmer, Ray Kinsella, who hears voices telling him to build a baseball pitch in the middle of his fields. In doing so he endangers his livelihood but he is compelled by a driving force to resist becoming like his father ('Life ground him down'), his desire to do something 'spontaneous' before it is too late, and his guilt at having rejected his father. Finally, of course, the film magically provides a resolution in which the quest for the father is satisfied and Kinsella and those around him are healed of their pain and suffering by his faith, vision and capacity to pursue his dreams. In the process, not only is the family romance central – in pursuing his vision his family will 'live' – but the narrative is also redolent of male romances built around sporting heroes, in this case the American working-class sport of baseball.[12] Where *Field of Dreams* seeks to recover a lost 'America', a heroic past of mythified figures of romance whether of baseball or of small-town communal values or of 1960s radicalism, threatened by the commercial values of Reaganite society, *Forrest Gump* (1994) offers the most comprehensive review of the American past since the 1950s. Gump wanders – or, rather, runs – innocently through iconic moments of American cultural and political history (Elvis, southern desegregation of the universities, the shooting of George Wallace, Kennedy, Johnson, John Lennon, Dick Cavett, Nixon, the Vietnam War, the Black Panthers, the anti-war Washington demonstration, Watergate). The interesting feature of *this* narrative is that it operates at a level of pastiche and a kind of postmodernist playfulness as does the narrative which permits Gump to fulfil the American dream of untold wealth through his capacity to run, play ping-pong and in his fulfilment of his promise to his dead, black Vietnam friend Bubba that he will set up in the shrimping business. In counterpoint to these narratives is the 'heart' of the film: Forrest's purity in his capacity to love, his loyalty to those who show him kindness and his ability to nurture, precisely because he 'ain't smart'. In a way the film sets out to undercut conventional images of masculinity and Gump ends up on the world stage of public identity obliviously and in carnivalesque mode (he tells Kennedy he needs a pee, his childhood gyrations are a model of the young Elvis, he shows his bum to Johnson, he telephones security because some guys in the Watergate Hotel are keeping him awake with their flashlight and so on). And all the way through, his one intent is to sustain his love unquestioningly for Jenny, his childhood friend. He repeatedly rescues her from her abusive father, lover, hippies, drugs and so on. He tells her, 'I'm not a smart man but I know what love is'; when they finally talk about Vietnam, she says 'I wish I could have been there with you' to which he replies simply 'you were'. Finally, their life-long romance is consummated and later fulfilled in marriage and her subsequent death from a mysterious virus (given her previous life of drugs and promiscuity, Aids? In which case ...? But that is not an issue which the film addresses). The film ends by displacing Forrest's father's absence (permanently 'on vacation') with his simple capacity for love, nurturing and fatherhood. Are these the virtues which are in men but which are repressed when they are, or try to be, 'smart'?

'Smartness', has a particular resonance within American culture in relation to masculine identity. It characterises the hard-boiled private eye from Hammett, Chandler and Spillane through to Robert B. Parker's monogamously inclined, chivalric Spenser, whose capacity for physical violence is more than matched by his wisecracking mouth ('I surely don't appreciate your snooping around here under false pretenses. "What other kinds of pretenses are there?", I said'). It is this kind of masculine persona to which Stanley Ipkiss aspires in *The Mask* (1994). To begin with Stanley is 'the nicest guy' who is easily exploited by unscrupulous women, garage mechanics or his landlady (he thinks of the wisecrack he should have made *after* she has slammed the door on him). Stanley finds an ancient mask floating in the river which has, at night time, the magical powers of the Norse God of Mischief and when he tries the mask on it transforms him into a potent figure of hypnotic force who overwhelms the landlady, garage mechanics, muggers, gangsters, police, the supermodel. As he puts it 'When I put that mask on I can do anything, *be* anything' but as Peggy tells him 'you, Stanley Ipkiss, are already all you'll ever need to be'. In fact, what he is is a romantic and the film again counterposes a postmodernist comic pastiche of computer-generated imagery of masculine power with a narrative which suggests that a repressed romantic self lurks within Stanley. In fact it is not the mask which will bring him success with women but the release into public being of his 'real' self.

Conclusion

In this chapter I have tried to explore in a fairly open way some ideas around popular narratives which represent masculine identity in relation to aspects of romance, of the family, sexuality, repression, nurture and love. In no sense do I wish to suggest that the argument is unproblematic nor do I have any interest in 'recovering' these fictions for some kind of 'new mannish' discourse. Indeed, I am sure it could be argued persuasively that such narratives are themselves inflected by the cultural production of the fabular 'new man' and by reaction to the incursions of feminism into Western cultures. All that I am seeking to establish is that the pleasures addressed in contemporary popular genres predominantly regarded as male are more ambivalent and complex than their common characterisation around action, violence and aggression.[13] Moreover, popular representations of men in relation to the family, domesticity and nurturing have had to be responsive to social and cultural change as well as contributing to changing perceptions of masculine identities.

Given the abuses to which the continued exploitation of male power and dominance gives rise in everyday social reality it is, of course, tempting to be dismissive of arguments which focus upon cultural representations of masculine romance, or of male psychological and emotional fragility or sensitivity. My question is, however, should we not look at popular genres in a more open way which reviews some of the more simplistic generalisations often circulated around the constitution of gendered pleasure?

Notes

1   John Cawelti, *Adventure, Mystery and Romance* (Chicago: Chicago University Press, 1976), p. 41, emphases added.

2   Bridget Fowler, *The Alienated Reader: Women and Popular Romantic Literature in the Twentieth Century* (Hemel Hempstead: Harvester Wheatsheaf, 1991), p. 8.

3   Seymour, *Harry's Game* (Glasgow: Fontana, 1986), *The Fighting Man* (London: HarperCollins, 1994).

4   Gerald Seymour, *The Heart of Danger*, (London: HarperCollins, 1995).

5   Seymour, *The Heart of Danger*, pp. 160–1.

6   John Le Carré, *Our Game* (London: Hodder & Stoughton, 1995), pp. 215–16.

7   The phrase 'exemplary masculinities' is drawn from a discussion of film in R.W. Connell, *Masculinities* (Cambridge: Polity Press, 1995), pp. 215–16.

8   Cited in Graham Dawson, *Soldier Heroes: British Adventure, Empire and the Imagining of Masculinities* (London: Routledge, 1994), pp. 11–12.

9   C. Mansueto, 'Take the toys from the boys', in D. Thompson (ed.), *Over Our Dead Bodies: Women Against the Bomb* (London: Virago, 1983), pp. 118–19. Cited in Dawson, *Soldier Heroes*.

10   Anthony Giddens, *The Consequences of Modernity* (Cambridge: Polity Press, 1991), pp. 21–9.

11   For a discussion of the anxieties and contradictions of white masculinity explored in such films, see Fred Pfeil *White Guys: Studies in Post Modern Domination and Difference* (London: Verso, 1995), pp. 1–36.

12   See, for instance, Eamon Dunphy's article 'Hail the new romantics', *Independent on Sunday*, (17 July 1994), in which Brazilian football is characterised as a game of the dispossessed played with a 'beauty' and spontaneity beyond the imagination of the professional coach. See also the *Independent*, (10 June 1995), in which, again, Brazilain footballers are represented as fulfilling 'romantic ideals'.

13   The films and film-scripts of Quentin Tarentino from *True Romance* to *Pulp Fiction* are an obvious absence in this argument. This was a deliberate choice mainly because these films seem to me so bound up with cinematic self-referential pastiche that it would have pulled the discussion in a different direction.

Filmography

Born on the fourth of July (dir. Oliver Stone, 1989).
Field of Dreams (dir. Phil Alden Robinson, 1989).
Forrest Gump (dir. Robert Zennekis, 1994).
Indiana Jones and the Last Crusade (dir. Stephen Spielberg, 1989).
Indiana Jones and the Temple of Doom (dir. Stephen Spielberg, 1984).
The Mask (dir. Charles Russell, 1994).
Raiders of the Lost Ark (dir. Stephen Spielberg, 1981).
Rocky IV (dir. Sylvester Stallone, 1985).

Notes on Contributors

The Editors

Lynne Pearce is a senior lecturer in English at Lancaster University. She is also a member of the Women's Studies Institute, and teaches mainly in the areas of feminist theory and women's writing. She is co-author (with Sara Mills) of *Feminist Readings/Feminists Reading* (Harvester Wheatsheaf, 1989/1996) and author of *Woman/Image/Text: Readings in Pre-Raphaelite Art and Literature* (Harvester Wheatsheaf, 1991); *Reading Dialogics* (Edward Arnold, 1994); and *Feminism and the Politics of Reading* (Edward Arnold, 1997). With Jackie Stacey, she also co-edited *Romance Revisted* (Lawrence and Wishart, 1995) and her other publications on romance are cited in her chapter in this volume.

Gina Wisker is a principal lecturer at Anglia Polytechnic University and teaches mainly in nineteenth- and twentieth-century women's writing, postcolonial writing and popular fictions. She has written for, and edited, *Insights into Black Women's Writing* (Macmillan, 1992); *It's My Party: Reading Twentieth-Century Women's Writing* (Pluto Press, 1994); and written *Empowering Women in Higher Education* (Kogan Page, 1996). Gina is currently writing a book on postcolonial women's writing.

The Contributors

Flora Alexander is a senior lecturer in English and member of the Women's Studies Group at the University of Aberdeen. She has published work on Iris Murdoch, Margaret Laurence, Alice Munro, Emma Tennant and Candida McWilliam, and her current research is on contemporary fiction by Canadian women.

Phyllis Creme is a senior lecturer at the University of North London where she teaches writing, media and cultural studies.

Barbara Creed lecturers in cinema studies at La Trobe University, Melbourne, Australia. She is the author of *The Monstrous Feminine: Film, Feminism, Psychoanalysis* (London: Routledge, 1993) and has published widely in the area of feminist film theory.

Maroula Joannou is a senior lecturer in English and Women's Studies at Anglia Polytechnic University. She is the author of '*Ladies, Please Don't Smash these Windows*': *Women's Writing, Feminist Consciousness and Social Change 1918–38* (Oxford and Providence: Berg, 1995) and editor of *Women Writers of the 1930s: Gender, Politics, History* (Edinburgh: Edinburgh University Press, forthcoming). She has edited *Heart of the Heartless World: Essays in Cultural Resistance in Memory of Margot Heinemann* with David Margolies (London: Pluto Press, 1995) and *The Woman's Suffrage Movement: New Perspectives* with June Purvis (Manchester: Manchester University Press, 1997). She is presently completing a book on contemporary women's writing for Manchester University Press.

Maria Lauret teaches American Studies at the University of Sussex. She is the author of *Liberating Literature: Feminist Fiction in America* (London and New York: Routledge, 1994) and is currently writing a book on Alice Walker.

Derek Longhurst is currently Dean of the School of Humanities and Social Sciences at Staffordshire Univeristy, where he is also Professor. Previous publications include *Gender, Genre and Narrative Pleasure* (London: Routledge, 1989) and articles and chapters on media theory, Shakespeare and popular culture, crime fiction and science fiction.

Nickianne Moody is a senior lecturer in Media and Cultural Studies at Liverpool John Moores University. Her main research field is popular fiction, cultural history, and empirical research methodology for cultural studies. The current research projects that she is involved with are an oral history of the 'Boots Booklovers' Library', and the representation of 'plague' across a range of media forms and genres. Nickianne has recent publications on women's science fiction, popular media and tourism, digital culture and the representation of disability in science fiction. She edits the newsletter and journal for the Association of Research in Popular Fictions and is currently convening a conference on 'Medical Fictions' for the association.

David Oswell lectures in the sociology of media, communications and culture in the Department of Human Sciences, Brunel University, West London. He is currently conducting research into constructions of childhood within Internet policy cultures.

Paulina Palmer lectures in English Literature and Women's Studies at the University of Warwick. Her publications include *Contemporary Women's Fiction: Narrative Practice and Feminist Theory* (Hemel Hempstead: Harvester Wheatsheaf, 1989) and *Contemporary Lesbian Writing: Dreams, Desire, Difference* (Buckingham: Open University Press, 1993).

Judy Simons is Dean of Humanities and Social Sciences at Leicester, De Montfort University, where she is also a professor. Her books include *Fanny Burney* (1987), *Diaries and Journals of Literary Women from Fanny Burney to Virginia Woolf* (1990), *Rosamond Lehmann* (1992) and, with Shirley Foster, *What Katy Read: Feminist Re-readings of 'Classic' Stories for Girls 1850–1920* (1995), all published by Macmillan. She is editor of the Macmillan New Casebook on *Mansfield Park and Persuasion* (1997) and, with Kate Fullbrook, of *Writing: A Woman's Business* (Manchester: Manchester University Press, 1998). She is currently working on a study of twentieth-century women's fiction, *Re-writing the Love Story*, also for Macmillan.

Patsy Stoneman is a senior lecturer in English at Hull University, where she has taught since 1966. Her main interests are the nineteenth-century novel and women's studies in literature, and she is convenor of an MA course in 'Women and Literature in English'. Her main publications are *Elizabeth Gaskell* (Sussex: The Harvester Press, 1987), the Macmillan New Casebook on *Wuthering Heights* (1993), and *Brontë Transformations: The Cultural Dissemination of Jane Eyre and Wuthering Heights* (Hemel Hempstead: Harvester Wheatsheaf, 1996).

Index